Negotiating Commercial Real Estate Leases

By Martin I. Zankel

Mesa House Publishing

A Division of Two Coyotes, Inc.
Fort Worth, Texas

Cover illustration and book design by Scott Anderson

Library of Congress Card Number: 00-103291

Copyright © 2001 by Martin I. Zankel

Editorial correspondence and requests for permission to reprint should be mailed to Mesa House Publishing, c/o Two Coyotes, Inc., 3228 College Avenue, Fort Worth, TX 76110. E-mail should be addressed to books@mesahouse.com.

This publication is intended to provide accurate information in regard to the subject matter presented. It is sold with the understanding that the publisher is not engaged in rendering legal, financial, medical, or other professional services.

ISBN: 0-940352-14-1

Printed in the United States of America

Table of Contents

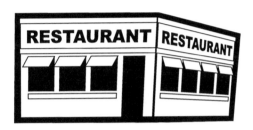

Acknowledgments

With much gratitude, I acknowledge that the original edition of this book could not have been produced without:

- Peter Bedford and Stuart Moldaw, two talents who, through their unexplained and quixotic faith in me allowed me to learn the grist of this material while, simultaneously, I was having a wonderful time. My good fortune in numbering these two giants as clients is living testament to the proposition that luck is more valuable than skill; and

- My wife, Maggi, whose saintliness is a fact the undeniable evidence of which is nearly 40 years of uninterrupted tolerance of the barely tolerable and support of the unsupportable (me); and who patiently, over many months, watched without complaint (could it have been relief) as I crept away to my computer directly after dinner, like a polite boarder; and

- Suzy Marroquin who, with the consummate ability I thanklessly took for granted, put these forgettable words into readable form; and Shirley Campagna who patiently and skillfully carried out my ever less rational revisions; and Angharad Jones who with beaming countenance, bountiful optimism and a positive attitude that would shame Norman Vincent Peale, witnessed the trials of a bloodied warrior on the battlefield of the conference table and prepared the results of most of the negotiations that form the matrix of this book.

To these and scores more, my thanks and more thanks.

Preface

I negotiated my first commercial lease in 1965. It was for a 2,400 square foot Stop 'N Go™ Market in San Rafael, California. I dare not contemplate what I agreed to 35 years ago. I looked at that tenant form lease as if it were engraved in stone. At that time I represented a landlord. Like all good standard form tenant leases, it was very brief. It was years before I was to learn the rule of thumb that landlord's leases are lengthy and tenant's leases are brief. I wouldn't have cared much in any event. I needed the money that I saw emanating from that lease like rays from the sun, which should not be directly examined.

I don't know whether I was taken advantage of or not. What I do know is that the lease transaction proved to be a profitable one. What I also know is that I knew nothing about leases or leasing. More important, I didn't know how to get help in a relatively uncomplicated manner without becoming a student or reading a 1,000 page tome, or, worst of all, hiring a lawyer. I signed and prayed for the blessings of blissful ignorance. I suppose I should have taken my luck in not suffering from my obliviousness as a religious augury. But I was too dumb for that, too.

Not one to let my lack of knowledge interfere with my training, I negotiated my first industrial lease in 1969 and my first office lease shortly thereafter. I did all of this first as a broker, then as a developer, then as a lawyer, and finally as a developer *and* lawyer. Psychoanalysis is the next logical step.

There are many good books about leasing commercial, office, and industrial space. There are relatively few that deal with the essential business issues that must be examined in each clause of the lease and about which I so desperately needed help 35 years ago. There are form books aplenty. How to draft clauses, with examples. They all assume there is nobody to negotiate against. I have always found it to be great fun to negotiate with oneself, or with a partner. One is never troubled with arguments this way. And one makes the most brilliant deals, as long as there is no one on the other side! However, alas, this isn't the way negotiations truly work. You have my word. This book is an attempt to forget the form books, acknowledge that there are two sides to each argument, and try to deal with the real economic questions.

What are the issues to which a business owner should pay attention? What are the ones he or she should leave to the lawyers? Although I am a lawyer, this book is not intended as a legal treatise. It is intended to be for the benefit of the real estate professionals and business people who struggle to find out which issues are important and which are not; what alternative solutions can be offered to solve a problem; and what alternatives would be palatable to the other side. If you see what you think is legal advice in this book, do yourself a favor and ignore it. Even better yet, see a lawyer.

I have sought to fill the need that I felt 35 years ago. What I hope to do is benefit the relatively inexperienced real estate broker or developer or landlord who is trying to find a way through the maze of legalisms and small print to fashion a transaction that is livable and that satisfies the needs of all the parties.

In doing this, my goal will be to set forth the critical issues faced, the position that each of the parties is likely to take, and the compromises that are frequently made. I will try not to favor the landlord or the tenant. I have, and do, represent both with regularity. If it seems that I tend towards the tenant's side, it is only because, in most situations, the landlord's form of lease is used as the foundation for negotiations.

In this book we will be threading a way through a lease negotiation. In so doing, I will, from time to time, highlight in bold type some basic negotiating advice that is not specific to lease negotiations alone. For example, "Never humiliate your opponent. They may get an opportunity to return the favor." I merely add these as dividends, to you the reader, for which I have paid in blood over many years.

CHAPTER 1

The Myth of the Standard Form Lease

"This is our standard form lease; there can be no changes."

One might look at the speaker of these words expecting to see a cassock and collar.

Contrary to popular belief, there is no such creature as a *standard form lease*. A lease is a complex document that contains hundreds of agreements. The idea that one party to the lease can present the terms of each of these myriad agreements in a manner that equally serves the interests of both sides is obviously absurd. The drafter of a lease represents one side or the other. Accordingly, the lease will be skewed that way.

I addressed a group of brokers one morning. Some of them had attempted, with difficulty, to alter the "form" lease of a landlord client of mine that they thought particularly tough. During the question session, one member of the audience asked if I would advise my tenant clients to sign this lease. I responded, without a trace of self-consciousness, that I would not, because I would not advise any client of mine, landlord or tenant, to sign any lease that had been drafted by the other side in a transaction without negotiation.

The first time I ever signed a lease I was a 22-year-old prospective apartment dweller in New York City. The Real Estate Board of New York drafts a standard form of apartment lease, which then lay in front of me. I diligently read the entire lease. (I do believe I permanently injured my eyes in the process, the type being smaller than even my youthful eyesight could abide.) At the time, I was appalled at the number of rules and regulations *I* would have to observe. But the persons who drafted that lease did not have my interests in mind. They had the interests of the landlord in mind. There is nothing offensive about this; landlords need protection. Tenants are not a sanctified class of beings. They are no

1

different from other human beings. They are full of faults, even as landlords are.

What I have since discovered is that all forms of leases can and should be negotiated. What I have further discovered is that those people who slap so-called standard form leases in front of you and ask for execution fully expect that you will respond with requests for changes.

This is not always true, however. Regional mall landlord leases are among the most difficult for a tenant to negotiate. Since a substantial portion of my law practice involves the representation of both landlords and tenants, I have negotiated on both sides of lease transactions involving regional shopping mall space. I remember an early experience that I had with a regional mall lease. I was approached by a small tenant who knew of some work our firm had done representing larger tenancies. We also had negotiated several small tenant leases in regional malls without any dramatic success. Our new client asked if we would represent him in the negotiation of his lease for a camera shop in a large regional mall. I told him to turn to the signature page at the back of the lease, sign it, and return it to the leasing manager of the mall with a letter stating that he had signed where he was asked to because he was sure that the lease incorporated all of the understandings he and the leasing manager had reached. I thought he would be better off with this approach than wasting his time trying to get changes the mall would not make for a small tenant.

Every large landlord has its own form lease. I represent one landlord that has 12 form leases. Every large tenant has *its* own form lease. There are gross leases, industrial gross, new, bond net, retail, industrial, office, full-service office, and short and long forms of each depending on term. All of these leases can be negotiated — some more than others. A form lease is like a cube of clay. Push on it and its form changes. Pull on it and its form changes again. A lease negotiation is about pushing, pulling, tugging, and pressing that cube of clay until it emerges into a shape that both parties can be comfortable with.

If a form lease can be negotiated, does it make any difference *whose* form one starts with? It can, but my experience tells me that a more important question is "Who *drafts* the lease?" because that person will control the negotiation. Usually (but not always) the lease is drafted by the party whose original form is placed into negotiation in the first place. For example, if the lease is to be based on the landlord's form, the landlord's attorney or representative generally does the drafting of any changes to the form. Similarly, if the tenant's original form is placed into negotiation, the tenant's lawyer or representative generally does the drafting of any changes. But if the landlord's form is placed into play with the agreement that the tenant's lawyer will draft the changes, then it is better to be in the position of the tenant's lawyer with drafting rights than to be in the position of the landlord whose form is that on which the final lease will be based. Why? Because the person who drafts the document will control the drafting of any concessions.

An active negotiation between two relatively equal parties can be an arduous, lengthy process, but sooner or later intelligent parties genuinely interested in making a business deal will want to stop negotiating and sign the lease. When that stage in the negotiation is reached, all of the minor outstanding points will end up being conceded by the party who does not control the document, simply because the party who does control the document refuses to make the final requested changes to it. For example, if the parties are arguing over a seemingly unimportant question like whether the holdover rent should be 125% or 150% of the rent at the end of the term, this becomes such a minor item on the battlefield that the party who is not doing the drafting will eventually concede the point as being an issue not likely to occur. Five years later when it becomes a real issue on expiration of the lease term, that battle will long ago have been lost — just an unnoticed body on the negotiation battlefield.

Therefore, my first piece of advice in any lease negotiation is **GET CONTROL OF THE DOCUMENT. The party who controls the drafting of the lease document will win all the small battles.**

With modern word processing and desktop publishing, incorporating any number of changes into a lease is no longer a problem. As a negotiating technique, however, to lure either a prospective landlord or tenant into believing that the provider of the lease form is unwilling to alter the form substantially, handwritten insertions and deletions are sometimes used. On numerous occasions, I have taken a lease form we have in the office for a client and inserted new material, crossed out existing material, drawn arrows and asterisks indicating midline insertions, or used addenda to add whole sections. None of this was *necessary* because the lease form was on a word processor. An original custom document could easily have been produced. Nonetheless, we used that technique (often called *cut and paste*) to indicate how reluctant we were to change the form.

Varieties of Form Leases

There are limitless varieties of form leases. Let's start with gross leases. The term *gross lease* generally means that the landlord pays expenses. Most often these leases provide limits to the landlord's patience and to its pocketbook. These limits are called *stops*. We will describe this in some detail in the course of the book. Sometimes there are no stops; sometimes the stops apply only to certain expenses. I have one client who has a gross lease, a full gross lease, an all gross lease, and a pure gross lease. To use all of these terms may seem fatuous, but each describes a different level of gross. Then there is the retail gross, the industrial gross, and the gross short form or long form.

Similarly, there are various varieties of net leases. Under a net lease, the landlord is the lucky party. The tenant has the opportunity to bear most of the expenses. If the tenant is to bear *all* of the expenses, the lease is called a triple net lease (meaning the tenant bears the three elemental forms of property expense: taxes, insurance, and maintenance). If tenant is to bear all of the expenses as well as the risk of condemnation and destruction, the lease is called a bond net lease. The permutations are endless.

Moreover, as with the gross lease, there are short and long forms for net leases. What is the difference? The number of pages, of course. How does one reduce the number of pages? Simple, reduce the responsibilities of the tenant. The shorter the form, the more beneficial to the tenant. Why would a landlord use a short form lease? One reason is because there is a desirable tenant who won't sign a long form lease. Another reason is so as not to frighten the universe of tenants available for a particular space. That universe may consist largely of small tenants who do not have lawyers and do not wish to read lengthy leases in fine print. (They have not got the money for the ophthalmologist, to say nothing of the legal fees.) Therefore, the landlord, to be competitive, cuts out as much of the hammer-and-anvil language in the lease as it possibly can, in return for which the tenant will receive only a short lease term. By agreeing to a short lease term with the short form, the landlord limits its exposure to the types of risk that may have been omitted from discussion in the lease.

For example, in its long form lease, a landlord may have an intimidating, uncompromising assignment and sublet provision to be sure that it collects all possible profits. However, if the lease term is to be only two or three years, the landlord may be willing to take the risk that there is not going to be much profit in the lease for the tenant. Thus, it will cut down the two-page assignment and sublet clause to a single paragraph.

This leads us to the general rule that lengthy leases favor the landlord and short leases favor the tenant. Why is this so? Is it because landlords are a group in need of protection? Hardly. Actually, the answer is exactly the reverse. Over the years the courts have felt tenants to be the group in need of protection. Much statutory and case law favors tenants. Therefore, the landlord, to overcome these tendencies in the law, drafts lengthy clauses clearly establishing the rights of the parties, rather than leaving it to a court to decide.

The very best lease for a tenant would simply say that the landlord leases to the tenant and the tenant hires from the landlord *x* property for *x* dollars a month on a month-to-month basis with an option to extend monthly for 120 months (ten years). This, in effect, gives the tenant a right to walk away from the lease obligation any time it chooses. Moreover, if there is an argument, the relationship of the parties — not having been thoroughly reduced to writing — is unclear, and off to court they go, where there is a good chance that the dispute will be settled in favor of the tenant.

Approaches to Negotiation

In negotiating a lease, where does one start? With the obvious, of course. In commercial leases, the "obvious" are the essential business terms of the lease — the rent, the location, the size of the space, the term of the lease, and the tenant improvements (if any) to be constructed by the landlord.

And after that? There are two approaches that are most common. The first is simply to start at the beginning of a lease and negotiate your way to the end. This is how this book is organized. I have simply followed the order of the lease clauses in the standard lease forms (can I still use that expression?) in my office.

A second technique often used is to take the most critical legal clauses, the business provisions having already been negotiated, and deal with them first. After that, proceed in order. For example, I have a tenant client who insists that the assignment and sublet issue be resolved along with the operating covenant, before any time is wasted haggling about other legal issues. The disadvantage of this technique is that if you obtain what you are seeking for the so-called critical issues, it may lead the other side to think, perhaps in error, that it can have the benefit of everything else because you apparently don't value the other clauses so dearly.

Regardless of which approach you follow, there are few rules of thumb to a lease negotiation. There is only experience.

Here, then, is mine.

CHAPTER 2
Premises

Describing the Property

We start with the essence of the deal, that which is being transferred for consideration: the property, or premises. The premises must be described in a manner adequate to permit persons with no knowledge of the transaction to locate them. If this can't be done, the entire transaction is in danger of foundering on the reef of vagueness. Courts won't enforce a lease if they can't definitely establish what's been leased.

Exhibits

Single Tenant

If a single tenant is renting the entire premises, most descriptions can be done without a lawyer's help. In that situation, it is simple to take the legal description from the deed or title insurance policy. A plot plan can be adequate if streets and dimensions are properly delineated. Remember the test: If a stranger can take your drawing and locate the premises with reasonable accuracy, then the description is adequate. The drawing doesn't have to be done by Lewis and Clark.

Multiple Tenants

While a written legal description *can* be used for multitenant properties (shopping centers, office buildings), drawings and plot plans are the rule. Landlords will want to use care, however, to limit the information that is on the plan. Names of proposed tenants, locations of buildings, and similar specifics can constitute legally binding representations unless expressly disclaimed. A landlord can unwittingly find itself in the position of needing to have a small tenant's permission for any reconfiguration of the building or common area! One marvels at the material that a tenant desperate to break an unprofitable lease can suddenly discover it must have relied on originally. There is no more disheartening assignment to a lawyer than being asked by his client to "get me out of this lease." Plot plan representations are high on the list of weasel methods.

Appurtenances

The premises clause should, if the tenant is paying attention, include references to *appurtenances*. These include rights to common areas, driveway easements, street vaults (for utilities), and other rights needed for the full enjoyment of the property. And don't forget to mention the basement, if it's in the deal.

Rentable/Usable/Leasable Areas

Unit Costs

As we shall see, in a negotiation, rents are often discussed in terms of unit cost, or cost per square foot. Eventually, that unit cost must be converted to an actual monthly rent figure for the premises. Thus, for example, the parties may agree that the rent is $10 per square foot per year. The question then arises: a square foot of what?

A method must be devised to calculate the square footage and, thereby, the monthly check that must be sent to the landlord as rent. For example, $10 per square foot per year X 4,000 square feet = $40,000 per year or $3,333.33 a month. To charge the tenant for rent on its share of the common areas (the *load factor*) a method must be established for allocating those areas among the various tenants, that is, converting the area actually occupied by the tenant (*the usable area*) to a figure representing the area for which the tenant is charged rent after the load factor is applied (the *rentable area*). Thus, we need a method for converting usable area to rentable area. This is generally done by use of a *conversion factor* or *R/U Ratio* (rentable to usable ratio).

The tenant may occupy 4,000 square feet, but when the load factor is applied to allocate common areas, the tenant may be paying rent on 4,600 square feet. How do we get there?

Rentable Area

The terms "rentable" and "usable" are office building terms. They are devised to allocate the common areas (corridors, lobbies, common bathrooms, and so on) among the tenants in a building. The industry bible for making the calculation is entitled *American National Standard Method for Measuring Floor Area in Office Buildings*, which is published by the Building Owner's and Manager's Association (BOMA)

International.[1] We'll call this the "BOMA Standard."

One starts, typically, by measuring from the inside surface of all outer walls on a floor, excluding vertical penetrations such as elevator shafts, stairs, and utility ducts used in common by tenants. Let's take a theoretical office building, which we'll call "Leaning Towers." Leaning Towers is configured in a square measuring 100 by 100 feet from the inside painted surface of the exterior walls. In the middle of each floor is a cluster of vertical penetrations (elevators, stairways, and so on) measuring 20 by 50 feet. The rentable area of the floor, therefore, is 9,000 square feet.

100 ft. x 100 ft.	=	10,000 square feet
Less Vertical Penetrations	=	-1,000 square feet
Equals Net Floor Rentable Area	=	9,000 square feet

If there are eight rentable stories in Leaning Towers (excluding the basement), all of which are in the same configuration (let's forget the lobby for the time being), the rentable area of the building will be 72,000 square feet (8 x 9,000 sq. ft.). Rentable area is usually calculated for each floor, so that full floor users pay for all corridors on their floors. However, under the 1996 revisions to the BOMA Standard, each floor is allocated a portion of building common areas such as lobbies, conference rooms, health facilities and the like that are located on one floor, but are for the benefit of all tenants in the building.

Usable Area

The usable area is that portion of the floor that is actually leased or held for lease for the exclusive possession of tenants or is building common area. The BOMA Standard goes to the inside finished surfaces of corridor or exterior walls, and to the center of a wall that separates two office spaces (*a demising wall*). There are other standards of measurement, in particular in New York, where the Real Estate Board of New York standard could yield a rentable area that exceeds the size of the building. Rentable area under these New York guidelines is left to the discretion of the owner and could include mechanical penthouses and freestanding power plants. Additionally, tenant space is measured to the corridor side of hallways, rather than to the inside finished surface. Thus,

---

[1] Building Owner's and Manager's Association [BOMA] International, 1221 Massachusetts Avenue, N. W., Washington, DC 20005. The book is publication number ANSI Z65.1-1996 and is available for $35 to nonmembers.

it is apparent that many variations are possible. But with few exceptions, such as the expectably creative overreaching of New York landlords, the BOMA Standard is widely accepted.

One can see that all floor common areas (but not building common areas) such as corridors, stairways, elevators, and elevator lobbies are excluded from the calculation of usable area. Only space subject to present or future lease or building common area is included.

Let us say, for example, that in Leaning Towers, ignoring those tenants who have leaped off their balconies in pairs to test Galileo's theory, we have a tenant (Pisa Nut, Inc.) that leases a space consisting of the entire third floor plus a portion of the fourth measuring 35 by 65 feet, or 2,275 square feet. Thus, Pisa Nut's usable area is 11,275 sq. ft. (9,000 + 2,275). Moreover, the usable area of all premises in Leaning Towers is calculated as follows:

Floor	Total Area	Vertical Penetration	Common Area	Usable Area
Ground	10,000 sq. ft.	1,000	1,500 sq. ft.*	8,500 sq. ft.*
2, 4-8	10,000 sq. ft. (x6)	1,000	1,500 sq. ft. (x6)	8,500 sq. ft. (x6)
3	10,000 sq. ft.	1,000	1,000 sq. ft.	9,000 sq. ft.
Total	80,000 sq. ft.		14,000 sq. ft.	68,500 sq. ft.

*Including a 2,400 sq. ft. lobby which is building common area.
**Please note that a full floor occupant will have more usable area by the amount of footage that on other floors would be devoted to common corridors, in this case 500 sq. ft. In other words, a full floor user, since it has no neighbors on the floor, uses the entire floor, including corridors, as its premises. Therefore, there is less common and more usable area on its floor.

Calculating Tenant's Cost of Occupacy

Allocating Costs

In any multiple tenant project, it is necessary to devise a method for sharing certain costs among the tenants, costs that are intended to be passed through from the landlord who has advanced those costs. Such costs are taxes, operating costs (offices), maintenance (shopping centers and industrial), and insurance. Once, probably before you were born (but, alas, not before I was born), the landlord paid all such costs and charged the tenant one "gross" figure. That was before inflation became a part of the normal expectancy of our economic life. Landlords with long-term, flat-rent leases, under which costs were borne by them, discovered that cash flow was disappearing through a gaping hole in their leases.

Not being a self-sacrificing variety of human being, the first line of defense for the landlord was to establish a *base year* or *base amount*, the costs of which the landlord would bear. This base is sometimes called a "stop," to reflect the fact that landlord's cost obligation is "stopped" at that amount. The risk of costs in excess of the stop would be passed on to the tenant.

The second and more complete line of defense for landlords was the establishment of the net lease, under which the tenant would bear all costs from the first dollar. Theoretically, the minimum rent would be proportionally reduced. To divide these costs among the tenants, it is necessary to formulate a method for calculating each tenant's pro rata share of total costs, the sum of which, in a fully occupied building, will total 100 percent. To accomplish this it is necessary to allocate among the tenants those portions of the project not originally intended to be leased: the common or joint facilities.

Rent Calculation

The R/U ratio conversion calculation (which follows) creates a rentable area for tenant's space on which minimum rent will be computed. For example, if Pisa Nut and the landlord negotiate a rental rate of $25 per square foot, Pisa Nut will pay that rate multiplied by its rentable area (11,887 square feet), not by its usable area (11,275 square feet). Landlords are meticulous about the distinction. We'll go through the calculation now.

Pro Rata Share

There are three methods of calculating Pisa Nut's pro rata share of operating costs.

R/U Ratio

The R/U ratio is the conversion factor we alluded to earlier. It is typically calculated on a floor-by-floor basis. We said that each floor has a rentable area of 9,000 square feet. (This totals 72,000 square feet in the building.) However, we must further consider that there are 2,400 square feet devoted to the lobby on the ground floor. Some landlords simply add the load for the lobby (building common areas) to the balance of the building by dividing the 2,400 square feet by the number of floors (in this case eight) for a total of 300 square feet per floor. Thus, the rentable area would be 9,300 square feet for seven floors and 6,900 square feet for the ground floor, for a total of 72,000 square feet.

	(1)	(2)	(3)	(4)	(5)	(6)
Floor	Rentable	Office Usable	Percent	Allocation of Lobby	Total Usable	Floor R/U Ratio**
1	6,600*	6,100	9.23	221.5	6321.5	1.0588***
2	9,000	8,500	12.86	308.6	8808.6	1.0588
3	9,000	9,000	13.62	326.9	9326.9	1.0000
4	9,000	8,500	12.86	308.6	8808.6	1.0588
5	9,000	8,500	12.86	308.6	8808.6	1.0588
6	9,000	8,500	12.86	308.6	8808.6	1.0588
7	9,000	8,500	12.86	308.6	8808.6	1.0588
8	9,000	8,500	12.86	308.6	8808.6	1.0588
	72,000	66,100	100.00	2,400	68,500	

*Excluding building common area (lobby).
**Divide column 1 by column 2.
***Include lobby of 2,400 in R/U calculation.

Others simply allocate building common areas on a pro rata basis, based on usable area.

The R/U ratio for a partial floor user, such as Pisa Nut on its partial floor, is calculated as follows:

$$\frac{9,000 \text{ (rentable on the floor)}}{8,500 \text{ (usable on the floor)}} = 1.0588$$

Thus, Pisa Nut's rentable area is as follows:

Floor	Usable	Pro Rata Lobby	Subtotal	R/U Ratio	Total (Rentable Square Feet)
3	9,000	326.9	9,326.90	1.0000	9,326.90
4	2,275	82.6	2,357.60	1.0588	2,496.20
					11,823.10 (16.42% of building costs)

Direct Usable Fraction

The second method of calculating Pisa Nut's pro rata share of operating costs simply ignores the R/U ratio conversion, as well as the necessity to use rentable area in the calculation at all.

$$\frac{11,275 \text{ (tenant's usable area)}}{68,500 \text{ (total usable area)}} = 16.46\% \text{ of building costs}$$

Load Factor

The last method of detailing a tenant's pro rata share of operating costs involves calculating a load factor and adding it to tenant's usable area.

Building size (10,000 sq. ft. x 8) =	80,000	total area
Usable area of offices	− 66,000	
Load loss	14,000	
Load factor (14,000 ÷ 18,000)=	17.5% of building costs	

Gross Leasable Area

This term is typically used in shopping center leases. It is the theoretical equivalent of, and uses the same principle as, the direct usable fraction mentioned in the previous paragraph. That is, all the space that is leased, or is available for lease, is totaled to arrive at the gross leasable area for the shopping center. The tenant's leased area is then measured, generally to the exterior surface of outer walls. Landlords prefer to measure to exterior walls, so the tenant can pay rent for the solid concrete portion of its space. It is a miracle that BOMA hasn't applied this profit-making theory to office buildings.

Construction

If the space to be leased is to be constructed by the landlord to a design agreed on by the parties, a situation is created that is far too complex for this primer. Careful draftsmanship by lawyers and the active participation of architects and construction people are required. There are several ways to deal with construction. All we will do here is outline briefly the issues to be covered.

Turnkey

In a turnkey situation the landlord performs all work of improvement necessary to put the tenant in possession (the build out). Theoretically, all the tenant has to do is to turn the key, open the door and commence business. No improvements to the premises are required of the tenant.

Shell Plus Allowance — Landlord Builds

As in a turnkey provision, under this arrangement, the landlord performs the build out; however, the tenant is responsible for all costs above an agreed level for the tenant improvement portion. The tenant improvement portion is that part of the construction beyond the skeletal structural shell. The landlord is responsible for building the structure, including bringing utilities to the space. All costs above this are tenant improvements (sometimes called *TIs*). The landlord provides an allowance for TIs, which is negotiated in the lease. Let's say the allowance is $25 per square foot. This should be based on rentable area because the landlord has factored the allowance into the rent.

Before construction commences, the TIs are put out to bid. If the landlord is the only contractor, the tenant had better check the figures with a consultant. If not, another visit from the tooth fairy should be sought. (See the section on excess costs for solutions when the tooth fairy fails to show.)

Shell Plus Allowance — Tenant Builds

This technique is primarily applicable to commercial (retail) leases. In this case, the landlord generally delivers the structure to the tenant "as is." Landlords love "as is," under the Three Monkey Theory (hear no evil, etc.). However, if the landlord knew, or should have known something adverse about the space and did not tell the tenant, the landlord may lose the benefit of the "as is" provision if the tenant could not have discovered the defect after reasonable inspection. Courts will willingly step in to decide what "should have known" means. That term means what the landlord could have known had it used reasonable care in the ordinary course of managing its property, by conducting prudent inspections of its own property before offering it for sale or lease to others.

Under the version of the shell plus allowance alternative in which the tenant builds, the tenant takes the shell and will construct its own TIs. Subject to certain limitations, the landlord will agree to reimburse the tenant for the TIs, but this reimbursement will have a limitation called the *allowance*. All costs over the allowance are at the tenant's risk. There will also be limitations on the *type* of costs for which the landlord will agree to reimburse the tenant. These limitations are related to whether the improvements will be usable by a successor tenant should, for instance, our example tenant, Pisa Nut, have difficulty paying the rent.

By illustration, so as to take advantage of the unique architectural features of Leaning Towers, Pisa Nut plans to install a pendulum from the balcony of its space to test certain ancient Tuscan theories. The landlord thinks this idea is religious heresy. That's what the landlord says, anyway. Actually, however, the landlord is not bothered by religious, philosophical, or moral principles. The landlord is more worried about how it will fob off the pendulum on the next tenant. Thus, the landlord will refuse to apply the allowance to the item because it is not generic, and thus will not be usable by future tenants. It is a special purpose improvement, limited in utility to this one tenant. This bothers the landlord greatly.

Build To Suit

This is simply a variant of the turnkey method. However, it is generally applied to freestanding buildings, that is, buildings that stand on their own sites and are solely occupied by one tenant. The creditworthiness of the tenant is of great importance in these cases. If Pisa Nut is creditworthy enough, the landlord may even install the pendulum, provided it can be wholly written off over the term of the lease and landlord can get credit from a future buyer for the rent he collects for such an exotic improvement — but more about that in a moment. A build to suit, as all other build-out methods, will either be *prebid* or be subject to a cost ceiling and approval of plans. If it is prebid, the parties put the plans for the improvements out for bid to several contractors before they bind themselves to a lease. In this way they seek assurance that costs can be borne economically within the agreed budgets. A method that subjects the lease to a cost ceiling and approval of plans is covered under Excess Costs, below.

Excess Costs

Under any of the methods previously described, some control of costs is required. Exceptions occur (1) in overbuilt markets, in which a landlord will do almost anything to sign a tenant, including fixing the rent without knowing the cost of the build-out; or (2) in underbuilt markets, particularly retail, in which tenants must agree to pay for everything over the shell cost to get the location. In both cases, the hangover will come later. More typically, the parties will want to reserve rights to opt out of the deal if it becomes too expensive.

Let's suppose that Mr. Galileo, who represents the owners of Leaning Towers, agrees to give Pisa Nut a tenant improvement allowance of $25 per square foot. He thinks that comes to $281,875 (11,275 square feet of usable area X $25). "I'm only going to give you an allowance to spend for the space you've leased," he says. But the representative of Pisa Nut, having read this book, rebuts, "I'm paying rent on 11,887 square feet. The rent includes a return on the build out; therefore, we want an allowance of $297,175."

Galileo, using the rational approach for which he is justly renowned, says, "Go to hell! My deal is to pay you $25 per square foot for improvements, not $26.35 per square foot." Pisa Nut's owner, using the excellent judgment that arises from an existing lease that is about to expire, caves in. The owner of Pisa Nut has violated a seminal principle of negotiation: **Never sit down at the negotiating table without the ability to get up and walk away.** Without this ability, pressed by the *necessity* for reaching an agreement, Pisa Nut will be disemboweled by the tenacious Galileo.

The plans are developed and bid. The bid comes in at $325,000. Who pays how much?

There are as many answers as there are creative people drafting leases. Here is a typical example of how this problem is dealt with in the lease negotiations, that is, before the bids are received.

The allowance of $281,875 is the base cost. The landlord includes that figure in its rental quote. Costs in excess of the allowance will have to be borne by the tenant one way or another.

The tenant may have several choices. First, it could pay the excess sum, in this case $43,125, in cash. All landlords accept cash.

Alternatively, the tenant could agree to an increase in its rent to reflect the landlord's increased investment. This solution presupposes that the landlord will want to amortize the excess costs over the term at an agreed interest rate, postulating that the improvements won't be worth anything at the end of the term.

Let's use 10 percent interest over a 10-year term, or a rental constant of 15.86 percent. That is the annual percentage of the original amount of the overage that the tenant will have to pay back to the landlord over the 10-year term for the landlord to receive all of its expenditure back plus a 10 percent yield. If the rent were increased by 15.86 percent of the excess cost of $43,125, the rent would increase by $6,840 a year, or nearly $70,000 for the term.

The tenant says this method is not fair (as if fairness were important!) because the landlord is borrowing money for the project from its permanent lender based on a 30-year amortization schedule rather than the 10-year term of the lease. The loan constant (that is, the constant annual payment that the landlord pays to its lender for each $1 of original loan amount) for a 30-year payoff is obviously much lower than that for a 10-year payoff because the period to repay the amount of the borrowing is so much longer. The loan constant for a 10 percent loan payable over 30 years is only 10.54 percent — 33 percent lower than that required for the 10-year payoff.

But the tenant is still not finished arguing for a better deal. Pisa Nut's owner points out to the landlord that he knows the landlord is a merchant builder who will sell the shopping center shortly after it is built and operating. In that case, the tenant knows that the landlord can sell the property tomorrow by capitalizing the income at the prevailing rates — say, 9 percent or thereabouts. One capitalizes income by dividing the income by the rate of return sought by the investor. If the additional income can be sold at a 9 percent capitalization rate, all the landlord has to receive is $3,881 a year of the excess costs to break even (0.09 X 43,125 = $3,881). This also means that if the rent is increased by the $6,840 that the landlord is seeking to increase the annual rent for the excess costs, the landlord can sell that increased income to an investor at 9 percent capitalization, or $76,000. Since the excess cost to the landlord is only $43,125, Pisa Nut can see that the landlord will realize a $32,875 profit. Pisa Nut argues that at a 15.86 percent rental constant, the landlord is profiteering on the tenant improvements, which are not supposed to be a profit center. Of course, underlying this argument is the assumption that a buyer will pay for an arbitrarily inflated rent, which, by virtue of the excess costs, may now exceed fair market rental value. As you can see, both Mr. Galileo and Pisa Nut have plenty of room to negotiate a solution.

Moreover, Pisa Nut states that it's not going to agree to be exposed to an unlimited cost overrun. Thus, the parties could agree that if costs exceed the allowance by a certain amount — say, 10 percent — they will negotiate to modify the plans to bring the costs to acceptable levels. If they fail, the tenant should have the right to terminate. Mr. Galileo will object to this because he may not want to lose the tenant. It can become a game of chicken. Pisa Nut may decline to pay any cost excess over ten percent and cancel. Mr. Galileo must then decide whether to (1) absorb the "excess excess" (that is, everything over 110 percent of the allowance, or $310,062) and rescind the cancellation of the lease; or (2) allow the deal to collapse.

Thus, to summarize the key points of construction, we have seen that

1. There is an arrangement to build out the space.

2. There is an amount of money budgeted for that purpose in the lease.

3. If costs exceed this amount, there is a system for recapturing those costs from the tenant.

4. If costs get out of control, the tenant can call a halt to the transaction or redesign the plan.

Delivery

Delivery date is the final critical issue for space to be constructed. We have already observed in our example that Pisa Nut is faced with impending expiration of its existing lease. It cannot operate its business without an office. It is every tenant's nightmare to have its lease expire while still awaiting delivery of new premises.

Landlords are similarly fearful of facing penalties or the loss of a tenant for reasons they cannot control, such as the bankruptcy of the contractor, strikes, or unavailability of special materials. (For example, the local pendulum maker may have gone out of business, causing one to have to be ordered from Transylvania, the gothic pendulum capital of the world.)

Thus, each party will approach this problem with care.

Construction Scheduling Checklist

The most efficient way to deal with delivery issues is to break the tasks down, then establish deadlines and notice provisions for each. This is a complex subject that cannot be covered thoroughly in this book, which is intended to deal with basics. The following, however, is a checklist of the issues to be covered:

1. Drawing preliminary plans

2. Approval of preliminary plans by other party

3. Preparation of working drawings (final plans)

4. Approval

5. Resolving a dispute by terminating the lease, submitting to an independent party, or setting a time limitation for action

6. Putting plans out to bid

7. Evaluating bids

8. Revising plans if necessary to reduce costs

9. Obtaining building permits

10. Commencing construction

11. Notice to tenant in advance of completion

12. Substantial completion (that level of completion sufficient to permit tenant to occupy the premises for its intended purpose)

Size of Premises

Words of Imprecision

Generally speaking, a lease will state the size of the premises in square feet. For example, "approximately 11,275 square feet of usable area" or "11,275 square feet, more or less, of usable area." These qualifying words "approximately" and "more or less" represent a huge hole through which the tenant can lose considerable money. There have been cases holding that when parties could actually see what they were getting, they had no cause for complaint when the property didn't measure what they'd thought, so long as what was delivered was what they'd seen, even if the size was off by as much as one-third! The outcome of such a dispute will, of course, depend on the facts of what each party thought were the elements of the bargain. But one should avoid this dispute at the outset, particularly, as with almost all nonresidential leases, when the rent is a function of the number of square feet in the premises.

The tenant will probably wish to tie its rent obligation to a measurement of the premises when delivered if the deal was originally made on a square-foot basis. Landlords don't especially like this, because they cannot take the lease to their lender for financing if the amount of the rent is uncertain.

Landlord Representations

As a matter of logic, the landlord should be able to make a representation of the size of the space because it owns the premises. This is particularly true when it is new construction and the landlord has architects and engineers running about with tape measures and other gadgets. Mr. Galileo, a man of some technical ability in his own right, to say nothing of being the possessor of an inquiring mind, will probably have had the work of measurement done by consultants. But remember, "as is" is the landlord's marching song.

Measurement

If the landlord can't be convinced to measure, and if the negotiating positions are such as they are in this case, in which the tenant seems to be more motivated than the landlord, then the tenant can reserve the right to have measurements done by a surveyor of its selection. If the figure calculated by the tenant's surveyor is different from the square footage stated in the lease, the tenant will want the rent adjusted. The landlord may take the position that it will not adjust for a minor change in size. The parties will have to negotiate how much money in rent is "minor."

No matter who measures, the figure must be subject to audit or recalculation by the other party's surveyor to prevent the measurement being based solely on the 11-inch foot on the landlord's surveying tape or the 13-inch foot on the tenant's surveying tape. If a serious disagreement ensues, (say, more than five percent) a procedure will have to be included for selecting an independent third party surveyor. Perhaps Copernicus would be interested in the job.

Once the parties agree on the figure, the rent and pro rata share of costs can then be calculated.

Substituted Premises

Retail

Landlord lease forms frequently contain provisions allowing them to move small tenants from one location within a project to another to allow leasing to larger tenants should adjoining space become available. Typically, shopping center or retail tenants will strenuously resist any such demand by landlords because one of the key issues in selecting a retail location within a shopping center is the proximity to other, compatible tenants. Giving a landlord a free right of space transfer means that tenants have waived, in effect, their right to select their own retail merchandise neighbors. The tenant will want to attempt to get its landlord to agree to a number of things before acceding to such a draconian provision. These are detailed in the section on "Logistics of Move."

Office

In an office complex such as Leaning Towers, this problem is less critical for the tenant, although still important. No tenant — whether retail, office, or industrial — should lightly waive its right to select its own location. Location is an essential element for which the tenant has bargained in any real estate negotiation. Although not subject to the compelling reasons that are present in a retail negotiation, in an office situation other critical issues will affect the tenant's reluctance to agree to this provision — for example, views, proximity to noise-producing elements (heating/ventilation/air-conditioning shafts, etc.), proximity to competitors, access to common facilities, and the like. However, the landlord, should it have a sufficient negotiating position, still has the same interest at stake. If there is an office tenant who occupies, say, 5,000 square feet and the landlord has in hand a prospective tenant for 20,000 square feet (two full floors), and further, if the only fully vacant floor is adjacent to the floor occupied by the tenant, then the landlord is faced with the prospect of foregoing a lucrative 20,000 square foot lease because it cannot move its half-floor tenant to another location. This is a bitter pill to swallow.

Logistics of Move

If the tenant agrees or, in the realities of bargaining, is compelled to agree to accept the possibility of a move contrary to its will, then the tenant will want to be sure of a number of things.

1. All costs of the move will be paid by the landlord.

2. The tenant will have the right to approve the new location. If not approved, the tenant should be given a suitable amount of time to locate other premises. The cost of the move to other premises, including any rent differential, should be paid by the landlord. Thus, for example, suppose the tenant is compelled to give up a lease at $1 per square foot that has three years to run and, because there is no other satisfactory location within the building, must pay $1.25 per square foot in a new location. Then not only should the landlord be asked to pay the moving expenses but also the additional 25 cents per square foot of new rental for the period of the overlapping term.

3. The tenant will ask the landlord to pay the costs that the tenant will incur for tenant improvements to the new premises into which it will be moving, at least to the extent that the present improvements were not amortized during the pretermination period. If there were three years to go in an original term of ten years, then the landlord will be asked to pay 30 percent of the new improvement costs because the tenant will, in fact, be receiving the benefit of an additional seven-year term over which to amortize its tenant improvements for the new space.

As an example, let's say the tenant paid $100,000 for TIs to its space when it originally signed the lease seven years ago. It now is compelled to move out three years early. Thus, it has not amortized $30,000 of its improvements. Because of inflation, the cost of the TIs for its new premises will be $150,000. The tenant should attempt to collect

$45,000 (30 percent of $150,000) from the old landlord to apply to its improvements of $150,000 in the new premises because the tenant would not have had to pay these expenses if the landlord hadn't relocated the tenant to obtain a more attractive prospect. If, however, the tenant is able to find suitable premises elsewhere within Leaning Towers, then the situation is different. In such cases, all costs for improvements similar to those in the tenant's original premises should be paid by the landlord, and the rent should be identical to that under the current lease. Thus, it is advantageous for the tenant to find acceptable premises within Leaning Towers.

Expansion Rights

Desirable tenants with negotiating strength may sometimes be able to bargain for the right to expand their premises within the complex at a future date. This is a proposition fraught with danger for the landlord. These situations typically arise in a tenant's market, in which landlords are competing strenuously for relatively few available tenants and the tenant is a growing company that anticipates requiring additional space during the course of its lease term.

Option To Expand

There are a number of ways to accommodate such a requirement. The least desirable from the landlord's standpoint is the option to expand. Under this scheme, the tenant has the same rights to expand its space as it has to extend the term (see Chapter 4). On specified notice to the landlord, the tenant has the right to demand that additional space adjacent to its current premises be made available for its use.

If the tenant has paid the original improvement costs, then the lease adjustment required at the time of the exercise of the expansion right is relatively simple. All that has to be done is change the legal description and the rent. The tenant's obligations for construction are already stated in the existing lease.

The difficulty for the landlord is obvious. It must keep that space available and vacant until the tenant makes up its corporate mind whether it will exercise the option or not. Accordingly, the landlord will want to seek numerous protections. The landlord may seek a period of time following commencement of the original lease during which the tenant cannot exercise the option to expand (for example, five years during which the space could be leased by the landlord to others, followed by a one-year window period during which the tenant could exercise its right to expand). In that way the landlord could have an opportunity to rent the option space for a short term. Alternatively, a period of time might be specified after which the option could not be exercised. Thus, for example, the landlord might be willing to take the rental loss for the expansion premises for a period of two years, after which the tenant would lose its option and the landlord would be free to lease the premises. In a stronger landlord's market, the landlord might even demand some partial rent for premises that are held available for the tenant. This arrangement, however, will limit the landlord's ability to lease the premises, because only tenants wishing to lease on a month-to-month basis will be prospects.

If the landlord is to perform the improvements, then more detailed arrangements must be made, for both the construction itself and paying the cost of that construction. If, for example, the tenant receives an initial allowance of $25 per square foot for improvements and does not exercise its option for five years, then is the tenant to receive the same $25 allowance five years later for the expansion space? Surely the costs for TIs will be more than $25, even if the improvements are identical. A formula could be developed that ties the original allowance into an index, but frequently, the parties do not wish to use a consumer price index adjustment, fearing that it will not accurately reflect the trend of construction costs. However, there are construction indexes available for this purpose.

Another issue is rent. If the option to expand is good for as long as five years, the landlord surely will feel that the value of the space will increase dramatically in that period. If the tenant has sufficient negotiating power to get the option to expand in the first place, it may be able to put a cap on the rent at which the option will be exercised. If this happens, the landlord will, of course, want to cap the construction cost obligation also. A more typical method of dealing with this problem is to use a fair market value adjustment (see Chapter 5).

Right of First Refusal

A second way to deal with a tenant's expansion requirements is to use a *right of first refusal*. Under this type of provision, the landlord is free to attempt to lease the space as quickly as possible. When an agreement is reached with a prospective tenant, however, the landlord then must disclose that agreement to the tenant who owns the right of first refusal. That tenant then has a period of time in which to either agree to accept the same terms the landlord has worked out with the prospective tenant or waive its rights to lease the adjoining space.

Any landlord would be highly reluctant to agree to such an encumbrance on his right to lease. The major difficulty is that anyone who gives another party a right of first refusal on property immediately clouds title to that property, whether it be a right of first refusal for sale or, as in this case, a right of first refusal for lease. If you were a prospective tenant interested in the space, especially if plenty of space were available in the marketplace, would you be willing to spend 30 or 60 days of your time negotiating a transaction and developing a space plan if you felt that all you were doing was setting up your proposal to be knocked off by the adjoining tenant? The likelihood is that you would not be willing to do so unless the landlord agreed to bear all of your expenses. Even then, you might not be willing to do so because you would waste valuable time that could be used to locate space that is, in fact, available for lease.

One way a landlord can reduce the problems inherent in a right of first refusal is to activate the first refusal right very early in negotiations with a prospective tenant instead of waiting until agreement has been reached. For example, instead of waiting until a lease is signed and a space plan drawn, the parties could agree that the present tenant's right of first refusal would commence on the execution of a letter of intent. On presentation of a letter of intent to the existing tenant, that tenant would have to agree to match those terms and incorporate them within its existing lease. This puts the prospective tenant at much less risk because letters of intent are frequently drafted after a limited expenditure of time by the prospective tenant. Therefore, all that is needed is a letter stating the essential terms of rent, term, tenant improvement allowance, options (if any), and any other specific business points. If the existing tenant agrees to those particular business points, they would be adopted for the new space, whereas all other terms of the existing lease would be as currently written.

A second protection for the landlord is a limitation on the amount of time allowed the existing tenant to exercise the right of first refusal. The shorter the period of time, the less encumbrance on the landlord's rights. Five business days favors the landlord; 10 or 15 days is probably evenhanded. Anything over 30 days is a severe disability for the landlord because a prospective tenant will not want to delay its space search for that long a time.

Right of First Offer

Of all types of expansion rights, this is the least evil from the landlord's standpoint. This usually applies when a tenant (let's say Tenant A) wishes to reserve the right to lease space that adjoins its own, that is presently leased to Tenant B. Tenant A wants the first opportunity to lease the adjoining space when and if it becomes available. If the landlord agrees to such a provision, it will not want to be compelled to offer the space to Tenant A before it offers the space to or enters into negotiations with existing Tenant B. A difficult situation can develop if Tenant A has a right of first offer on the space of adjoining Tenant B. For example, when Tenant B's lease expires, the landlord and Tenant B can be negotiating an extension, only to discover that they cannot extend Tenant B's lease term without giving first opportunity to lease the space to adjoining Tenant A. This would be poor practice on the part of the landlord and an unfortunate situation for existing Tenant B. Therefore, existing tenants and even, if possible, other adjoining tenants should be excluded from the terms of the right of first offer.

Under the right of first offer, when space becomes available, or is to become available, the landlord is obligated to make a good faith proposal to lease to Tenant A, who has bargained for this right, stating the essential terms and conditions under which it proposes to offer the space to others for lease. Tenant A then has a period of time in which to agree to lease the space on those terms and conditions. If it fails to do so, the landlord may then proceed to market the space as best it can. Suppose the landlord is unable to obtain the terms and conditions that it originally offered to tenant A, but has to settle for something less. Under the provisions of a right of first offer (unlike those under a right of first refusal) the landlord has no obligation to go back to Tenant A to give A an opportunity to match the terms of the final offer.

Let's look at an example. On expiration of an existing lease, the landlord tells Tenant A that it will offer the space for lease at $1 per square foot for ten years with consumer price index adjustments every three years and a tenant improvement allowance of $25 per square foot. Tenant A refuses these terms, whereupon the landlord attempts to market the space. After several months of failure, the landlord finally receives a proposal, which it is prepared to accept, for rental of 90 cents per square foot with a $30 per square foot tenant improvement allowance and consumer price index adjustments every five years. Under a right of first refusal, the landlord would be obligated to go back to Tenant A to offer Tenant A an opportunity to match the terms that the landlord finally obtained. However, under a right of first offer, so long as the original first offer proposal was made in good faith, the landlord would have no such obligation. Tenant A with the right of first offer would simply be out of luck. As a practical matter, under the facts stated above, Tenant A probably would have made a counterproposal that could have been the subject of a fruitful negotiation; provided, of course, that the landlord desired to undertake further leasing with that tenant.

CHAPTER 3
Use

The use clause provides the landlord with a means for controlling the activities conducted upon its property. Smart, involved landlords (as opposed to rent collectors) take a rigorous interest in the purposes for which their tenants are using their property. You wouldn't want to lend your car to someone only to find that he or she was entering it in a demolition derby or ferrying contraband to and from Central America or carrying service equipment for dirt bikes. Landlords have similar interests.

Office and Industrial

The use provision is of relatively little importance in office and industrial leases. Unless there are competitive or security problems to be dealt with, the clause should be left to the attorneys to pick nits at your expense.

Shopping Centers

Shopping center or other retail leases are another matter. The use clause is critical to the control of the merchandise mix of the integrated retail operation that constitutes the project. In strip centers (supermarket, drugstore, and shops), the use clause is moderately important because ownership of these centers is primarily real estate driven. That is to say that the location of the real estate is a prime driver of value. In community-sized centers (200,000 square feet or more, including, generally, a junior department or off-price store), the clause becomes increasingly important as more discretionary merchandise is sold. For regional shopping centers (generally consisting of two to five department stores and having a gross leasable area in the one-million-square-foot range), the use clause is critical because regionals are more of a merchandise-driven business, meaning that the prime driver of value is the quality of the merchants.

Before we get into the factors to consider in negotiating a use clause, a word should be said about regional center landlords. As a group they represent the most unbending, irrational, power-wielding negotiators of any commercial landlords. They rank right along with New York office building owners as purveyors of the unconscionable. But, as in many cases in which one side acts imperiously, there may be a reason for it, other than the occasional raw demonstration of power. As someone who has negotiated on behalf of, as well as against, regional shopping center landlords, I can attest to the verity of this fact.

In the case of the regional center:

• There are only a few in a given region;

• They take an enormous amount of time and money to build; and

• Retailers often need to be in that particular center if they want to be represented in that market area.

Regional shopping center owners feel that they need to maintain the strictest control over their tenants because they have gone through a lengthy development process fraught with risk to get the center built. While doing so, they have hocked themselves to the teeth to their lenders, given away the department store sites, and paid cash to department store operators to attract them. For these reasons, the shops represent do or die for the landlord. Regionals are financially viable only if the shops can deliver the rent by making sales. Thus, the landlords take what may be seen as a psychotic interest in exactly what merchandise is being sold from which location in the mall.

This does not excuse them from culpability for some other egregious lease language that they will indelicately jam down the throats of tenants. However, at least one can understand their sensitivity, even while they seem impervious to any idea of fairness or reason.

Restrictions on Use

For the reasons just mentioned, and others that we will discuss later, landlords want to restrict the permitted use of the premises as narrowly as possible. The tenant, on the other hand, wants to make the clause as broad as possible so it will be able to make alterations to its merchandise lines or assign the lease to another party should it be unsuccessful and wish to reduce its liability.

Consider what might happen if a cookware shop has a use clause (see Drafting the Use Clause, below) restricting it to the sale of cookware. Let's take as an example a chain called Got Woks.

The chain consists of 40 stores located in malls around the country, all having approximately the same use restriction. The chain has a net worth of $20 million. Along comes an offer from Neck to Toe Corporation to buy the chain for $30 million. But Neck to Toe also sells table linens. Now there's a $10 million profit in jeopardy because Got Woks must obtain lease amendments from 40 landlords to obtain a use clause that will permit the sale of table linens. The landlords, I promise, will make a material dent in the $10 million profit, if they are willing to permit the transfer at all (see Chapter 11, Assignment and Subletting).

Percentage Rent

Another reason landlords will want to restrict the tenant's use of the premis es is to maintain control over percentage rent rates (see Chapter 5). Different retail businesses pay varying percentages of gross sales as additional rent, depending on profit margins that are general for the particular type of business. For example, a full-price apparel store might pay six percent of gross sales as percentage rent, whereas an off-price apparel store would pay two percent or three percent. A furniture store might pay eight percent to ten percent of gross sales. Now let's say that an off-pricer wants to go out of business. It finds a full-price furniture store prepared to take over the lease. If the landlord is not able to prevent this, it will be faced with never realizing percentage rent from this store because a low-volume, high-profit-margin operation (furniture) will occupy space under a lease with a percentage rent factor intended for a high-volume, low-profit-margin retailer (off-price apparel).

Conflicts and Competition Within the Center

Shopping center landlords also maintain control of conflicts or outright competition within a center by restricting the uses permissable under the terms of the leases. Consider the case of Got Woks, once again. Got Woks (premerger) is doing tremendous volume. As a result, it has been making sizable percentage rent payments to the landlord for several years. An arch competitor, Pots 'n Things, is eyeing a location in the shopping center that is available for sublease and that is close to Got Woks. In the absence of landlord controls, good old cutthroat competition would result in two tenants sharing business that previously only one had, resulting in the immediate loss to the landlord of its theretofore dependable percentage rent from Got Woks. There is only a certain volume of specialty cookware business that can be expected at the shopping center. If two tenants share it, the original tenant will be knocked out of the percentage-rent-paying category. Tenants have an awe-inspiring confidence that they can outsell and outmerchandise their competition. This is a confidence landlords do not share, with understandable good sense.

Frequently, a landlord, to attract a prized tenant, grants that tenant the exclusive right to sell certain merchandise in the shopping center. Unless the landlord controls all uses within the center, it may risk a violation of the exclusive right if another tenant, over whom it has inadequate control, starts selling the proscribed merchandise. For example, suppose the landlord lands a high-rent-paying liquor store on the promise of an exclusive right to sell alcoholic beverages in the shopping center. However, two years later, the shopping center's supermarket changes its previous "no alcohol" policy and commences to sell liquor. Now, not only will the landlord lose its liquor store percentage rent but it also may gain a lawsuit from the liquor store operator for promising what it cannot deliver. Exclusives also may give rise to problems with antitrust laws; but that's a subject too advanced for this discussion.

Drafting the Use Clause

The wisest policy for a landlord is to utilize the narrowest possible use language with a statement banning any other uses. For example, "The retail sale of quality cookware at upper price lines and for no other purpose whatsoever."

The favored language for a tenant would be the broadest possible, with use specified in terms of purpose or intent. For example, "The parties intend that the premises be used for the retail sale of kitchenware." Because courts interpret such clauses as being permissive rather than restrictive, in effect, this is not a restriction at all.

Range of Restrictions

What follows is a selection of use clauses ranging from the most restrictive (most favored by landlords) to the least restrictive (most favored by tenants).

1. *Very Specific:* "For retail sale of quality cookware at upper price lines and for no other purpose."

2. *Slightly less specific:* "The retail sale of cookware and for no other purpose."

3. *A right to change the use with landlord's consent:* "The retail sale of cookware and for no other purpose without the landlord's consent first had and obtained in landlord's sole and absolute discretion." In some states there is a question whether the landlord would have to act in good faith with the qualification "absolute discretion."

4. *Landlord's consent — less definite:* "The retail sale of cookware and for no other purpose without the landlord's prior written consent." There is an argument in many states, under the rules of good faith and commercial reasonableness as applied to real estate leases, that seems to indicate a court would hold the landlord to a standard of reasonableness as to any change in use. This is a considerable advantage to a tenant. In those states in which the rule of commercial reasonableness applies, a request by the landlord for more money has been held to be unreasonable on its face.

5. *A right to change the use:* "The retail sale of cookware and for no other purpose without the landlord's prior written consent, which shall not be unreasonably withheld."

6. *Tenant allowed to alter its merchandise:* "The retail sale of cookware and such other merchandise as the tenant carries in its other stores in the State of _____ from time to time and for no other use without the landlord's prior written consent, which shall not be unreasonably withheld."

7. *Nonrestrictive:* "The parties intend that the premises be used for the retail sale of cookware. Tenant covenants that it shall not use the premises at any time for nonretail purposes except as may be ancillary to the use of the premises as a retail store."

Nonselling Purposes

In those retail leases in which the landlord expects to receive percentage rent, the landlord will want to restrict the amount of area that the tenant devotes to nonselling purposes. For example, if the landlord is leasing the premises based on an expected volume per square foot, it would be greatly disappointed to find out that 40 percent of the premises is to be devoted to the regional offices for the tenant's other stores in the chain or for a storage area to supply inventory for other stores in the chain. Thus, some limitation on the amount of square footage that can be devoted to nonselling purposes would be included in the lease.

Hazardous Uses

It is important to include language restricting uses that would present a hazard to other tenants in the shopping center, increase the rate of insurance, or present a threat of air, soil, or water contamination.

Miscellaneous Restrictions

Other restrictions generally included in the use clause are nuisance, noise levels, floor loads (particularly in uses where there is a threat of heavy equipment or machinery vibrations), distribution of handbills in the common areas, and the like.

CHAPTER 4
Term

It is simple to reach an agreement concerning the length of a lease term. The fun is in trying to figure out when the term begins, when it ends, and if there are any rights to extend or renew.

Beginning the Term

Existing Tenants

Often the landlord and tenant enter into lease arrangements while an existing tenant is still in occupancy. All is well *nearly* all the time. Nearly. There are always risks, however, when one's promises are based on reliance on a third party, such as the existing tenant. Be fairly warned that if the existing tenant (let's call the tenant "Who me?") has attempted to negotiate to extend its term, there is an excellent possibility that you will have a recalcitrant occupant on your hands. "Who me?" runs great risk of a substantial damage claim for failing to vacate as required by the lease. However, that will not prevent "Who me?" from staying put, to everybody's detriment, if it can show that there had been negotiations with the landlord, that the negotiations had dragged on as a result of the tenant's being misled by the landlord or that its position was jeopardized by the landlord's behavior. "Who me?" is sure to make one or more of these claims whether it can prove them or not, especially if the new tenant is a competitor.

For these reasons most leases contain language that exonerates the landlord for delays in commencement of the term in the event the landlord is unable to deliver possession because the premises are not available.

Such language does not help a tenant who must have premises available by a certain date. Sooner or later that tenant has to have some place to move to. If not, a right of termination is needed. Even this is not an adequate solution to a tenant who must wait around for premises it thought would be available, only to find that it faces a substantial delay.

Construction

Construction is, without a doubt, the most difficult problem one faces in negotiating provisions with respect to term. The landlord and the tenant have differing objectives.

Landlord's Objective

The landlord wants to start the term as soon as possible. Frequently the landlord seeks to have the term commence, even if the rent doesn't. Such an arrangement is generally called a *preliminary term* or some similar name. During the preliminary term, the lease obligation is in force without, however, the obligation to pay rent. Even though the rent does not begin, there are advantages to the landlord in commencing the term early. Such obligations as insurance, indemnity, and the like, go into effect. Most important, use of this preliminary term often can shift the burden of delayed construction to the tenant, even if the landlord is performing the construction work. We'll discuss this in more detail in Remedies for Late Delivery.

Tenant's Objectives

Commencing Business — The tenant has a more serious problem than the landlord. All the landlord wants to do is collect rent. The tenant has to conduct its business. Therefore, the tenant's principal objective is to gain occupancy by a definite time, so it can meet its seasonal opening requirements.

Selling Seasons — Let us say, for example, that there is a retail apparel chain called Rags to Witches, which, in addition to a normal complement of women's apparel, carries special lines in black attire and a separate pumpkin pie department. Like most apparel chains, Rags to Witches does approximately 25 percent of its volume and earns nearly all its annual profits during the Christmas season. In its particular case, as you might expect, the Christmas season starts on October 20. This date is critical to its opening.

The Moving Train — One must bear in mind that although the landlord has a construction obligation to meet after signing the lease but before the opening of the store, the tenant also has a legion of tasks to accomplish, all of which need adequate lead time. These include ordering merchandise, ordering furniture and fixtures, hiring personnel, placing advertising, arranging promotions and similar preopening tasks. To accomplish all of these tasks in a timely fashion to be ready for the opening date in late October, the lease must be executed in April.

On execution of the lease, events are put in motion that can be likened to a moving train. The lease is executed for premises in California. Rags to Witches executives immediately telephone their buyers in New York, who place orders for merchandise suitable for the Christmas season. The merchandise is to be processed in two of New York City's largest boroughs, Hong Kong and Kuala Lumpur.

The mythical train starts out from New York in May or, at the latest, June. Along the way other tasks and persons climb aboard the train. Personnel must be hired, black hats must be ordered for the salespeople, brooms must be ordered for the opening day sale, telephones installed, supplies, furniture, fixtures, advertising placed, promotions organized.

Even for office and industrial tenants, movers must be organized, personnel replaced if the distance from the old location is substantial, stationery printed and the like. The moving train gathers speed as it crosses the continent. It will arrive at the leased premises on approximately October 1, to allow the tenant time to install fixtures, as well as to stock and staff the premises. If the premises are not delivered as scheduled, there is going to be a train crash. Did you ever try to sell pumpkins in June? Did you ever try to open a store on December 23? Who is going to pay all those salaries? What is going to happen to the out-of-season merchandise? As you can see, serious problems will arise. How can we deal with these issues?

When the Landlord Constructs the Premises

Commencement of Construction

What is *commencement of construction*? This issue is no different from everything else in life: everybody has an opinion. It is best to reduce these opinions to written specifics. For example, if a new building is to be constructed, perhaps the excavation of the foundation or pouring the foundation slab could constitute the definition of commencement. If it is an existing building and interior construction is all that is required, then perhaps it is the day on which the general contractor places trades people on the premises for the purpose of commencing work under the terms of the contract.

The tenant will want to place provisions in a lease requiring the landlord to commence construction by a certain date. The landlord's view is that *completion* of construction is the critical issue. Thus, it will not want to be under compulsion to commence on any particular date. However, the tenant will be placed in serious jeopardy if the premises are not ready when promised.

This jeopardy will be reduced, to the benefit of all parties, if the tenant receives advance notice that the premises won't be ready so it can reduce its commitment. Suppose that Rags to Witches intends to take possession for fixturing on October 1. To make that possible, the landlord needs 120 days of construction time (or 180 or 240, depending on whether the building has to be built or remodeled). Therefore, construction must commence by June 1. If the tenant has that much advance notice of the landlord's inability to deliver, it can take steps to reduce the losses it will suffer. It can cancel orders, reroute merchandise, abort the hiring of personnel, and take other similar actions.

There is much to be done before construction can commence. We have seen (in Chapter 2) that construction plans and specifications must be agreed on; put out to bid to keep prices within budget; and submitted to the appropriate governmental agency for building permits, often the most time-consuming procedure of all. Delays in any of these procedures can threaten the promised completion date.

For example, Rags to Witches may think that pumpkins containing lit candles would add a nice touch to its opening day decor. The code requirement for special materials required to house these pumpkins may be a surprise to the parties. This surprise may require alterations to the plans and a delay in issuance of the permits. The extra cost involved may cause the construction costs to soar substantially *above* the budget. The landlord and the tenant will have to meet with the architects to attempt to effect cost reductions elsewhere to bring the project in at acceptable cost levels.

A delay in commencement of construction, unless met with a willingness to incur overtime, can delay completion and cause the tenant to miss a selling season and, perhaps, to elect to forgo the deal. For these reasons the tenant wants to know as soon as possible, and constantly throughout the construction process, if the landlord is adhering to the schedule. The first test is commencement of construction.

Completion of Construction

This is the critical date. What is completion? Lawyers sometimes use the term *substantial completion*. Generally this means the date on which completion has been accomplished to a sufficient degree to allow the tenant to commence its business. In other words, only a minor amount of work remains to be done; if necessary, Rags to Witches could open the store, even though the landlord is not entirely finished. The tenant will want to be sure that its obligations under the lease do not commence until it can truly operate its business.

One potential oversight is the common areas. If the Rags to Witches premises is completed sufficiently to permit the installation of its fixtures and commencement of business, but the parking area is not paved, Rags is not going to get many customers. If Pisa Nut's premises on the fifth floor of Leaning Towers are all completed and ready for occupancy, but the passenger elevators have not been placed in service, that is not going to be an exciting prospect.

Unacceptable Delivery Periods

Frequently there are certain periods of the year during which a tenant will not want to move or open its business. In a retail context, the Christmas season is one obvious time. If a tenant needs 30 days to prepare its store after substantial completion by the landlord, and if that tenant needs to be open by October 20, then the tenant is going to refuse delivery of the premises between October 1 and, say, January 15 (assuming that February 15 is the next satisfactory opening date). If the tenant were to take delivery within that period it would miss a substantial part of the season on which it depends so much.

In the office context, an example could be an accounting firm named Goodby, Oversight, Offtrack, and Feckless, a professional corporation ("GOOF," for short). GOOF may refuse to take new premises between January 1 and April 15, a period during which a substantial part of its tax practice commands the time of all personnel in the firm from the lowliest clerk to the senior partner.

Thus, the negotiators for the tenant will want to proscribe certain periods during which they are not obligated to accept possession from the landlord. The landlord, on the other hand, will vigorously strive to narrow these periods as much as possible. It may say to Rags to Witches that it will not take the penalty of delayed rent after expending the time and money to get the store constructed, just because the October 31 date is missed.

First, the landlord can suggest that the tenant put its fixture installers on the premises while the landlord's construction workers are still there. The two groups of workers can then work together at the end of the construction period, thus narrowing the 30-day fixture-installation period. Further, the landlord will state that even if October 20 is missed, there is still the customary Christmas season available, which usually doesn't start until approximately Thanksgiving Day (says the landlord). Landlords tend to have a constricted view of the Christmas season because theirs lasts all year long, rent checks being the same on June 1 as they are on December 1.

Force Majeure — Once the landlord commences construction, numerous events outside the landlord's control can occur to cause delays. The usual list includes strikes, casualty (fire, earthquake), bad weather, and other events over which the landlord has no control. The list can be quite lengthy. The landlord says, "I may have promised you October 1 but it's not my fault that the carpenters went on strike on August 1 for two weeks." It will want to extend the October 1 promised completion date to October 15 to allow for the strike period. The tenant's view is that Christmas season is Christmas season no matter what happens.

This is a question of allocation of risk to be negotiated between the parties on the basis of 10 percent reason and 90 percent negotiating strength. The tenant will insist that if it must concede some amount of *force majeure* delay, as it surely will, that it will not abide an unlimited delay. Therefore, Rags to Witches will insist that it have some remedy, notwithstanding fault, if the delay extends beyond October 28.

GOOF has a similar problem if its lease on its existing premises is about to expire. No matter what the reason, GOOF must move before its lease expires. If its space is not available, even if there have been 40 days and nights of rain, it is going to be subject to severe problems. It will have to locate emergency space or be subject to a substantial damage claim from its existing landlord.

A form of delay for which the landlord will insist it be given the benefit, no matter how long it takes, are delays caused by the tenant. Such delays customarily arise out of change orders required by the tenant. Further, the landlord will insist that this time be deducted from the actual completion date in calculating the date on which rent commences. For example, if the landlord is delayed 30 days by tenant change orders and delivers the premises 30 days late, then rent would start on the date it would have started had there been no delay caused by the tenant.

Remedies for Late Delivery

Rollover Date

The so-called "rollover" is generally applicable only to retail tenants, although it could also be obtained for GOOF. Under this remedy the tenant insists that if the premises are not delivered by the October 1 promised date, it need not accept the premises or commence rent until the next acceptable period (say March 1, because no retailer likes to be open in January or February). Thus, the landlord loses three months' rent on premises that it has completed and fully paid for. But the tenant has bargained in advance not to be compelled to open its business too late for its main merchandising season. Similarly, if GOOF's space cannot be delivered by December 15, GOOF would rather wait until May 1 than move during tax season.

Termination by Tenant

This is a drastic remedy. If the landlord has invested its money in the premises, particularly if there is anything in the construction that is unique to a particular tenant, the landlord will not permit lease termination except under the most exigent circumstances. The landlord's argument is that having purchased the improvements needed by the tenant, it must not be left without a source of repayment unless the degree of its negligence borders on the wanton. However, tenants in a good negotiating position should be able to get some termination right, even if delivery is only slightly later than the promised date, and certainly if it is substantially delayed.

Damages

Because the tenant will suffer the aforementioned train crash if the premises are not ready, it will incur substantial losses and will want to be made whole, if possible. The landlord, on the other hand, does not want to be responsible for anything that happens if it has made a good faith effort to meet its obligation. One method of bridging this gap is to decide on a fixed sum payable to the tenant if the landlord fails to meet its delivery date obligation. This is referred to as *liquidated damages*. The question is whether a fixed sum can be agreed on. Frequently it is a function of some multiplier of the agreed rent.

Temporary Quarters

A variant on the damages issue is the provision of temporary quarters to an office tenant whose lease is expiring. At some point, when it becomes plain that the promised completion date will not be met, the tenant may place the landlord under the burden of providing temporary quarters or, at the very least, paying for the move to the temporary quarters for a temporary period. Frequently tenants will also attempt to get landlords to pay for the move from the temporary quarters to the new space; however, this has the suspicious appearance of a double dip because the tenant must move at least once, even if everything goes according to plan.

Tenant Construction

When the tenant has agreed to construct its own premises, generally (but not always) subject to reimbursement of an allowance by the landlord, many of the issues described above are avoided because the speed of construction is within the control of the tenant. Accordingly, the risk of delivery will have been transferred to the tenant, so long as the landlord has delivered the space ready for either demolition or commencement of construction, in a timely fashion and free of any previous occupancy. The only issue after delivery of the space ready for construction (in a structurally sound condition with all utilities in place) is completion of the common areas.

End of Term

Generally speaking (and nearly always in the case of office and industrial leases), it is a matter of simple arithmetic to calculate the end of the term once the beginning of the term is established. As a small concession to simplicity many parties choose to state that the term ends on the last day of a month by stating that if the lease term commences on other than the first day of any month, that partial month is not counted in computing the term. Thus, if there is a ten-year term that commences on October 15, 2001, it will end on October 31, 2011. In this way the first 15 days are not included in the term for purposes of calculating the length of the term.

Using the example I have just given, and relating it to Rags to Witches, you can immediately see a problem for the tenant. The term will end 15 days before the witching season! There are big bucks to be made during the witching season. For this reason Rags to Witches negotiators will want to specify that the lease term will end on January 31 following the expiration of ten years. In this way it will get the full benefit of the witching and Christmas seasons in its final year. The extra 30 days is needed just to arrange an orderly evacuation of the store.

The landlord feels that the space will lose its attraction for a new retail tenant if it can't deliver the premises to that successor tenant for that Christmas season. Thus the landlord is not without risk in this situation even though, at least in theory, the space will be occupied by a rent-paying, sales-producing tenant. There is some protection available to the landlord in such circumstances. It could, for example, give the tenant the right to extend its occupancy for this *tail* period only if tenant had been paying percentage rent during the previous three lease years.

Options to Extend the Term

Although options to extend the term of the lease are customary, they are of no advantage to a landlord, other than as a marketing necessity to attract tenants. Because an option is a grant of a right to the tenant, to be exercised, if at all, at a later date in the tenant's sole judgment, the landlord cannot know whether the lease term will be extended or not. Therefore, the additional term does not bind the tenant and cannot be the basis for financing; and the potential rental stream cannot be sold.

For the tenant, on the other hand, the opposite is true. Options contain all of the promised delights of paradise. The tenant does what it chooses with another person's property without consulting the owner of that property. If the tenant is doing well at the location, it exercises its option and stays. If not, it leaves. If it is not doing well, but the space is worth more than the lease rent, the tenant simply makes some money on the option. But there are qualifications to this statement, as we shall see.

Option Provisions Other than Rent

To mitigate the effects of this unhappy provision for the landlord, several precautions will be taken.

Notice

Landlords will insist on adequate advance notice from tenants about whether the option will be exercised. With the requirement for notice, the landlord can make provision for releasing the space if the tenant elects not to exercise the option. In a dead market, if the tenant elects to exercise, the landlord may want to plan to hire a nightclub for a party for family and friends. In an overheated market, the landlord might consider jumping off a bridge if the tenant elects to exercise.

Occasionally a tenant may forget about its option until a date after the date on which it was required to give notice. In some circumstances, and in some states, the tenant will be allowed such an inadvertence if the landlord has not been injured as a result. This is the "What the hell" legal theory: "Aw shucks, just because the contract says 90 days' notice doesn't really mean that — what the hell!" Courts in some states ignore contract language with impunity. But in other states, in which contract language is given weight by the courts, particularly if the mistake is egregious, the tenant will be out of luck.

A reminder to exercise an option five or ten years after the original lease was executed can easily be misplaced or mislaid by a clerk.

Therefore, unless a careful and organized system is in place, tenants will want to use care to ensure that they don't forfeit their option rights accidentally. Some tenants will insist on a provision in the lease stating that the option right will not be considered to have lapsed until the landlord notifies the tenant that the time period is about to expire. Naturally enough, landlords already stung by having had to grant the option in the first place don't want to be charged with the task of reminding the tenant that it holds a club with which to beat the landlord over the head. A contractual obligation to be a masochist may be depraved, but is not illegal, yet.

Options Personal

The landlord should try to restrict the assignability of the option. (For assignment provisions in general, see Chapter 11.) The landlord will want to take the position that it made this deal with Rags to Witches in preference to other tenants and that it would not have agreed to do so with some unspecified tenant. Because Rags is financially obligated for the base term to the lease, the parties have effectively agreed to assignability of the base term. However, Rags is not obligated for the option term until it exercises, and the landlord may be unwilling to permit assignment of the option term. The landlord will argue that the options are personal to the tenant that originally executed the lease and are not transferable along with assignment of the lease to a third party. My guess is that the landlord's chances for success in obtaining this provision are one in ten in a balanced market.

Option Provisions Involving Rent

This is by far the most important element of the option provision. There are three primary methods for establishing the rent during the option term.

Fixed Increases

The parties may agree to an absolute amount of rent payable during the option term. The parties may calculate this sum by assuming an increase in the value of the space over the initial term. For example, suppose the rent is $10,000 a month, and the parties are willing to assume a five percent per year increase as being within the tenant's planning guidelines and the landlord's estimate of the risk it is willing to take on price. Then the rent after five years (assuming the initial term to have been five years) will increase to $12,500 a month — unless the parties compound the five percent increases, in which event the rent will be $12,763. The fixed increase method of calculation is generally considered to be favorable to the tenant because it sets a firm amount to be paid and permits accurate budgeting. It is less favorable for the landlord because the ceiling on the tenant's expense translates reciprocally into a ceiling on the landlord's income.

Cost-of-Living Adjustment

This method provides that the rent will be calculated at the time the option period commences based on the change in some easily ascertainable index, for example, the Consumer Price Index or the Wholesale Price Index, if the tenant's business is more truly related to wholesale rather than to retail values. The index selected, whichever one it happens to be, is compared with the index at commencement of the term. One suggestion for simplicity and avoidance of arguments is to agree upon the exact index number that will be the *base* for all future calculations. For example, "The Base Index is agreed to be 300 at commencement of the term." The change is translated to a proportionate change in the rent. The object is to preserve the purchasing power of the rental dollar collected by the landlord. This has nothing to do with market values. It has to do with attempting to give to the landlord an amount of money that will purchase the same basket of goods that the rent purchased at commencement of the term. As far as the landlord is concerned, it is a purely defensive device.

The tenant, one can argue, has now lost the predictability of its rent because runaway inflation can multiply the rent obligation if the option is exercised. Thus, there are a number of variants on the pure cost of living index. Some of these can be described by use of illustrations.

- Cost of living not to exceed five percent per annum;

- Cost of living not to exceed eight percent per annum compounded, but not less than two percent per annum compounded (the landlord will attempt to get this minimum increase if it is going to bargain away a ceiling on the amount it can receive);

- Seventy percent of the change in the cost of living (the tenant attempts to limit the unlimited nature of the increase by agreeing to pay only a portion of the change in the cost of living); or

- Any of the above, provided, however, that the rent shall not decrease from the rent previously in effect. In this case the landlord is not willing to take the risk of a deflation, that is to say, a reduction in rent as a result of a decline in the index. The landlord's argument is that the property cannot be financed if the lender sees that a rental decrease is possible. No lender will base its loan on an income stream that can diminish by contract.

Another variant on this theme is to compute the change in the cost of living on an annual basis, rather than over the period of the initial term in order to eliminate decreases in any single year of the initial term. For example, suppose the provision states that the rent change is to be computed annually. If the cost of living increases by 10 percent per annum (for simplicity) for the first three years, decreases by 10 percent in the fourth year and doesn't change in the fifth year, then, under a cumulative computation (forget compounding for the moment) the landlord would be entitled to a 20 percent increase. (See Table 4.1, Column A.) If, however, the provision states that the computation is to be made annually but not placed into effect until exercise of the option, and that in no event would the rent computed hypothetically for each year decrease below that for the preceding year, then the parties would be counting only the increases. Therefore, the rent would increase by 30 percent because decreases are ignored (see Table 4.1, Column B).

Table 4.1 *Increase (Decrease) in Consumer Price Index*		
Year	**A**	**B**
1	10%	10%
2	10%	10%
3	10%	10%
4	(10%)	—
5	—	—
Total	**20%**	**30%**

Fair Market Value

The fair market value method of adjustment is the one that will reduce the landlord's risk the most because, theoretically at least, rent will be the same as if the space were placed on the open market and leased to a third party. Thus, the most offensive element of the option provision (to the landlord) is considerably mitigated; at least the landlord will receive a fair market rent and not be obligated to settle for a bargain transaction.

There are numerous ways of computing fair market value. They revolve around appraisal, arbitration or, in some cases, the nebulous admonition to "negotiate." Courts may try to make the parties place a market value on the property, even if proper procedures for doing so have not been placed in the lease. Courts are not reluctant to establish a market value. It is important that the lease provide specific procedures for establishing a market value. If it does not, and you decide to go to court, by the time the market value has been established the lease will have long since expired, and your bank account will be substantially diminished.

The tenant will want the definition of market value to reflect the facts that the landlord will not be placing any improvements in the property, that the landlord will not be paying a commission, that the lease restricts the use of the premises and to consider any other factors that tend to constrict the value.

The landlord, on the other hand, will want the market value established as if the lease didn't exist, so that the property will be valued at its highest and best use. Whatever the parties negotiate, however, should be expressed in the lease.

The provision in the lease should include a specification as to the type of person who will be selected to do the valuation. Is it to be a real estate appraiser? If so, are certain specific credentials to be required? Can it be a real estate broker with a certain minimum number of years' experience? Should that experience be specific to the area and type of property that is the subject of the lease? Are there limitations on the amount of time the appraisers may take to make their decisions?

Let's examine two common methods of establishing fair market value:

1. <u>One Appraiser</u> – The first method is commonly referred to as the baseball arbitration technique. This has become popular as baseball has become more and more of a financial subject rather than a national pastime. Under this technique, the parties attempt to negotiate for a limited period of time during which each puts on the table its own opinion of rental value for the extended term. If they are within a certain percentage of each other (say 5 percent or 10 percent) the values can be averaged; that average becomes the rent. If they are farther apart than that, then a procedure is established for selecting a qualified independent appraiser unaffiliated with either the landlord or the tenant.

An independent agent, such as a judge or arbitration group, can be charged with the task of appointing the appraiser. Alternatively, one party can be designated to present a list of qualified appraisers to the other party, who will choose one from that list. Both parties present their arguments to this appraiser during a limited period of time; the appraiser then delivers his or her opinion. The opinion is not as to the rental value of the premises but, rather, as to which party's proposed rental value most nearly resembles that of the appraiser. Thus it's a winner-take-all proposition. Either the landlord's or the tenant's opinion of value becomes the rent. This prospect is supposed to have a sobering effect on both parties and cause each to want to be close to true market value to avoid having the other party's opinion of value selected.

2. <u>Multiple Appraisers</u> – Under this system, if the parties are unable to reach agreement in a limited negotiation period after exercise of the option to extend, then each selects an appraiser. If their appraisals are within a certain percentage of each other, the two appraisals can be averaged; that average becomes the rent. Failing this, a third appraiser is selected by the two originally selected appraisers. This third appraiser can be directed to do one of the following (or any other variant):

- Simply select one of the two original appraisals, using a variant of the baseball appraisal;

- Submit an appraisal of its own, which is accepted as the fair market value;

- Average its appraisal with the two original appraisals;

- Throw out the high and low appraisals and select the one in the middle as the fair market value; or

- Throw out any appraisal more than x percent higher or lower than the middle appraisal, and average the others.

CHAPTER 5

Rent

Just as the *premises* are the essence of the transaction for the tenant, so *rent* is the essence of the transaction for the landlord.

Reduced to its simplest terms, a lease transaction is one in which the landlord gives the tenant the right to possess property in return for the payment of rent. You recall that the premises paragraph can be simply stated once a method of calculation is established, so long as there is no construction to be done. Similarly, the rent paragraph can be simply stated so long as the procedure for calculation is established, unless it is a retail lease subject to percentage rent.

Method of Calculation

Fixing the Rent

As a rule, rents are quoted by the square foot in multiple occupant premises. This method of fixing the rent pertains to all types of commercial occupancies (office, industrial, retail). Thus, for example, the parties may agree that the premises are to be leased at $1 per square foot. It now remains only to measure the square footage to translate that unit rental cost to a monthly rent for the premises (see Chapter 2).

Rental Adjustments

We discussed the establishment of rent during an option term in the preceding chapter. The methods for rent adjustment during the fixed term are identical.

If the parties enter into a 10-year lease in which the rent is fixed for the first two years but is thereafter subject to adjustment to reflect the change in the consumer price index (CPI), that adjustment is calculated as previously discussed in Chapters 2 and 4.

Sometimes the parties use a combination of adjustments, changing every several years. As an example, let's assume there is a 10-year lease with adjustments every two and a half years. The parties might agree that there would be a CPI adjustment after two and a half years, a fair market value adjustment at the end of the fifth year and another CPI adjustment after seven and a half years. The landlord then might become more willing to enter into a longer term lease because it can adjust the rent to reflect market value at least every five years and protect the purchasing value of the rental dollar in the interim.

Cost Reimbursements

Some people consider cost reimbursements to be rental adjustments. I do not. Additional revenue to cover, dollar for dollar, additional costs is a reimbursement, not income. And please spare me the accounting rules. However, to the extent that such revenues are a profit center (I can refer you to the famous New York porter wage clauses), having little to do with operating costs, one could consider them a rent adjustment. This subject will be discussed in Chapter 10, Operating Costs, rather than in this chapter on rent.

Offset or Abatements

A tenant frequently desires to offset against its rental obligation any costs it has incurred that should have been borne by the landlord, for example, costs incurred in repairing the roof, which the landlord should have repaired under the terms of the lease. Landlords feel rather strongly that under no circumstances should the tenant be the sole judge of whether it has the right to reduce its rent obligation. The landlord feels that the idea of its tenant acting as both judge and jury is unhealthy, un-American, and smacks more of social reform than of business practice. Moreover, their lenders don't like it. Lenders look to the income stream from the lease as a source for repayment of the mortgage obligation. Any interruption in that income stream jeopardizes the lender's source of repayment. Lenders are finicky about such things.

The tenant responds to such an objection, while wringing out its handkerchief, by saying that it fully understands the lender's position. Therefore, it will agree to limit the amount of its unilateral right to offset to several months' rent. Depending on the relative negotiating strengths of the parties, this may be adequate, because the tenant will now be in the position of having satisfied the landlord's stated objection.

There are two factors at work that tend to mitigate this argument.

First, the tenant usually will want to limit this remedy to solving only relatively small problems, as discussed above. The tenant is normally willing to settle for this limited deductibility rather than taking the matter to court, because smaller arguments are customarily settled before the parties get into a courtroom. For a breach that involves substantial sums of money, however, the tenant will probably be satisfied only by going to court. The single exception to this rule occurs when there is to be a construction reimbursement. In this situation, the tenant has expended funds that the landlord is supposed to reimburse. If the landlord does not do so the tenant will want to open all the spigots on every remedy to get that money back. One of the most accessible remedies is the right to offset construction cost against rent, to the extent of the landlord's breach of its obligation to pay the tenant improvement allowance. This is the only sure source of repayment in which the tenant can have confidence. One possible approach for the tenant to assuage the landlord's nightmare fear of a *repair and deduct* remedy is to agree that no deduction from rent shall be made unless and until an arbitration proceeding (of a relatively prompt nature) described in the lease is completed with a finding against the landlord.

Second, my experience in representing tenants for 25 years (I have represented landlords for much longer) leads me to the conclusion that when there is a landlord default, this remedy is more of a negotiating card than a real solution. If the tenant has a valuable lease, it will not want to place that lease in jeopardy by deducting rent, thereby subjecting itself to a three-day notice and an unlawful detainer action. It may find that in the perfidious courtroom the judge will find that the landlord was not in default, and the tenant will be threatened with the loss of its lease. For this reason tenants are extremely cautious in exercising a right of offset.

Negotiation of rental offsets is as pure a power element as there is in the lease negotiation. A strong landlord will resist to the death (almost) giving the tenant the ability to make a unilateral incursion into the rental stream on which the landlord relies for payment of the mortgage, establishment of the true value of the property, and making installment payments on the Porsche. It is a persuasive tenant indeed who will be successful in such an undertaking.

Cotenancy

In a retail project, landlords use the enticement of *anchor* tenants to attract other major tenants, to say nothing of small shop tenants. Let's call one of these anchor tenants "Magnet." Not only is the landlord using

Magnet as an attraction, it is also basing its rent on the lure of traffic to be generated by Magnet. Once having taken the bait, the tenants attracted by Magnet will want the landlord to deliver on the lure. Therefore, if Magnet for some reason ceases operating in the shopping center, the tenants who were attracted find themselves in the position of having incurred an obligation to occupy a shopping center they no longer want to be in, at a rent they would not have paid were it not for the fact that Magnet was to be a cotenant, which it is not. Tenants with any strength will seek the right to terminate their minimum rent obligation and, if Magnet is not replaced in a reasonable period of time, to terminate their leases. Needless to say, our landlord, a former paving contractor who is making a valiant effort to look like he comes from Malibu, and his lender, a faceless agglomeration of pension investors called a "conduit," will view this request with some incredulity. This can make for a very active discussion.

Free Rent

As this revised edition is published, the real estate markets are very tight and free rent is not on anyone's mind. But time will take care of that. It always does. Think back to the the latter part of the 1980s, when, courtesy of the Savings and Loan industry, one of the most serious instances of nationwide overbuilding occurred. As a result, vacancy rates in many large cities skyrocketed. Offering free rent for a designated period was one of many lures used to attract tenants from competing buildings. Why would a landlord offer free rent instead of simply reducing the contract rent? The theory is that once the higher rent is activated, after expiration of the free rent period, the building will show a higher income and cash flow, which can then be capitalized for sale at a higher price than if the rentals had, from commencement, been simply lower. The effective rent is the same. The landlord's hope that he might sell this higher rent stream to an investor who will ignore the method by which the rent got so high is sometimes referred to as the "Greater Fool Theory."

A second reason is that since tenants are highly inconvenienced by having to move, they would be inclined to exercise an option to extend the term at a rent that is higher than tenants would otherwise pay. Therefore, the free rent, with a higher rent becoming effective after expiration of the free rent period, is a one-time benefit. The landlord may stand to profit when the tenant, motivated by inertia, elects to stay in the premises at a higher rent rather than to undertake the dislocation and upset involved in a move. Let's take an example.

If the effective market rent is $13.25 per square foot and the tenant makes a deal for two years free rent (in a five-year term) with the balance of the term at $24.00 per square foot, the effective rent using a present value interest rate of eight percent is approximately the same as the effective rent in the marketplace. The tenant also has a five-year option. The option, however, will be based upon the $24.00 rent. Moreover, it will probably be subject to some adjustment, such as the Consumer Price Index adjustment discussed in Chapter 2. If the tenant wants to exercise its option, it will have to pay that higher rate.

The flaw in all of this for landlords is that an industry has developed among tenants who sign these leases and simply vacate to go to other premises after the free rent period has expired and make another deal for another two years free rent. A lot of landlords have learned the lesson that they would have been better off collecting partial rent during the entire term rather than going to an arbitrarily inflated rent for the final portion of the term in order to attempt to create an artificial and unbelievable property value based on the overstated rent (e.g., $24 per square foot). No sophisticated buyer will give a full $24 value in its cash flow analysis to a lease for which 40 percent of term (or 20 percent or 10 percent) has been represented by a free rent period. Landlords are just fooling themselves. The Greater Fool Theory depends on the mistaken assumption that there will always be a greater fool to be found to extricate the previous owner from his or her mistakes.

In our example, our landlord may very well have been better off charging $10 to start and increasing the rent over the term to get to the current effective market rate. At least the landlord would have been collecting rent from the start, which would give the tenant a vested interest in staying.

Percentage Rent

A good shopping center landlord is expert in finding ways to participate in all the good things that may happen to a tenant. But only the good things. The percentage rent clause (occasionally called overage) is one of the landlord's favorite ways of doing this. In effect, the landlord is saying that it has spent a lot of time, money, and effort putting together a shopping complex that will attract customers. If, as a result of creating this shopping environment, the tenant does well enough to exceed reasonably profitable sales goals, the landlord should share in the good fortune that it played a part in creating.

Tenants do not object to this, under the theory that they will pay the rent if they are doing sufficient volume to be making plenty of money. Under those conditions they will share some percentage of the gross with the landlord. As a general principle, tenants can make enough profit to justify operating a store without ever reaching percentage rent. If they do reach a level of gross sales sufficient to pay percentage rent, they have no objection to parting with some of it in favor of the landlord.

The percentages will vary depending on the type of operation involved. Low-volume, high-profit operations (furniture, jewelry, liquor) pay high percentages, whereas high-volume, low-markup operations such as discount stores, off-price stores, supermarkets, and giant drugs pay relatively low percentages. The amount of percentage rent to be paid is occasionally a subject of negotiation between a landlord and a tenant, but not often. There are industry standards to which the parties usually will conform, although these standards are subject to inroads from the largest and best of the tenants in each category, which might be able to bargain for lower percentages.

Gross Sales

The essential element of percentage rent is *gross sales*, the sum against which the percentage is applied to arrive at the additional rent that is due, if any. The definition of gross sales should be the subject of careful discussion. The landlord will want all revenue of any type or nature included in the definition. If anything, the landlord will demand that all revenue that could be remotely attributed to this location should be included in gross sales. However, the tenant will want certain specific exclusions, usually related to that portion of the income that is a pass-through (sales taxes, for example) or that is not profit producing. Here, without discussion, is a list of some of the exclusions aggressive tenants will seek.

- Returned merchandise
- Casualty loss recoveries
- Bulk sales (such as to a succeeding tenant or to a liquidator in a going-out-of-business operation)
- Sales or other taxes
- Negotiating Commercial Real Estate Leases
- Receipts from public telephones and vending machines (which would be paying percentage on a percentage)
- Bank card discounts
- Interest and carrying charges
- Sales of fixtures (sales not in the ordinary course of business)

- Sales to employees at discount
- Revenue from nonprofit operations (such as delivery and alterations)
- Bad debts
- Subrents

Calculation of Percentage Rent

Customary and Historical Breakpoints

Having established the level of percentage that is applicable to the particular operation in question, it should now be possible to compute percentage rent. Let's consider a jewelry store operation called Ice in the Summer. It has agreed to pay seven percent of gross sales as percentage rent. Its minimum rent on a 4,000-square-foot space is $4,000 per month, or $48,000 per year. If we take the minimum rent paid by Ice in the Summer ($48,000 per year) and, assuming no additional cost offset, divide it by seven percent (the percentage rent according to the lease contract), we get the figure of $685,714. This figure represents what is known as a natural breakpoint, that volume of gross sales that results from dividing the minimum rent by the percentage rent. That is the theoretical real estate break-even point.

In actual fact, as I have discussed previously, tenants will make money at a lower gross sales volume than this. Therefore, when active competition for space develops in a shopping center, landlords can sometimes bargain for an *unnatural breakpoint* (please pardon the expression), that is, a breakpoint that is not the result of dividing the minimum rent by the percentage rent but is some arbitrary figure perhaps higher, perhaps lower. As an additional lure to the landlord, the tenant may offer to pay percentage rent before it would otherwise have done so under a natural breakpoint calculation. For example, Ice in the Summer may be willing to start paying seven percent of all gross sales in excess of, say, $550,000, to bridge some negotiating hurdle with the landlord. If Ice in the Summer thinks it will be making adequate profits at $500,000, it may very well be willing to make this concession.

The reverse situation also could occur. A tenant may agree to pay more minimum rent than it feels the site justifies at the moment of lease execution because it may feel that over time, it will do a very fine volume at this location. In return for paying higher rent than it thinks it ought to, Ice in the Summer may bargain for an unnatural breakpoint that is higher than the natural breakpoint. For example, the landlord may concede that no percentage rent will be due until a volume of $800,000 per annum is reached.

But let us assume, in our example, that our lease calls for a natural breakpoint. This year, Ice in the Summer has been doing sizzling volume and has attained sales of $275 per square foot, or $1,100,000 in gross sales. Multiply this by seven percent and we can see that the rent due is $77,000. However, Ice in the Summer has already paid $48,000 in minimum annual rent. Thus, $29,000 in percentage rent is due the landlord.

Another way to come to the same conclusion is to go back to the natural breakpoint, which we had calculated to be $685,714. Deducting the natural breakpoint from the actual volume of $1,100,000, we arrive at $414,286 as the amount of gross sales subject to percentage rent. Multiply this gross sales figure by seven percent and guess what we end up with? $29,000!

Offsets and Reimbursements

As we have just discussed, percentage rent is offset by the minimum rent paid. We have also talked about the principal exception, unnatural breakpoints. What other offsets, if any, are available to a tenant? One can review the history of percentage rent and retail rents in general to attempt to make sense of the percentage rent concept. It was once rational. Once upon a time, as we alluded to in Chapter 2, there was no such thing as *net rent*. Rent was paid to the landlord, who then paid the taxing agency, the insurance premiums, and the operating costs — the balance being the landlord's profit. With the advent of serious inflation, this system changed to build in cost protection for the landlord and evolved into the net rent system we have today.

Originally, under the gross rent system tenants deducted their rent from the percentage calculation, as Ice in the Summer did. The difference from the original system, however, is dramatic. The rent that Ice in the Summer deducted was the net rent *before* payments to the landlord for reimbursements of taxes, insurance, and common area maintenance. Thus, to make the historical calculation match the modern calculation, Ice in the Summer would have to seek to reduce its percentage rent by the amount of the cost reimbursements that used to be paid by the landlord and are now paid by the tenant as well as by minimum rent. Aggressive, strong tenants will get tax and insurance offsets. Smaller tenants will not. Thus, in the past 20 or so years, landlords have derived still another profit center: the refusal to grant tenants an offset for all of the rent that they pay, including cost reimbursements.

Advances — Percentage rent offsets can include other expenditures made by a tenant for which the landlord does not wish to pay, at least at the front end of the term. For example, there may be a cost overrun in preparing the space. Let's say the landlord gives a tenant with 4,000 square feet of space an allowance of $20 per square foot, or $80,000. The costs, however, amount to $90,000. The parties may agree that the tenant will bear the additional $10,000, subject to its right to recapture that sum from the first percentage rents due under the lease. This may not happen for a few years but, for the tenant, it's better than not getting anything.

Lease Year

A lease year, like a fiscal year, is any 12-month period that the parties decide on as the unit for calculation of gross sales. Retail tenants, who tend to have a fiscal year that does not conform to the calendar year, frequently want the lease year to coincide with their fiscal year so that no additional accounting has to be done. As long as it includes twelve months, it really should not matter, although regional shopping center owners typically will fight to keep a December 31 year-end for all of their tenants to make their accounting simpler.

The real issue is not which 12-month period is selected as the lease year but, rather, how to calculate percentage rent for a partial lease year at the beginning or at the end of the term. Remember Rags to Witches? It opened its store for business on time, you will be happy to know, on October 20. As we previously mentioned, it anticipated doing 25 percent of its volume during the Christmas season. Let's say its natural breakpoint is $200 per square foot. Rags to Witches proceeded to do $50 per square foot during the two months after it opened. If Rags does its partial lease year percentage rent calculation the way the landlord wants it to (assuming a calendar year as a lease year), strictly on a pro rata basis, it will have volume extrapolated to $300 per square foot ($50 for 2 months = $300 for 12 months). They will end up paying percentage rent for this two-month "year," even though retail tenants seldom reach percentage rent before their fifth year of operation. For this reason, active negotitions should take place between the parties regarding calculation of percentage rent for the partial year at the beginning and end of the term.

Various solutions are available. To satisfy an alert tenant, these discussions should all be based on 12 consecutive months, rather than two months multiplied by six. Thus, for example, a fair clause would state that notwithstanding the partial year, no percentage rent shall be due until 12 months of the term have elapsed. The gross sales for that period can then be prorated for the partial year. For example, Rags' sales amounted to $50 per square foot in the first two months because that represented the Christmas season. For the actual *entire* first year, however, its volume was an excellent $165 per square foot, very satisfactory for the first year, but not adequate for percentage rent payment as $300 would have been. If we take the $165 per square foot in actual annual volume and simply multiply this by 2/12, the fraction of the year in which Rags was open, we get a volume of $27.50 per square foot instead of the $50 the landlord would like. Since the breakpoint for the partial year is $33.33 per square foot ($200 X 2/12), there is no percentage rent payable, whereas by extrapolating the partial year, preferred by the landlord, percentage rent would be payable on $16.67 per square foot ($50 in actual sales less $33.33 of breakpoint).

The landlord's objection to this is purely academic, because the landlord has no practical good answer. The academic answer is that if percentage rent is due, the landlord will receive that rent ten months later than it otherwise would have because a full year must be permitted to elapse rather than just the partial year in question. This reasoning will indicate the lack of seriousness that some parties bring to the negotiating table since the likelihood of a tenant paying percentage rent in the first lease year is negligible.

Miscellaneous Issues

Frequency of Payment
Tenants would like to pay percentage rent as seldom as possible. This means annually. The landlord would like to receive percentage rent as frequently as possible. This means monthly. The parties could bargain for quarterly payments, semiannual payments, or any other variant. The landlord will want the payments to be discrete, that is to say, calculated in separate units. In this manner, if figured by the month, when the tenant reaches a monthly volume sufficient to pay percentage rent, it pays. When it does not, it doesn't pay. When the volumes for two consecutive months are totaled, that total may indicate that there was not adequate volume. But the tenant may have already paid percentage rent for one of the two months. This is advantageous to the landlord. If a tenant has to pay more frequently than annually it will want to be sure that all payments are cumulated and that no monthly calculation is discrete. The tenant will want all monthly calculations to be on a year-to-date basis so as to receive the rent benefit of low-volume months. Table 5.1 is an example of how this difference in calculation might work.

Table 5.1. *Ice in the Summer*						
	Gross Sales					
Month and Sales as % of Annual Volume	*If Calculated By Individual Month*			*If Calculated Cumulatively*		
	Breakpoint	*Actual*	*Due*	*Breakpoint*	*Actual*	*Due*
Jan. 4%	$57,143	$32,000	—	$57,143	$32,000	0
Feb. 4%	57,143	32,000	—	114,286	64,000	0
March 9%	57,143	72,000	1,040	171,429	136,000	0
April 8%	57,143	64,000	480	228,572	200,000	0
May 7%	57,143	56,000	—	286,715	256,000	0
June 6%	57,143	48,000	—	342,858	304,000	0
July 6%	57,143	48,000	—	400,000	352,000	0
Aug. 8%	57,143	64,000	480	457,143	416,000	0
Sept. 10%	57,143	80,000	1,600	514,286	496,000	0
Oct. 9%	57,143	72,000	1,040	571,429	568,000	0
Nov. 12%	57,143	96,000	2,720	628,572	664,000	2,525
Dec. 17%	57,143	136,000	640[1]	685,714	800,000	5,475
	$685,714	$800,000	$8,000	$685,714	$800,000	$8,000

Assumed sales as % of annual volume.

[1]The small payment compared to the large sales volume shown in December (for sales calculated by individual month) reflects the fact that tenant has been overpaying during the year, as finally calculated at year end.

Records

Landlords will insist that retail tenants keep accurate records at a place available to the landlord and near the shopping center for a reasonable period of time after the close of the fiscal year. Landlords could reasonably demand that records be kept for three years, because, in any event, that is the period of time tenants must keep the records for income tax auditing purposes. If an error is found, landlords also will insist that the tenant should pay for the landlord's audit. Since tenants will not want to absorb such a cost if the mistake is minimal, the amount that will give rise to this obligation is negotiable. Landlords will also insist on a provision that if there are multiple errors or if the error exceeds a certain percentage (five percent, six percent, seven percent), the landlord has the right to terminate the tenant's lease. This is a radical remedy that the tenant will resist. However, the landlord has a right to be dealt with honestly by the tenant. The landlord is justified in feeling that it shouldn't have to hire a detective every year to find out what the tenant's sales truly were.

Covenant of Continuous Operation

To give value to the percentage rent clause, landlords will insist that the tenant promise to operate its retail business continuously and in a manner that will maximize gross sales. If the landlord has given a tenant a good space at a good rent, based on the anticipation that the tenant will (1) develop foot traffic for the other tenants and (2) pay percentage rent in the future, and then finds the tenant has closed its doors, the landlord will feel stupid. No one likes to feel stupid.

Tenants with sufficient negotiating strength will not agree to a covenant of continuous operation. They want the right to decide to keep the store open or close it, based on their business judgment. Tenants take the view that the decision to operate the store or not is an internal decision. Moreover, tenants argue they should not be obligated to operate a store at a loss that exceeds its rent obligation.

The question often arises in court of whether a percentage rent tenant who actually does sufficient sales volume to pay percentage rent has, by this performance, obligated itself to continued operation. This is a so-called *implied covenant of continuous operation*. That is to say, it isn't expressly stated in the lease but is implied by the intent and performance of the parties. Tenants will want to avoid this implication by expressly negating it in the lease. At the very least, this will cause the issue to be faced squarely by the parties in their initial negotiation.

Finally, there is the question of remedies for a breach of a covenant of continuous operation. Landlords will insist that leases should include appropriate remedies because there is some question as to whether a court will specifically enforce this covenant. Courts are loath to issue an order that involves supervision of an ongoing business. Landlords, therefore, will be wise to include either a remedy in liquidated damages (a certain dollar amount per day, for example) or some other specific damage remedy.

Radius Clause

If the landlord is relying on percentage rent in the future, it will be sorely disappointed if the tenant who has broken into the percentage rent bracket decides the following year to open another store nearby in what the tenant perceives to be a better location. The landlord will then probably witness a precipitous decline in gross sales from the tenant's present store and the evaporation of percentage rent. To avoid this, landlords may require a so-called *radius clause* specifying that the tenant will not operate another store within a certain distance, called the *radius*, from the premises. There are antitrust implications to this restriction.

CHAPTER 6
Taxes

In negotiating the tax paragraph one must define terms so that everybody is thinking about the same thing. In the course of the initial business discussions, the parties will decide whether the lease is to be net or gross, with tax stops, or with caps (which means expense ceilings). However, the question is whether the parties think they've agreed to the same thing. Similarly, the parties will probably agree that if the tenant is to pay taxes in multiple occupant premises, it will pay a pro rata share. What does that mean? Pro rata share of what? Let's find out.

Net vs. Gross

In Chapter 2, Premises, we briefly discussed how all leases were once gross. Once upon a time (as in a fairy tale), the landlord paid all operating expenses for the property. That was called a *pure gross lease*, which no longer exists except as a museum specimen. Landlords lost their collective virginity in the boudoir of inflation. Thus, some provision for increased expenses is nearly always present in modern leases. The choices are to use a *net lease* or a *gross lease* or a variant of these.

Net means simply that the rent stated in the lease is received by the landlord net of *all* expenses. This means that the tenant pays all of the operating expenses. This term is now, also, an abbreviation of the terms *net, net, net* or *net, net*. This used to refer to maintenance, insurance, and taxes, in that order. In general practice, however, these terms have fallen out of favor in most areas. They have been replaced by the term *net*, which has replaced *triple net*, and the term *industrial gross*, which replaces the old *net, net* lease (i.e., tenant pays insurance and maintenance). For purposes of this chapter, the term *net* simply means that the tenant pays the taxes for the premises.

Gross means that the landlord pays expenses from the rent revenue. Under such a scheme, however, landlords will demand that tenants pay all such expenses above a certain level. As we discussed in Chapter 1, this level is called the *stop*.

Net

Include Everything

If the landlord has bargained for a net lease, it must be sure that the definition of taxes includes all of the possibilities, not just the taxes that the parties know about now. Proposition 13 was passed by the people of California in 1978. This constitutional amendment restricted the values against which taxes could be assessed. The result was a severe constriction of the tax base from which municipalities could collect revenue. Local governments attempted to make up their losses through increased user and development fees. However, I don't know a single real estate lawyer in California who did not dread all the possible schemes a government could devise to increase revenues, including rental taxes, taxes on the lease transaction, license fees, gross receipts taxes, and others. The idea is to include all possibilities, whether or not now in effect, whether in substitution for existing taxes or in addition to them, and whether they are called real estate taxes or not.

A landlord might be distressed to discover two years after signing what was purported to be a net lease that a government agency has enacted a new form of tax nobody had thought of before. Let's say it's the new Flush Tax assessed against all rent-producing properties in the jurisdiction. (You know they wouldn't dream of assessing such a charge against the single family property owners who sired Proposition 13 and its progeny.) The Flush Tax is predicated on metering all toilets in income property buildings in order to levy a tax on each flush. Our landlord had forgotten to include the Flush Tax in its lease and may no longer have the net lease it thought it had. Its rental profits are about to go down the you know where. Better get it all.

True Net

No, this doesn't refer to an old John Wayne film. This simply means the landlord is trying to cover all the possibilities to prevent getting nailed by the Flush Tax. One could easily envision, for example, our elected representatives perceiving that their constituents, few of whom are commercial landlords, might relish the prospect of socking it to the evil rich people who collect all those rents. Not exactly a novel idea. Accordingly, the lawmakers proceed to include in the Flush Tax enactment a provision that states that under no circumstances will landlords be entitled to pass any such tax on to their tenants for reimbursement. A landlord might want to provide that in such an event, the base rent will increase by an equivalent amount. I have no idea if that will work, but it would be worth a try.

Caps or Ceilings

Caps are limits, pure and simple. A not-to-exceed number agreed to by the parties. For example, the landlord may be about to sign a net lease for its new industrial/office park in the desert called Greased No Palms. (We'll call the landlord GNP for short.) GNP has located a hot new warehousing tenant named Plain Pipe Rex for 20,000 square feet. Rex is delighted at the prospect of moving to this high-class facility with his combination wholesale plumbing supply and ladies fashion operation. It has even agreed to sign a net lease. But Rex's owner is nervous about moving in the stylish circles that the landlord says will be locating in the park. What if the taxes on the building are higher than the landlord estimates? It might wipe out the profit on a month's sales of P-traps.

To be cautious, Rex insists that if taxes in the first year exceed 50 cents per square foot of rentable area of premises, the landlord will pay such excess not only in that first year, but every year thereafter. For example, if taxes are assessed at 55 cents in the first year and 65 cents in the second, then the landlord will pay 5 cents in each year (the amount of the first year excess). Rex will pay 50 cents in the first year and 60 cents in the second and grudgingly at that, because Rex did not anticipate a 20 percent tax increase. Rex had budgeted 50 cents for taxes based on what the landlord said, and he's not happy.

To avoid the unpleasant little surprise of the second year increase, Rex might, if it had a good enough bargaining position, negotiate a limit on the amount of any future increases in taxes. For example, it could require that the landlord absorb any increase in excess of five percent per annum in the same manner that it got the landlord to swallow the first-year jolt.

Gross

Stop Level

The amount of the so-called *stop level* is the critical element in any gross lease negotiation. That is the level above which the tenant commences to reimburse the landlord. There are two principal methods for approaching this problem: base year and base amount.

Base Year

Under this procedure, the parties agree that the amount assessed as taxes for the first year will be borne by GNP (the landlord). If the amount assessed for the second year is greater than for the first, then Plain Pipe Rex will reimburse the landlord the amount of the increase only. Using our example above, since the first-year taxes are 55 cents per square foot, that is the amount of the landlord's obligation for the balance of the lease term. However, Rex will be stuck for the full 10-cent increase in the second year.

Rex will want to be cautious when it comes to defining the first tax year. Let us say that it is to locate in a multitenant building of 100,000 square feet, of which Rex occupies 20 percent. Let's further say that Rex is the first tenant to occupy the building. Thus, in that first year, only 20 percent of the building has had tenant improvement work installed. If Rex has foolishly agreed to pay 20 percent of all increases in taxes over the first year, it will find itself paying taxes on the value of the tenant improvements subsequently installed for the benefit of other tenants.

If Rex's owner can get his mind off wrenches and hemlines for long enough to pay attention, he will see the problem and insist that the base year not commence until 90 percent of the building is occupied; or, alternatively, insist that a system be devised for calculating base year as if the building were 90 percent occupied.

Base Amount

Both parties might wish to opt for certainty by agreeing to an actual amount of taxes that would represent the level above which the tenant would reimburse the landlord. In our example this amount would be $10,000 per year (20,000 square feet for Plain Pipe Rex multiplied by 50 cents per square foot). Any amount of real estate taxes assessed against the property for which Rex's allocable share exceeds $10,000 would be Rex's responsibility. When Rex's share comes in at $11,000, it must reimburse the landlord $1,000.

The landlord may express a preference for such a scheme because the program eases its financial planning, having eliminated the guesswork as to how much tax will be assessed against the property that it will not be able to pass through to tenants. The landlord's tax cost is now firmly fixed. The risk of the assessment is removed.

Rex might also feel this to be an advantageous system, but only if it can get the base amount high enough so that it doesn't feel as if it is acting as a guarantor of the assessment for the landlord. It also avoids the argument over what the level of taxes should be if 90 percent of the tenant improvements have been performed, or the corollary argument over what should constitute the base year, i.e., what level of occupancy or of improvements.

What Tax Bill?

If the premises is part of a larger property, such as a multitenant building or a shopping center, then a question arises as to what amount should be allocated among the occupants. An additional question often arises as to whether the entire amount of that bill is properly chargeable to the occupants. Let's examine these questions.

Separate Assessment

If the premises that is the subject of the lease is sitting on its own site, such as a freestanding building (a freestanding building is one that is located on its own parcel of land, unattached to any other structure), it is often, but not always (depending on the local tax assessor's policies), possible to have the property separately assessed so that a separate tax bill is received just for this parcel. Thus it is possible to avoid squabbling about the appropriate pro rata share or how much of the assessment should have been included in the allocable tax bill. If Rex's 20,000 square foot premises is in a separate building on its own land parcel, but part of a five-building complex originally assessed as one parcel, it might be possible to have the parcel separately assessed and thereby avoid the argument about the value of the tenant improvements built for a neighboring tenant.

Similarly, even if the building is not free standing but is part of a large single-story structure, it may still be possible to have the assessor assess the premises separately (once again, depending on the policies of the local assessor). This often is done for larger tenants in shopping centers. Assessors are becoming less and less cooperative in making life easier for landlords and tenants this way, but it can happen if the parties supply proper platting and other data.

In such a case, the parties may wish to arrange to divide the outside areas as well, such as parking, landscaping, and driveways. If the subdivision plat presented to the assessor indicates such a division of the common areas, it can be assessed this way. If not, then landlord and tenant will arrange, if possible, for the common areas to be assessed separately and the bill for those areas to be prorated among the users. If this is the agreed solution, the common areas, for tax purposes, become a separate tax lot receiving its own tax valuation and billing. The valuation would be based on land value plus the parking lot improvements. Since such improvements are usually uniform, the argument about one party being assessed for special improvements made for the particular benefit of another tenant is eliminated.

Exclusions

You will recall how we discussed the care that GNP will want to apply to the drafting of the definition of taxes so that all possibilities are included. GNP will want an all-inclusive definition. Rex may not agree. There are a number of matters that Rex will want to be sure are not included in the tax amount on which the reimbursement is based. What are some of the issues Rex may want to explore?

Change in Ownership

For those states that have followed California's example, tax valuations that can be placed against a property are restricted until there is a *change in ownership*. For example, the valuations in California are locked in at 1975 levels, plus two percent per year, unless there is new construction (and then the increase is restricted to the value of the new construction) or a change in ownership. What a change of ownership is can be a complicated question. Let's simply agree that it is intended to cover a transfer of the property to a third party or where the true ownership changes hands.

If a tenant leases space in an old building that has been in the same family for years, it will find the applicable taxes to be quite low because there has been no reappraisal since 1975. In such a case, the tax valuation bears no rational relationship to the true value. The tenant prepares its occupancy cost budget accordingly. A short time after its lease term commences, the head of the landlord family dies, leaving not only a large estate but also a large estate tax obligation to the heirs. To raise money to pay this obligation, the heirs sell the property. The tenant, who has had nothing to do with all of this, now finds that its tax reimbursement obligation has multiplied many fold; its occupancy cost has increased unexpectedly and dramatically. What to do? Unless provision has been made in the lease, there is nothing it can do.

For this reason, many tenants who are paying attention will require that any increase in taxes caused by a sale to a third party and not related to regular and customary reappraisals or changes in rates, be excluded from the tax billing for which they will be responsible for reimbursement.

Tenant's Argument — The tenant will argue that the premises were represented as having an occupancy cost, including rent and cost reimbursements, of a certain amount and that it relied on this representation when comparing the space with others it was looking at before it decided to enter into this lease. If, through no act on the tenant's part and no action that had any benefit to any occupant of the building, the property is sold simply to solve the estate tax problem of the landlord and the tax obligation skyrockets, then it is no longer the economic deal that the tenant thought it had. Although the tenant is prepared to pay for increased taxes in the ordinary course of business, it is not willing to subsidize the landlord's profit-making activities that do not benefit the property.

Landlord's Argument — The landlord will argue that the tenant is receiving the exclusive benefit of below market valuation reflected in a lower tax bill. This represents nothing but a windfall for the tenant, who should expect to pay taxes as if the building were just built or purchased at fair market value. The fact that the taxes are lower is a benefit that the tenant has no right to expect to be permanent. Moreover, the landlord will observe that any exclusion from the tenant's tax obligation effectively acts to increase the landlord's operating cost as far as a new owner is concerned, thus reducing by a capitalization factor the amount of purchase price available to be obtained for the property.

For example, suppose the tax bill increases from $5,000 to $12,200 per year — an increase of $7,200 — and the tenant is not responsible for reimbursement because the increase resulted from a change of ownership that the tenant had bargained to have excluded from its share of taxes in its lease. You can see that the amount of cash flow or income that the landlord has to sell to a new owner is $7,200 per year less than the selling landlord had been receiving before the tax increase. If the sale price is structured to reflect a nine percent capitalization rate, the landlord will suffer a price reduction of $80,000 ($7,200 divided by 0.09).

Possible Solutions — If the tenant has been getting the benefit of taxes that have been assessed at less than fair market value for a number of years, its arguments are less compelling. However, if the tenant was attracted to the premises because the landlord promised a low occupancy cost born of the artificially low taxes, then some relief may be in order. The landlord will not want to give blanket protection because of the large reduction in the market value of the property caused by such relief. But some partial solution may be indicated, such as locking in the tax valuation for some limited period of time.

For example, the parties may agree that the tenant will not pay tax increases that result from a sale during the first three or five years of the term, or will not pay tax increases that result from a sale for three to five years from *commencement* of the term, or will pay only 50 percent of such increases, and so on, with the number of variations limited only by the limits of intelligence.

The landlord, if it must concede anything at all, will favor the solution that specifies abatement for a finite period. Such a solution allows the landlord to preserve the value of the premises less only the actual amount of the tax relief, rather than the amount of the annual tax relief capitalized at market rates. The landlord will be reluctant, however, to grant any such relief for a new building or a fully valued building, arguing that the tenant has no vested right to the permanent benefit of an artificially low tax bill.

Unrelated Taxes

Bearing in mind that our landlord has included in its lease form a broadly inclusive definition of taxes, the tenant will want to continue whittling away by addressing itself to taxes that have no relation to the property: inheritance or estate taxes, income taxes, gross receipts taxes. As a rule, landlords will not have a problem excluding death duties. They will want to limit the exclusion for income taxes to those taxes levied against the *general income* of the landlord from all sources, as opposed to the landlord's income from the lease or property, which the landlord definitely will want included. Gross receipts taxes, if in the nature of an income tax on the general income of the landlord, are subject to the same comment.

Management Fees

As we will discuss in Chapter 10, Operating Costs, landlords will want to add a management or administrative fee to the various reimbursements from the tenant to cover its costs of doing the bookkeeping and otherwise valiantly fighting for the tenants' rights. After all, the rent can hardly keep the landlord's staff of sons, daughters, nieces and nephews in Porsches, let alone permit a profit. The tenant, however, is likely to resist the charitable impulse to pay the landlord a fee for sending the tenant the tax bill. The landlord will argue that it is carefully monitoring taxes, hiring a consultant to verify the fairness of the bill, even appealing to the taxing agency, if necessary, its concern for the tenant's welfare knowing no bounds.

New Construction

Two issues are presented when discussing new construction: first, the additional valuation added to the taxable base; second, the undetermined quality of the improvements. The second issue will be discussed under "Allocation" below.

New construction almost invariably is for the benefit of the landlord. Either the landlord is building the additional space to rent or it has already rented the space being built out. In either case, it's for the landlord's benefit. The landlord could argue, most easily in the shopping center context, that the additional space will enhance the integral shopping unit or the attractiveness of the project. The tenant, however, will be impervious to this reasoning, insisting that it will not agree to pay more taxes just because the landlord decided to speculate on some additional space. The tenant will argue that any construction occurring after the date it moves into its space should be excluded from the tax bill of which the tenant is to pay its share. When the landlord starts complaining of stomach trouble caused by ungrateful tenants who do not appreciate its labors, the tenant may fall back to the position of agreeing to include the new space only after it is leased and occupied, at least avoiding additional tax charges during the construction and lease up period. The landlord will have convinced the tenant that as long as the denominator of the pro rata fraction increases, the tenant will not suffer a larger tax bill.

GNP is so pleased with the tenant's compromise agreement that it proceeds to tell Rex that "in any event, if we have a beautiful, elegant new building, it will enhance the entire project." At this point, the light suddenly flashes in Rex's owner's brain, that the new construction will likely be of an expensive variety, perhaps dwarfing the value of Rex's building, saddling Rex with a pro rata share of a disproportionately enlarged tax bill. Rex promptly rejoins the fray and withdraws his initial agreement. The landlord deserves the ignominy of this negotiating defeat for harping on an issue that had already been conceded. **Any experienced negotiator knows that as soon as the other party concedes a point, shut your mouth and move on. Do not discuss the issue further.**

The Tax Parcel

It is important to understand what property is to be included in the tax bill of which the tenant will pay its share. Is it the five-building complex of which Plain Pipe Rex leased one building? Does Rex pay 20 percent of the tax bill on those five buildings? What if one building is sold and a separate tax parcel is created? Rex's lease may provide that the tenant is to pay 20 percent of the tax bill, but the remaining tax parcel now contains only four buildings and 80,000 square feet. Rex is occupying 25 percent of the premises in the new tax parcel, but paying only 20 percent of the bill, as stated in the lease. Unless the landlord has provided for this contingency, it will have a problem on its hands.

What if GNP decides it can squeeze another building onto its land, ending up with six 20,000 square foot structures? Reciprocally, unless Rex negotiated carefully, it may end up paying 20 percent of the tax bill for occupying 16.67 percent of the property (one 20,000 foot building out of six). These problems can be solved by a proper delineation of how the tenant's pro rata share is to be computed, accompanied by a careful statement of exactly what real estate is to be included in the tax amount to be allocated.

Allocation

The question of allocation arises only with respect to multitenant premises, whether it is a building that is shared or a parking lot or other common facility. When this question does present itself, there are, as usual, a number of issues to look out for.

Leased vs. Leasable

Landlords are always striving to transfer risks to the tenant. The oft-repeated argument is that having signed the lease, the landlord has no way to recoup unexpected expenditures, whereas the tenant can always raise the prices of its wrenches and mini-dresses. This, of course, assumes that the governing factor behind the price of a wrench or a dress is the additional rent that arises out of tax reimbursements.

The diaphanous quality of this argument will not prevent the landlord from attempting to lease the building on a net basis. How does one do this? Very simple. Pass the risk of vacancy on to the tenant. But how?

You remember that Rex occupies 20,000 square feet in a complex of buildings that consists of 100,000 square feet in the aggregate, all of which are included in one tax bill. To allocate the taxes among the tenants of the complex, GNP's form lease states that Rex's pro rata share is represented by a fraction, the numerator of which is the area leased by Rex and the denominator of which is all leased areas within the complex.

Now let's further presume that the landlord has met a bit of market resistance in its leasing program. As a result, it has only leased one other building. Now the tax bill arrives. Naturally enough, it covers all five buildings and 100,000 square feet. What percentage of that tax bill will

Rex be responsible for? The calculation will look like this:

$$\frac{\text{Leased by Rex} = 20,000}{\text{Leased in Complex} = 40,000} \quad = 50\%$$

Rex has agreed to absorb a substantial part of the landlord's risk of vacancy by inadvertently (we are, after all assuming, so far without any basis, that Rex is a rational, economic person) agreeing to pay a share of costs based on what the landlord has *leased*, rather than what is *built* or what is *leasable*.

What most tenants prefer to do is to say that the pro rata fraction has as its denominator the entire leas*able* (rentable) square footage in the complex, whether leased or not. In this case, the calculation would appear as below and Rex's share of project taxes drops from 50 percent to 20 percent.

$$\frac{\text{Leased by Rex} = 20,000}{\text{Leasable in Complex} = 100,000} \quad = 20\%$$

Thus, the landlord has all of the pleasure of bearing the entrepreneurial risk of vacancy to go with the rewards of earning rent while sleeping. Is it no surprise to you that landlords don't see it that way? I thought not.

GNP's problem is that it has no rational argument with which to support its position. The only way it will prevail is with power, intimidation, and a landlord's market. Take, for example, the longest-running example of a landlord's market in existence — the regional shopping center. (You will recall our previous discussion in Chapter 3.) Regional landlords will insist that the denominator of the fraction be the area actually leased. The absence of a rationale will not impede them one iota in their insistence.

Typically, the negotiating battleground forms over the issue of how much vacancy risk the tenant should be asked to bear. Remember that, with rare exception, tenants have little negotiating room in a regional shopping center situation once the tenant's business managers have decided this is an area in which they want to have a store located. Having made that decision, the store negotiator will have limited choice as to other locations, because regional shopping centers tend not be located too close to each other, and only occasionally in the same market area.

Accordingly, the tenant will attempt to bargain for a limit on the amount of vacancy that will be included in the denominator of the fraction. For example, the tenant might agree to having the leased area constitute the denominator, provided that, for purposes of the calculation, at no time will the denominator of the fraction be less than 90 percent of the leasable area in the shopping center. In this manner, the tenant will avoid paying the additional share arising out of a huge vacancy.

Both tenant and landlord will have enough problems if that unfortunate circumstance arises.

Improvements to Other Premises

We have discussed how the landlord justifiably (just in case any one thinks I'm bearing down a bit heavily on this class of necessitous persons) will allocate the burden of real estate taxes among its tenants to give substance to the agreement either to net the leases or to transfer the risk of cost increases to the tenant. We also have seen how the parties will bargain over the computation of the fraction to be borne by the tenant. Now we will consider the possible tax implications of improvements to other premises.

Let's say that Rex is successful in getting *leasable* as the denominator of its fraction. Rex, you will recall, is using the premises as a warehouse for its wholesale operation. Let's just suppose that Rex uses 95 percent of its premises for warehousing purposes and five percent for offices. GNP leases the next building for approximately the same purpose. However, Building No. 3 is leased as a research and development building — in this case meaning it has finished flooring, ceilings, and enough electrical wiring and power to launch Mariner V. The cost, rental value, and tax value of this building is approximately double that of the building that Plain Pipe Rex occupies. Then, to add insult, Building No. 4 is leased to a food broker as its home office facility, complete with plush private offices, built-in bars, a shower for the boss' secretary, who jogs on her lunch hour, and other amenities that serve to triple the cost compared to Rex's building. Of course, these amenities are reflected in much higher rent. But, that isn't going to be much consolation to Rex when it finds out that it is paying 20 percent of a tax bill that aggregates all of these costs and values. Rex is going to end up paying taxes on values all out of proportion to the value of the building it has leased.

Rex will want to be sure, at the time of the lease negotiation, that it is protected against taxes for buildings with improvements considerably greater than its own. This can occur in any type of commercial real estate. The apparel tenant in a shopping center (remember Rags to Witches?) will not be happy to have its tax bill lumped with that of the restaurant next door. It's bad enough that it must put up with the customers of the restaurant falling asleep over coffee while using valuable parking, but the final insult occurs when Rags to Witches discovers it is paying taxes on enough plumbing to reflood the Red Sea.

Relative Cost

Solutions to the problems outlined in the preceding paragraphs are almost always complicated. For this reason, among others, landlords, not prone to welcome complications that don't carry a mark-up, are loath to agree to any but the simplest calculation, i.e., a straight pro rata share. When the tenancies are small, one can perhaps sympathize with the landlord. After all, are we going to get everyone's cost sheets and compare? What about subsequent alterations? Who's going to keep score? How much will it cost to argue? Is the cost of administration out of all proportion to the potential savings?

All of these are valid questions. Two possible solutions are often used when tenants have enough negotiating power and enough potential savings are involved to be worth the trouble.

1. *Replacement Cost.* First, the tenant can request that its share of the tax bill be calculated based on its pro rata share of the replacement cost of the entire complex rather than on a pro rata share of square footage. Let's use the following example:

Building	Cost	
Rex	$1,000,000	($ 50 per sq. ft.)
#2	$1,000,000	($ 50 per sq. ft.)
#3	$1,500,000	($ 75 per sq. ft.)
#4	$5,000,000	($125 per sq. ft.)
#5	$1,200,000	($ 60 per sq. ft.)
	$9,700,000	

Rex's share, if based on square footage, is 20 percent of taxable value or $1,940,000.

Rex's share, if based on costs of construction, is 10.3% of taxable value, or $1,000,000.

2. *Assessor's Worksheets.* Another alternative is to require that the allocation of the assessment among the tenants or occupants of the complex be based on calculations made in the initial instance by the

assessor for the taxing entity that is levying the taxes. This is not as easy as it seems and depends very much on the cooperation afforded to the parties by the assessor, the care or sloppiness with which the assessor does the work, and the willingness of the parties to rely on his or her work product. The least you can say for it (one hopes it is the least), however, is that it is the work of an impartial party who doesn't care which of the parties pays what.

When Payment Is Due

Most often landlords will seek reimbursement, or rather remuneration, from the tenant on a monthly basis, in advance, subject to adjustment to reflect the actual bill when received. The landlord frequently estimates the bill based on the previous year's billing from the taxing authority. Further, the landlord will reserve the right to estimate an amount greater than the previous year if, in its best judgment, there are grounds to believe that taxes will increase. This is not an altogether novel proposition.

Landlords feel the need to collect monthly on an estimated basis, in advance, for two reasons. First, hardened by experience, they remain coolly skeptical of tenants' promises to pay promptly when the tax bill is received. Second, they may have an obligation under the terms of their borrowing contract with their principal lender to *impound*; that is, to set up a type of sinking fund account with the lender for the purpose of paying the annual tax and insurance bills when they become due without the necessity for having to come up with a large lump sum of money. You can be sure that the landlord will resist the possibility of becoming a lender for what, in the end, is the tenants' obligation, i.e., the payment of such operating costs as taxes, insurance, and common area charges. Were they not to collect in advance, they would, in fact, be compelled to advance the money for the tenant to avoid a tax lien. Who can blame the landlord?

The tenants with negotiating strength, however, will take a much different view. Tenants will object to being obligated to pay in advance for any expense. Why, they will argue, should they pay the landlord in January for an obligation that the landlord does not have to pay to the taxing authority until the ensuing December? One reason is that the lender may require it. Tenants may theoretically answer that this is the landlord's problem, although this is merely a theoretical argument, because most people recognize that to get the project financed one must put up with these eccentricities of lenders.

However, if there is no lender requirement or if tenants are strong enough to tell the landlord that they are uninterested in the lender's requirements, then, in such event, tenants will insist that they be obligated to pay only when the landlord is obligated to pay the taxing authority. As a concession, they may concede to pay 30 days in advance to give the landlord some comfort. But no more, say the tenants, and they will advance the same argument as the landlord: They are not interested in becoming lenders to the landlord by giving it money months in advance of the date that the landlord is obligated to pay it to the taxing authority.

CHAPTER 7
Maintenance

Maintenance issues present themselves frequently in industrial and retail leases, but only rarely in the customary office space lease in which the obligations are most often borne by the landlord. In this chapter, we will try to get an understanding of the terms that are commonly used, the negotiating concepts, and some special issues that often arise in connection with this clause.

Understanding Terms

Interior vs. Exterior

Although this seems straightforward, there are some items that are clearly exterior but that custom and practice have dictated to be interior (and thus generally the responsibility of the tenant). The most obvious example is the storefront of a retail store, which is nearly always the responsibility of the tenant, even if the maintenance responsibility for the exterior of a building lies with the landlord. Windows are another example. But as a rule, the differentiation applicable to the terms *interior* and *exterior* is the same as you will find in the dictionary.

Structural vs. Nonstructural

The distinction between structural and nonstructural is more complicated, unless the terms are defined in the lease, because the courts have had a great deal of difficulty in being consistent. Inconsistency arising out of widely varying court decisions is not rare, unfortunately.

You might think that the term *structural* would have something to do with the structure. It just shows how naive you are. And that, of course, is the problem. Some courts will decide whether a matter is structural or not based on whether a "substantial" amount of money is involved; others on whether the improvement is an intrinsically important element of the building; others, believe it or not, actually will decide the issue based on whether or not the improvement in question is a structural member. Neither party should like the first possibility. The tenant prefers, or should prefer, the second possibility because it affords

75

more certainty than the first, while being broad enough to include such elements as plumbing, electrical, ceilings, and the like. The landlord prefers the last because it is the most narrow and therefore favors the landlord, who usually (but not always, as we shall see) is burdened with the obligation for performing structural repairs.

One could convincingly argue that the term *structural* should mean what it says: any load-bearing member or any member that supports a load-bearing member; for example, posts, beams, trusses, joists, foundations, and the like. If the tenant can bargain to expand the landlord's responsibilities, so be it. But the parties should understand who is to do what.

Roof or Roofing

In the most typical situation, one of the parties is assigned the responsibility to maintain the roof. Most people take this to mean both the structure and the roof covering material (polyurethane, tar and gravel, metal, and so on). However, the party with the repair burden might very well decide that what it really meant by the term *roof* is the structure of the roof and not the roofing material; or vice versa, depending on whose ox is to be gored. The better way is to state that the maintenance obligation includes both roof and roofing.

Repair vs. Replacement

Capital Cost or Operating Cost

Frequently, an obligation for ongoing maintenance and repair will fall to the tenant, whereas the obligation for capital repairs is borne by the landlord. In such a case, the tenant may want to draw a distinction between operating repairs and capital repairs. The latter would include replacement.

Let's take as an example a drugstore tenant that is negotiating to locate in a new shopping center. The name of the company is Aspirins 'R Fun, Aspirins for short. Aspirins is a major tenant because it will take 35,000 square feet in a new strip shopping center to be built by the U.S. real estate subsidiary of a noted Colombian agricultural enterprise, called Casa de Oro de Colombiana, COCO for short. For the moment, at least, COCO for some reason doesn't seem to need institutional financing.

COCO is run by a mysterious gentleman who does not make public appearances. Accordingly, his interests are represented by various underlings and hirelings who allegedly carry out his wishes.

Aspirins will seek to negotiate a 10-year lease with several options to extend the term. The parties agree that Aspirins will maintain the HVAC (heating, ventilating, and air-conditioning system). Aspirins is prepared to undertake this obligation, provided that COCO installs a high-quality system at commencement and gets a good warranty from the manufacturer and installer. Generally, a quality unit can command a five-year warranty on the most important elements, such as the compressor or condenser. Aspirins will insist on the manufacturer's warranty because installers tend not to be permanent fixtures on the American industrial landscape. If and when the time comes to call upon the installer to make good on its promise, Aspirins could be disappointed.

COCO may agree to all of this because it is probably going to include the cost of the warranty in the construction cost, which forms the basis for its rent quotation to Aspirins. Moreover, if something goes wrong, it is not the landlord who is answerable, it is the manufacturer. One can hear the landlord applying the famous Oscar Wilde aphorism: "Nothing you do to my traveling manager can intimidate me!"

Allocating Capital Costs

However, Aspirins is not through with shaving the edges of its obligation. It then raises the issue of what will happen if the HVAC expires before Aspirins' lease term does. If Aspirins has the unqualified obligation to maintain the HVAC, then clearly it will have to replace the system if replacement constitutes the reasonable course of action with an HVAC in that state of repair. But suppose the lease has only one or two years remaining and Aspirins does not intend to exercise an option to extend because the location is no longer satisfactory. It is not difficult to see that Aspirins may feel it to be a compounding of the insult of the poorly performing store if it must install a brand new system for the sole benefit of some unknown successor tenant just before it departs. Accordingly, Aspirins may insist that whereas it will perform normal ongoing repairs and will agree, further, to pay for a maintenance contract with a reputable HVAC servicing company during the entire term, it will *not* agree to replace the system. The landlord, says Aspirins, should bear the burden of replacement. COCO representatives make threatening gestures, contrary to the advice of its attorneys, who are cautioning restraint.

Settlement Alternatives

Let's look at the possible settlement alternatives when a landlord and a tenant are at loggerheads over the burden of making a capital replacement, such as the HVAC, the roof, the parking lot, or any other major element of the premises for which the tenant may have the responsibility for ongoing maintenance.

1. Aspirins must replace. "You used it up, you replace it," says COCO.

2. Aspirins replaces, subject to reimbursement from COCO for the unamortized portion of the cost. Let's say that the parties agree that an HVAC system should last 10 years, or 120 months. Aspirins installs the new system in the ninth year. It will derive one year — 12 months — of benefit from the new installation. Therefore, COCO will pay for 90 percent of the cost. COCO will then try to get this back from the successor tenant. Aspirins' argument is that if the system isn't replaced, COCO will have to either replace it for the benefit of the new tenant or get less rent to allow for the fact that the new tenant will have to do so.

   However, the parties will want to take into consideration what would happen if the tenant were to elect to extend the term by exercising an option. There are several possibilities.

   • If Aspirins exercises an option to extend the term, it gets no reimbursement because the substantial benefit of the improvement will have been derived by them.

   • COCO can refuse to reimburse Aspirins until the last date for exercise of the next ensuing option to extend.

   • Aspirins' repayment of COCO's overpayment (occasioned by tenant now having an additional period for which the tenant must pay the amortization) is a condition precedent to termination of the tenant's lease obligations. A condition precedent is a condition that must be satisfied before an obligation is due or terminates. In this case, Aspirins must pay COCO if it wants to be relieved of the obligation of the lease. This is a valuable remedy for COCO only if it does not have a successor tenant lined up at the end of the term.

3. COCO performs the replacement subject to an increased rental payment from Aspirins. The landlord's argument here, as in all cases in which it must come up with unexpected sums after the rent is set, is that the lease rent has been firmly established at the commencement of the term. COCO has no way of increasing its

revenue, unlike Aspirins, which can reprice its merchandise every day if it wishes to ignore the competition. The landlord will demand that the cost of the replacement be amortized at a current interest rate over an agreed term.

COCO will ask that the agreed term be the remaining term of the lease. This will evoke a good-natured guffaw from Aspirins, who, if it is willing to accept the principle of the amortized cost at all, will insist that the amortization be based upon the reasonably useful life of the improvement. In our example, it is 120 months. If the cost of the replacement is $60,000, the current borrowing rate is ten percent, and the agreed useful life is ten years, then the annual constant payment is 15.86 percent and the monthly payment will be $793.20.

But Aspirins will want to be cautious about making any concessions whatsoever. Aspirins may not be sure of the ability of COCO's representatives to make concessions. Do they have authority? Never make concessions to the other side in a negotiation if its negotiator does not have authority to commit its principal to make concessions to you in exchange. If Aspirins makes this mistake, it may find itself continually making concessions without getting anything in return.

Aspirins, therefore, professes to be unimpressed by this solution. Aspirins knows full well that COCO can take that increased rent and sell it (along with all other income from the property) at a capitalization rate much lower than 15.86 percent.

Remember our discussion of excess construction costs in Chapter 2? Let's go through that arithmetic again. If, for example, the income can be capitalized at nine percent, that means that COCO can sell and derive $105,760 from its $60,000 investment ($793.20 x 12 divided by .09). Aspirins will say that the unexpected breakdown of the HVAC, or the roof, or an unexpected governmental requirement, is not supposed to be a source of profit to the landlord. Therefore, Aspirins offers COCO $450 per month (.09 x $60,000 divided by 12). Aspirins argues that COCO already makes enough money in agriculture, transportation, and even real estate. COCO will take the position that no informed buyer will pay a full price for such contrived income, particularly if the new rent does not accurately reflect the real rental value of the premises. The positions being set, we will now leave the happy group to their deliberations. When last heard from, the COCO representatives had just offered the Aspirins representatives a smoke as the attorneys stole out of the room.

Special Problems

Hidden Plumbing and Electrical

It will come as no surprise to you to learn that tenants look on plumbing and electrical lines that are set into the concrete slab floor as part of the foundation and, therefore, a structural matter within a landlord's maintenance jurisdiction. You are by this time hardbitten enough to know that COCO finds this view outrageous, ungrateful, and unpatriotic. "Plumbing lines do not a structure make!" shouts COCO's representative poetically in his native dialect. This is a knotty problem to be resolved like all others — by resorting to power negotiations.

Aspirins' point is that COCO has installed the plumbing and electrical conduit in the initial instance in the wet concrete. If anything has to be repaired because it was defectively installed, it is not fair (talk about irrelevancies!) to ask Aspirins to pay.

COCO will argue that plumbing and electrical lines are the tenant's responsibility, no matter who arranged the installation in the first place, and no matter whether located in, on, or above the foundation. The way to resolve this, assuming the parties to be of relatively equal negotiating strength, may be through the landlord's warranty.

Construction Warranty

This is a double-edged sword. COCO will seek to make Aspirins assume maintenance responsibilities when the premises are accepted. Aspirins will refuse, saying that COCO should at least be responsible for what it built. This is not all bad for the landlord. COCO will then bargain for a limit on the amount of time for which it will be responsible for the correction of any construction defects: six months, one year, two years, or any other agreed term. Thus, while taking on maintenance responsibilities arising out of construction flaws for a period of time (why not, COCO was responsible for the work), COCO will at the same time put a "drop dead" date in the lease, after which even construction flaws become the responsibility of Aspirins, who didn't even supervise the construction.

COCO will, on the other hand, want Aspirins to accept the premises as delivered on the date of commencement of the term. "What you see is what you get," COCO's representative intones unoriginally.

Acceptance and Punchlist

When COCO has substantially completed its work in preparation of the premises, it will expect the tenant to accept the premises, thereby completing COCO's obligation. At this time, COCO hasn't got a clue whether or not the job has been finished properly. As we have learned by now, this will be no impediment to the landlord's making a demand on the tenant. Understand that what COCO has in mind is that its architect will write a letter to Aspirins stating that the landlord's work has been completed, and that Aspirins will simply say "I accept!" Perhaps, as long as it is at it, the tenant will want to roll over onto its back, exposing its belly for a scratch.

But alas, Aspirins is merely entertained by this exercise in naive insouciance on the part of the landlord. "How do I know you haven't shoved dry ice into the HVAC, or used the latest imitation plastic pipes, or black paint instead of tar on the roof?" These are questions full of pith and moment. Not only that, Aspirins isn't about to accept something it can't fully see, test, touch, or watch in operation.

Aspirins truly does not want to accept anything. However, it might agree to do so if COCO remains liable for defects or incorrect performance of the work. But this is exactly why COCO wants the work accepted, so as to escape further worry about returning to correct the contractors' work. Thus, Aspirins is looking to keep COCO liable for the term of the lease, whereas COCO is looking for the fastest way possible out of the responsibility for repairs, corrections or maintenance.

So long as COCO is to remain responsible for its own faults, there will be little problem. But once COCO insists on Aspirins taking "as is," a confrontation is established. If both parties agree on the limited period of responsibility for the landlord, both will want to promptly arrange for an inspection of the premises for the purpose of establishing exactly what remains to be done to complete all of COCO's work. COCO will want this inspection to take place immediately on notice from the contractor that the work is complete. Aspirins will want to wait until it has had a chance to "live" in the premises for awhile to see if all the moving parts are working. Thus, Aspirins will want something like 30 or 60 days after commencing business in the premises to provide what is commonly known in the construction business as a *punchlist*. And even then, Aspirins' construction people may not be interested in a joint tour for the purpose of listing defects. Rather, Aspirins may insist on composing its own list for submission to COCO. Moreover, Aspirins will want to demand some remedy if COCO does not complete the punchlist work within a reasonable time, such as a right to deduct from rent (get the smelling salts).

Levels of Tenant Responsibility

If we assume the obvious, that is, that Aspirins will have some maintenance responsibility, then there will be at least four differing levels of obligation, more or less, depending on the type of lease, as shown below.

1. *Full Service.* This occurs in a typical downtown office lease, in which the tenant is responsible only for negligence. The landlord will agree to do all the other maintenance except for damage caused by the tenant. You may think this is a magnanimous act on the part of the landlord. If so, please return your text to the teacher and leave school. Actually, these costs are included in the base amount we discussed in Chapter 6. To the extent that the landlord's costs exceed the base amount, the tenant will pay its pro rata share. In this manner the landlord retains control of the care of its building by having the work performed under its supervision at the tenant's expense. Because the landlord has a high degree of interest in the care and maintenance of its investment, this is a good method, in most instances, of assuring an elevated level of maintenance.

2. *Gross-Industrial.* In the typical industrial gross lease, which is also frequently applicable to office parks, the tenant is obliged to maintain the interior of the premises, excluding structural portions that the tenant did not damage. The landlord will be obligated for the exterior, structure, and roof.

3. *Net-Industrial.* The industrial net lease adds the obligation for nonstructural exterior maintenance to the tenant's burden. Painting, parking lot repairs, and the like, are included. It is not unusual for this burden to be increased by having the tenant bear the onus for structural and roof maintenance, particularly if the tenant is the first user. This is a market force question.

4. *Bond Net.* Under the terms of this type of lease, sometimes referred to as an absolute lease, the tenant assumes most of the indicia of ownership, including responsibility for all maintenance, whether it is structural or nonstructural, interior or exterior. These leases generally arise under the circumstances of a sale-leaseback transaction in which the tenant builds the building in the initial instance; or, alternatively, where the parties have agreed upon a sale, but for certain reasons (usually related to the Internal Revenue Service), do not want the actual transfer of

funds and title to occur just yet. Thus the tenant, for all practical purposes, behaves as if it is its own landlord. For the tenant this would be a heavenly state, were it not for the cost.

Tenant Remedies

Aspirins has now moved into its premises and had a wonderful grand opening. The company executives are busy congratulating themselves about the splendid location they have selected and the marvelous landlord they have never met. Suddenly, in the midst of a busy weekend selling day during Christmas season, the roof gutters back up and the water comes pouring through the black paint that COCO had meticulously arranged to place on the roof. After notifying the shopping center manager (who demonstrates decisive executive ability by shouting "Buckets, buckets!"), Aspirins had emergency repairs performed to the roof. It then demanded that COCO fix the leak. How has the lease treated this?

Repair and Deduct

Aspirins will want to be sure there is a landlord default clause, just as there is a tenant default clause. In that clause, the parties agree that if COCO does not meet its responsibilities within some agreed period of time, perhaps 30 days, Aspirins may do the work of repair. No peep from COCO thus far. Aspirins continues: "And if you don't pay us back the cost within 10 days after we bill you we can deduct it from the next rents coming due under the lease." Suddenly, COCO's representative rises from his seat. He is clutching his chest and asking for a doctor. As he is placed gently down on a nearby sofa he is heard to mutter, "My rent, my rent," his voice trailing off. (See Chapter 5, Rent, for a discussion of the medical [and negotiating] phenomenon we have just witnessed.)

Repair and Sue

This is not a comedy team, but rather one possible alternative to a staunch refusal by COCO to bargain over the deductibility of repair charges against rent. Aspirins simply does the work and sues COCO for the cost. You might think Aspirins already has this right under the law, and so it does. However, the clause will shorten the time that Aspirins has to wait before being able to go to court.

Constructive Eviction

This is a most unsatisfactory remedy that is available at law to a tenant in any case in which a landlord has failed to provide the tenant with premises that can be used for the purposes for which they were leased. For example, if COCO refuses to fix the offending roof of which we spoke earlier, and if exposure to the elements makes the premises unsuitable for use, Aspirins can simply move out and sue for damages. It must do so promptly, however, since the courts do not like tenants to sit on their rights while being harmed in this manner. Such delay simply indicates to the courts that the harm wasn't so bad after all.

Constructive eviction is most unsatisfactory for a tenant, because the tenant must vacate to take advantage of this remedy. In some cases, the tenant may wish to get out of its lease obligation. In such situations, this remedy is perfect. But in those cases in which the tenant wishes to stay at its location, this is unsatisfactory. One can hardly see the virtue of destroying a valuable lease at a profitable location for a few thousand dollars in damage.

Governmental Compliance

It is now five years after the term of the lease commenced. Aspirins is doing well. Nobody has seen COCO, but it is presumed that COCO has forgot it owns the place. The City Council of Cocaigne (now don't be smart, this is named after the famous painting by Breughel) has just passed a life safety ordinance requiring that storefront glass in all retail stores must be strong enough to withstand an earthquake of 7.5 on the Richter scale. "You mean like the windows in my car?" asks the landlord when he is located.

In the lease negotiation, the landlord wanted Aspirins to be responsible for all costs of complying with governmental orders after the commencement of the term. Aspirins, however, expressed a lack of interest in the breadth of this mandate. Aspirins states that it will accept responsibility only for those governmentally mandated repairs or alterations caused exclusively by its particular use (a drugstore), and not for any such changes required of the entire shopping center or all retail establishments. Aspirins says these generic requirements are COCO's problem.

At this time COCO's representative can launch into his tried and true soft-shoe routine about not having a source for return on the landlord's investment because its rent income under the lease is set. (Remember that routine? It is number 23 in the list of stock answers.)

There are a number of possible approaches to this problem. Two of them are listed below:

1. Aspirins pays for all governmentally mandated alterations except for structural alterations (unless caused by tenant).

2. Aspirins pays for structural alterations, but only on an amortized basis over the reasonably useful life of the improvement without interest. In this case, Aspirins may want to put a cap on the rent increase that may result from having to add such a sum to its monthly rent. If the increase exceeds the agreed cap, it can reserve the right to terminate the lease, unless COCO agrees to pick up all costs over the cap. COCO may agree to this but will certainly try to get an interest rate included in the calculation because, like most landlords, it will have to borrow the money to perform the work.

For example, the windows cost $50,000 to replace, have a reasonably useful life of 20 years, and the current interest rate is 10 percent. The monthly payment will be $537.50. If Aspirins has bargained for a cap of $400 per month, COCO will have to absorb the balance or Aspirins will be able to cancel the lease.

One of the cute asides in such a negotiation is to try to be the one who is last to exercise the right to decide on an action when there are excess costs. Make the other party commit first to any required action (terminate, bear the cost, and so on). If COCO makes Aspirins commit first, Aspirins may be unwilling to gamble on losing a good lease for a few dollars, and may agree to pay the entire cost over the cap rather than risk having COCO decide to go into the rental market with the store space. It is a game of chicken. Is Aspirins (or, for that matter, the landlord, if COCO was the one who became burdened with first choice) willing to take a chance that its counterpart may terminate the lease and take its chances in the marketplace, when the other party could have come up with a few dollars extra to preserve its lease?

Hazardous Waste

This relatively new subject of negotiation must be treated with considerable care. The law is changing rapidly with both new legislation and new case law coming down almost daily, interpreting the new statutes. The spectre of strict liability for the horrendous cost of clean up hovers over every deal. Each party will attempt to burden the other with broad responsibility for the cost of clean up of contamination. It is easy to agree that the landlord will be responsible for what it caused and the tenant will be responsible for what it caused. The question comes down to contamination caused by third parties. For example, what if the contamination pre-existed the ownership of the property by the landlord. Another possibility is that the property has been contaminated by a migrating plume from adjoining property. The tenant's position will be that the property has to be cleaned up whether the tenant is there or not. Therefore, it is the landlord's problem. The landlord's contention is that it doesn't want to be compelled to undertake a clean up that it may want to contest; or may want to seek a source of funds by pursuing the polluter before accomplishing the remediation. Thus, the overriding issue in any discussion of hazardous waste is who is responsible for third party contamination. If the parties agree that neither is responsible, than the tenant will want to reserve the right to terminate the lease if timely remediation is not accomplished since the tenant will not want to be exposed to any liability (to say nothing of danger to its employees should the contamination not be cured).

Landlord's Position

In negotiating provisions related to contamination and hazardous waste, the landlord will take the position that:

- Only tenants actually operate businesses at the premises.

- The tenant can do whatever investigations it wishes prior to executing the lease or taking possession.

- The tenant should indemnify the landlord against any contamination that occurs on the premises.

- The tenant should conduct regular testing to establish compliance with law and safety standards.

Tenant's Position

The tenant, on the other hand, will want to receive assurances and indemnities from the landlord that:

- The premises will be free and clear of any contamination or hazardous material (including asbestos-containing materials) at the commencement of the term.

- The landlord assures the tenant against contamination of the premises by any adjoining tenant of the landlord.

- A substantial negotiation will then occur, in the course of which each party will seek to limit its liability. The elements of settlement will involve trying to relate responsibility to fault; limiting the dollar amounts to be spent in cure of contamination caused by others; and requiring testing and monitoring on a regular basis.

CHAPTER 8

Alterations

Since the tenant is the one whose business is actually located in the premises, it would like to reserve the right to perform alterations to improve the method by which it carries on its business. On the other hand, the landlord is understandably very interested in what the tenant, or anyone else, is doing to the landlord's property. The tension around alterations in any lease agreement is created by the tenant's desire to carry on its business in an efficient manner and the landlord's insistence that its property be handled with care. We will examine in this chapter how the parties resolve this conflict.

Landlord Approval

Alterations are rarely permitted to the premises without the landlord's approval. This is true even in the so-called bond, sale-leaseback type of lease (see Chapter 7) because even in that case the investor would anticipate that he or she might have to take the property back at some time, either by expiration of the term or by default. Every landlord has a legitimate interest in knowing not only what's being done to its premises but also the exact type and quality of the improvements. Accordingly, it is unusual for a tenant to be able to make any material changes to the physical premises — certainly not structural changes — without the landlord's prior written consent.

Approval of Plans

Any landlord will require that the tenant submit a plan of the work of alteration to be performed as a condition to granting any approval. This will permit the landlord, either directly or through its consultants, to review the plan to ascertain the degree and quality of the improvements. The landlord will look to see how these improvements will affect the premises when the lease expires or is terminated by default. If the alterations will have a negative impact on the future marketability of the space, the landlord may become moody, churlish, and even say "no."

If the improvements will affect the integrity, structural or otherwise, of the building, the same result may ensue.

Minimum Amount Without Approval

If the landlord finds the tenant desirable, the tenant may be able to bargain for some dollar level of alterations to the premises that it may perform without the landlord's consent. The tenant's argument is that it should be able to paint the interior of its premises or recarpet or perform other decorative work without having to go through a bureaucratic maze with the landlord or the landlord's staff. The parties may agree on some figure, such as $4 or $5 per square foot, that the tenant may expend on alterations without seeking the landlord's consent. If the landlord does agree to this arrangement, it will nonetheless insist on receiving either a plan or a detailed scope of work so that it at least knows in advance what is being done to its property. The landlord perceives this as its right, as we discussed above. It is hard to argue with this view.

Structural vs. Nonstructural

Even if the landlord agrees to permit the tenant some minimum level of improvements without its consent, and many will not, it is a rare landlord indeed who will permit *structural alterations* to the premises without its express written consent, no matter what the amount of money spent. While the landlord might allow repainting or recarpeting or other similar nonstructural alterations to be performed without its consent (but with its prior knowledge), one can understand the landlord's fear of finding some structural steel beams replaced by laminated wood beams, or a huge pit dug in the concrete slab foundation for an employee swimming pool. Such changes affect the structural integrity of the building, materially affect the future marketability of the space, and may cause the landlord considerable expenditure of funds to effect repairs when the premises are vacated by the tenant. The critical issues the landlord will consider in its review of any alteration request are as follows:

- The effect of the proposed change on the structural integrity of the space;

- The potential costs to re-alter the space for future use; and

- The potential effect on the future marketability of the space.

Conditions to Consent

If and when the landlord does consent to the tenant's alteration request, the landlord may enforce specific conditions. In fact, the landlord is likely to have insisted that these conditions be placed in the lease, to be satisfied before entertaining a request for alteration. Such conditions would include:

- *Insurance.* The tenant may be required to supply builder's risk, worker's compensation, comprehensive public liability, and other insurance against occurrences during the course of construction.

- *Bonds.* If there is enough money at stake or if the tenant's financial condition is of some concern, the landlord may require that all work of alteration be bonded, naming the landlord. The bonds would include performance, labor, and materialmens bonds to assure (1) that the work is timely completed and (2) that when completed it is paid for.

- *Mechanic's Liens.* Language will surely be included in the lease under which the tenant will covenant not to permit any mechanic's liens to be filed against the property. A mechanic's lien is a lien against the property filed by a builder or contractor to secure its right to payment for services rendered. This is of critical importance to the landlord, who will brook no discussion of this subject. Such a lien clouds the landlord's title. The tenant might feebly insist that the mechanic's lien should be permitted to stay in place while the tenant proceeds to argue a given contractor or subcontractor. No landlord with any intelligence will abide such an argument. The landlord is uninterested in whether the tenant's argument is meritorious; it simply wants the lien removed. There is always a legal procedure of which the tenant can avail itself to expunge the lien while it continues its argument with the contractor or subcontractor. The landlord has visions of attempting to refinance its property for millions of dollars, only to find out that a lender will not place the loan because there is a $5,000 claim arising out of work done for a tenant that clouds the title.

- *Quality.* The landlord will insist that the work be performed with first-class workmanship and new materials. All of this, however, should be dealt with during the plan approval process. Language would be included to cover lesser instances for which approval is not required.

Tenant Conditions

The tenant, believe it or not, will want to place some conditions on the landlord as well. Why not?

Reasonable Consent

First, in addition to requesting the right to make interior nonstructural alterations without the landlord's consent, the tenant will insist that the landlord be reasonable in exercising its consent. This seems like such a benign request. Nonetheless, the landlord may not agree, at least regarding structural alterations. The landlord may state that it is uninterested in having a third party (the equivalent of a standard of reasonableness) tell it what type of structure it should own. As to nonstructural, decorative alterations, however, this is a rational request, because most often such improvements will be removed or destroyed when the lease is terminated.

Promptness

Second, the tenant will want to request that the landlord act expeditiously, perhaps even insisting on some time limitation for a response to its request for approval. The tenant may insist, for example, that the landlord respond within 5, 10, or 15 days following submission of a complete set of plans. Moreover, the tenant may insist that if the landlord denies its request, such denial will only be valid if it is accompanied by a written response setting forth in detail the reasons why the request has been denied. Only in this manner can the tenant respond to the landlord's objections. This also avoids obfuscation by a landlord who is simply trying to be obstructive. You don't think this is possible?

No Obligation To Remove

Finally, the tenant will want to have the right to walk away from the premises at the expiration of the term, leaving all of its alterations in place. Alterations are seldom transferable. Trade fixtures, yes. Tenant improvements, no. Thus the tenant will wish to leave all of its alterations (partition walls, doors, cabinetry, and the like) at the premises and not incur the expense of demolition or removal.

The landlord may have a different view. The landlord is thinking about the appearance of the space to a future tenant. If the improvements make the space look as if it is a special purpose space or as if the new tenant will have to spend money to reorganize it, then the landlord will want to insist that the improvements be removed. The tenant's argument is that the landlord approved the alterations; therefore, the tenant should not have to remove them. If this is the tenant's argument, the landlord may respond that it will agree to this proposition, provided, however, that it retains the right, at the time it approves the alteration, to condition that approval on removal of the alterations on expiration of the term. In this manner the landlord can view alterations case by case and decide, at the time it approves the plans, whether it will want those alterations removed on expiration of the term to make way for a new tenant.

CHAPTER 9
Common Areas

In this chapter we will discuss those areas of the building complex that are not leased to any tenant, but without which the tenant could not get that use of the leased premises for which it bargained. These are called the common areas. These areas are held for enjoyment by all the tenants in the complex, their clients and customers. Although the landlord does not specifically lease the common areas to a specific tenant, the landlord must be repaid for the costs of operating and maintaining the common areas. How all parties get what they are looking for is the subject of this chapter.

Definition

The *common areas* are supposed to be those areas of the building complex that are available to all tenants and their clients, visitors, and customers for the convenient operation of the business in the building. Parking areas are the most obvious example. However, there are many other areas besides parking that are held for the common benefit of all occupants: walkways, stairways, elevators, corridors, lobbies, landscaping areas, loading areas, and the like.

Some landlords like to define the common areas as all areas not leased for the exclusive benefit of a given tenant. The landlord in this way can attempt to saddle the remaining tenants with the cost of operating vacant premises. This again hinges on the difference between leased and leasable areas. In Chapter 6, Taxes, we explained that whenever the tenant pays a fraction of the costs of the complex in which the denominator is *leased* area, the tenant is effectively agreeing to bear the risk of vacancy. The tenant would always prefer to pay based on *leasable* area.

A better definition for the tenant would be: *"All areas of a complex not leased or held available for lease to others, which areas are available for the common use of all tenants, in the project."*

A tenant should not have to accept as common areas any areas that are held for the exclusive benefit of any one tenant or group of tenants. Why should a tenant pay any portion of the expense incurred for the exclusive benefit of another tenant? If the landlord assigns exclusive parking places to each tenant in the building, it could argue that so long as everybody receives a pro rata share, there should be no problem with aggregating the cost of maintaining those parking areas and dividing the cost pro rata. This would be a rational argument; however, it is rarely the case.

Exclusive Parking

Frequently, tenants demand rights to exclusive parking spaces for their own benefit. In office buildings, it is a matter of prestige to paint the name of the head of a particular office on his or her own parking place. Setting aside matters of ego gratification, it may be necessary for the tenant to have exclusive parking places for use by its clients and visitors. In a shopping center situation tenants may demand exclusive parking in spaces directly in front of its store for its own customers. All of this sounds unthreatening and logical. However, a landlord who agrees to such exclusivity does so only with the greatest care and at its own peril. The two problems that the landlord must recognize are

1. Enforcement, and

2. Plot plan commitments to other tenants.

Enforcement

It is nearly impossible to enforce exclusive parking for the benefit of one tenant. In a large complex in which there are many tenants, no matter what type of complex it is, there is no way for a landlord to assure that some other tenant or the customers of another tenant or the suppliers of another tenant, or any strangers at all will not park in the parking spaces exclusively designated for the favored tenant, unless there is a policeman standing on the parking space. The landlord should agree only to *allot* that parking space, perhaps even to paint the name of the tenant on the parking space. It should under no circumstances imply an obligation to enforce the exclusivity, let alone express one. That obligation must rest with the tenant. Any attempt to evict a tradesperson from a reserved parking place in which he or she has just parked a pickup truck is to court a black eye and/or an earful of unpleasantness.

Plot Plan Commitments to Other Tenants

Almost every lease in a multitenant complex contains an exhibit depicting the site plan. Typically, the site plan delineates the location of the buildings and the design of the parking area, including a demarcation of the parking spaces. Should the landlord be unwise enough to allocate exclusive parking within that parking area, it could be in violation of this plot plan exhibit, which other tenants may take to be a representation unless specifically disclaimed in the lease. We will explore this subject at more length when we discuss altering the common areas.

Uses

Because the landlord is the manager of the common areas, it will want to restrict the type of uses to which each tenant can put the common areas. For example, in a shopping center the landlord will not want the toy store to use the common areas for its annual magic show. Filling the parking lot with young children and their mothers is a good way to:

1. Court accidents;

2. Clog the driveways with fearful drivers afraid of knocking someone over;

3. Infuriate the other tenants whose customers are trying to park and shop; and

4. Raise insurance rates to the stratosphere. Indemnity and liability aside, it is simply not worth it.

In industrial parks, landlords will not want tenants to use the common areas for their annual wholesale clearance sales of unretreaded tires or, even more likely, for the storage of trash or the temporary storage of disassembled machinery until ready for reassembly. All these possibilities are unattractive to landlords. Accordingly, landlords will restrict tenants to use of the common areas for parking, ingress, and egress. If there are common trash accumulation areas, they will be so designated.

Tenants, on the other hand, have equal concerns that the common areas not be used by a landlord for purposes that would interfere with the tenants' use of the areas for their proper purposes. For example, in a shopping center, a tenant may not want the annual Christmas tree lot, the blood bank truck, a politician's speech stand, or kiosks placed in front of its store. An easement for theater parking, for which the landlord is collecting rent from the movie theater across the street, will be equally undesirable. Unless they are of specific benefit to its business, all of these activities will be unattractive to the tenant.

If the landlord intends to derive any income from the common areas, the tenant will want to be sure that income so derived is applied to common area charges that are to be allocated. Tenants are not attracted by a landlord who attempts to make money from the common area that tenants are financing with their monthly common area cost reimbursements. The landlord, however, may insist that the use of the common areas for such activities be "for the general benefit of the shopping center." If so, the stronger the tenant, the more possible it is that it will negotiate to have those activities conducted on portions of the common area that are far from its store. The tenant will say "It's a terrific idea to conduct the blood bank next week at the shopping center. Very community minded, very cooperative, I am all for it. Just be sure that it's not within 500 feet of my store."

Changes in Configuration

Landlord's Perspective

As a rule, commercial leases in shopping centers, office buildings, and industrial buildings run a minimum of three years. They more commonly run five or ten years with options to extend for another five, and frequently run for ten years with options to extend even further. Thus the terms go from three years up to thirty years, and perhaps even more. If the landlord has made the fatal mistake of attaching a plot plan to the lease that indicates a particular configuration of parking areas, driveways, and other common areas and then wishes to alter those in the future, it will have to get permission from every tenant who relied on that plot plan *unless* it has reserved in the lease the right to make alterations to those areas.

Unless the landlord has expressly reserved the right in the lease to make changes to these common areas, pleas of altered circumstances at the building complex, new tenancies, or new uses would all be to no avail in countering the arguments of a recalcitrant tenant who claims the right to control those common areas because, it says, the landlord promised that the common area would always look like it did originally. "Just look at the plot plan attached to my lease and you can see!" For this reason, all landlords will, or should, insist that they have a right to make alterations to the common areas in the future, if for no other reason than to protect themselves against unreasonable tenant demands.

The landlord may be faced with the necessity or desirability of altering the common areas to provide for a reorientation of driveways necessitated by a new traffic light at the interchange, to reconfigure the parking spaces to allow for more compact cars, more SUVs, or for any of numerous other reasons. The most important reason, however, could be that there is more than enough common area to take care of the needs of the complex and still permit the construction of additional buildings. If the landlord lost this ability, this would be costly indeed.

Any landlord who has gone to a tenant to ask for that tenant's gratuitous agreement to a plot plan alteration — no matter that the alteration has no possible relationship to the tenant's business — has without a doubt learned a costly but valuable lesson. Few people who ask for something for nothing get their way. It's better not to have to ask in the first place.

Tenant Protection

In circumstances in which the landlord demands the right to make alterations to the common areas, as any sensible landlord will, the tenant will want to be sure that he or she doesn't grant an unrestricted right. Common areas offer ingress, egress, lobby areas, and parking for the benefit of the tenants. If the landlord is to alter those areas, it should be for the benefit of the tenant. If the landlord is to do additional construction for its own benefit, it should not adversely affect present tenants, who have a right to expect a certain level of delivery of common services. There are three critical elements that tenants will want to preserve: access, parking, and exposure (for shopping center tenants).

Access

The tenant should insist that no changes to the common area impede access to its premises. The construction of a kiosk in front of the tenant's store will act as a hindrance, an impediment to customers. The construction of a fast-food stand in the lobby of the office building may obstruct access to the elevators and, further, may smell up the lobby.

Parking

Construction of buildings or reconfiguration of the parking areas may result in a reduction of parking available for a tenant and its customers. Moreover, it could result in customers having to park farther away from the tenant's premises. Tenants frequently demand that any change to the parking areas not reduce below a certain level the number of parking places within the proximate area of the tenant's location. Thus a tenant may demand that in no event shall there be fewer than X number of parking places within 100 feet of its premises. In an office building the tenant may require that at no time shall the size of the visitor parking area decline below a certain level nor shall the parking ratio (the number of parking spaces per square foot of rentable area) decline below a certain specified level. These levels vary from use to use. Shopping centers have in the past typically used such ratios as 5 or 5 1/2 parking spaces per 1,000 square feet or 3 square feet of parking area for each one square foot of building area. Office buildings frequently use a ratio of a certain number of parking spaces for each 1,000 square feet of rentable area.

Exposure

Retail tenants are particularly concerned about the exposure and visibility of their stores to potential customers in the shopping center or customers driving on surrounding roadways and freeways. Thus, some tenants may request a clause like the following: "No such alteration to the common areas of the shopping center shall materially impede the access to the tenant's premises by its customers, nor obstruct the exposure of the tenant's premises to the surrounding streets of the shopping center, nor reduce the number of parking spaces within 200 feet of the store to fewer than 50, without the tenant's prior written consent."

Common Area Costs

The costs of operating, maintaining, administering, repairing, and replacing the common areas are included in operating costs for office buildings (see Chapter 10) and in the allocation of common area costs in shopping center and industrial building leases. In the case of gross leases, all costs above the base amount are charged to the tenants of the building. In the case of net leases *all costs* are charged to the tenants who, after all, receive the benefit of the upkeep of the common areas because they, not the landlord, are the users of the common areas. A number of questions are presented, just as they are in the other cost allocation paragraphs of the lease (taxes, insurance, maintenance). What is included in common area costs, and how are costs for the common area allocated?

What Is Included?

For our present purposes we will exclude office buildings in which the landlord undertakes the operation of the entire building, including the tenant spaces. That subject will be treated in the next chapter. We will restrict ourselves here to shopping centers, office buildings in which the tenants do their own janitorial work, and industrial buildings. Further, for simplicity, we will assume that we are dealing with net leases. The discussion will be the same as for the gross leases with stops, with the minor exception that the landlord bears the base amount. (See the discussion in Chapter 6.)

The landlord wants to include everything possible in common area costs. It will want to use broad language that is illustrative but not inclusive.

The tenant, on the other hand, wants a narrow definition. The tough, strong, desirable tenants will try to make their list exclusive. That is, they will want to list the items that are includable and exclude any items not on the list.

Typically included, without dispute, on the list of permissible common area costs are cleaning the common areas, lighting, security, striping, landscaping, common area utilities, operating repairs, payroll (but only for employees on-site whose activities are restricted to the project), and liability insurance. This is an illustrative list. There are other items that are characteristically included. One such item is an administrative or management fee.

Management Fees

The landlord will insist that management of the common areas is a time-consuming undertaking for which it must be compensated. This is an unexceptionable position. What tenants object to is the landlord's turning the reimbursement of its staff time into a profit center. If the landlord charges a percentage of common area costs for an administrative fee, this, in itself, should be acceptable to a tenant. The fees acceptable to tenants will run anywhere from 5 percent to 15 percent of common area charges.

In some cases, the landlord includes administrative fees for taxes and insurance in the common area charges. Many tenants will object strenuously to paying the landlord for merely processing a bill. The landlord, on the other hand, will argue with equal vigor that it is not merely processing a bill. It is reviewing the bill carefully, objecting to it, negotiating to get it reduced, and so on. If the landlord has its project 100 percent leased, or the functional equivalent of 100 percent leased, the landlord may not be motivated to try to control costs because it is receiving reimbursement for 100 percent of whatever expenditure it makes. The tenant should not lose sight of the landlord's motivation to ensure that its costs are competitive with competing projects to keep its project attractive to tenants.

In addition, tenants want to be sure that the landlord doesn't include management fees in common area costs, instead of charging an administrative fee amounting to a percentage of common area costs. The charge for management fees is ordinarily based on the rental revenue derived from the project. This revenue has no relationship whatsoever to common area costs and represents a profit center. Anyone should be able to figure out that while management fees may run only 3 percent, administrative fees run 10 percent or 12 percent or 15 percent. This is because management fees are based *on rent*, while administrative fees are based *on common area costs*. Rents are 10, 15, or even 50 times greater than common area costs. Thus, the management fee method of charging results in a greatly higher expense to the tenant than fees based on common area costs.

Capital or Replacement Costs

This argument is similar to that presented in Chapter 7 for maintenance. The tenant is transitory. It will leave at the end of its lease term. The tenant does not want to rebuild the landlord's common areas, particularly if its lease is about to expire. One can sympathize with a tenant who has one year remaining in its lease term and discovers that all of the light standards in the parking lot are to be replaced with a new, more modern variety. The landlord will spare no expense that the tenant must bear. The solutions to this problem are the same as those described in Chapter 7, i.e., amortization of the expense over the useful life of the improvement, caps or ceilings on the expense to be borne by the tenant, and increases in rental.

Allocations

We discussed allocations at length in Chapter 6, Taxes. There are, however, several features unique to the discussion of common area costs: heavy users, special service allocations (which will be discussed in Chapter 10), and cost caps (discussed in Chapter 6).

In a shopping center, certain users of the common facilities, such as theaters and restaurants, make a greater demand on those facilities than do other tenants. Accordingly, the broad spectrum of merchandise-selling tenants may insist that those people, be charged something more proportionate to their use.

I have seen leases (and have written some) in which, for example, the fast-food chain whose building occupies an outparcel of the shopping center in a free-standing manner is charged 150 percent of its pro rata share of common area maintenance charges to reflect the extra cleaning costs that are involved in cleaning up after the customers of that tenant. The revenue derived from that tenant is applied to reduce the common area charges, and the reduced level is then allocated among the remaining tenants.

Estimates

The landlord will want to estimate the amount of the current year's common area expenses and collect that amount in advance, usually monthly, from the tenant, to avoid becoming the financier of what is, after all, the tenant's expense. The tenant will not object to this proposition, as a rule, because it would rather pay the bill in installments than be faced with a huge annual payout.

Miscellaneous

Charges for Parking — Tenants do not want the landlord to charge for parking. This is elemental. One of the attractions that lured the tenant to locate in the building was the availability of parking. During the energy crunch of the mid-1970s, however, government regulations were discussed that would have required parking fees to be charged to discourage the use of automobiles and thus reduce energy consumption. The landlord must, of course, comply with the law, just as the tenant is required to do. Accordingly, landlords generally put a provision in their leases that states that they are permitted to charge for parking. The tenant will want to narrow this down to permit charges for parking *if required by law*. In addition, the tenant will want to be sure that all the revenue derived from the parking charges is applied to common area costs.

The landlord may argue that he should have the right to charge for parking as long as it is uniform throughout the project. Tenants will resist this fiercely. They want parking to be provided for their customers and employees without charge. If there is to be any parking charge, then such charges must be customary in the area and subject to validation, and all income must be applied to reduction of common area costs otherwise allocable to the tenants.

Security — Landlords frequently, and with justification, require that tenants' employees park in areas designated by the landlord. They will frequently also require that tenants provide the license plate numbers of employees to monitor the enforcement of this restriction. The reason is obvious. The parking places in a shopping center are first and foremost for the customers, not the employees. However, once the landlord has designated an area in the outermost regions of the shopping center as that in which employees may park, the tenant may require that the landlord provide adequate security in those outermost regions because sales employees of retail tenants tend frequently to be women. The prospect of women returning alone to their cars late at night is unattractive, to both employees and tenants. It is also unattractive to the landlord, who would most certainly be named in a lawsuit arising from inadequate security. Accordingly, the tenant may request that any such area be well lit and adequately patrolled. The landlord will vigorously resist the latter requirement.

What Is Excluded?

Tenants generally seek to exclude from common area costs painting the exterior of the buildings (unless all the buildings are done at the same time), capital expenditures, landlord's overhead, and all other costs which, while they may be incurred in respect of the shopping center, are not related to maintenance of the common areas.

CHAPTER 10
Operating Costs

As a rule, the term *operating costs* is applicable only to multitenant office buildings in which the landlord provides the full range of property services for the tenant, including janitorial services and provision of utilities. This is distinguished from business park offices, shopping centers, or industrial buildings in which separate utility meters are provided and the tenant provides its own janitorial service. Although there are exceptions to these generalizations, the exceptions do not occur frequently enough to invalidate the generality.

Definition

Landlords want the definition of operating costs to be as inclusive as possible. This arises out of the same reasoning expressed in Chapter 6 concerning taxes and other reimbursable expenses. If the landlord has omitted to include a cost within operating costs, it will be burdened by a directly related reduction in cash flow and income and thus suffer devaluation of the property. A landlord pays a high price for any inadvertent omission. Operating costs will form the basis for reimbursement to the landlord whether the premises are on a net or a gross basis. As I pointed out before, whether the lease is on a net or gross basis goes only to the issue of whether the landlord bears a certain minimum amount of *initial* expense. The risk of *increases* in expenses is borne by the tenant in either case.

The landlord will want to include a generalized statement that all costs related in any way to the complex, whether in respect of ownership, maintenance, repair, or operation, will be included in operating costs. For example:

- Fuel
- HVAC
- Electricity
- Relamping and reballasting lighting fixtures

- All utilities (water, gas) not chargeable to specific tenants by reason of extraordinary consumption
- Labor and/or wages and other payments or costs of personnel hired exclusively for the building (janitors, caretakers, engineers)
- Wages and wage costs for the building manager
- Managerial and administrative expenses
- Costs of independent contractors hired to perform repair, maintenance, or operation of the building
- Supplies
- Window cleaning
- Telephone
- Accounting and legal services
- Inspection and consulting services
- Elevators, porters (see the final paragraph of this chapter)
- Security
- Directory board
- Amortization of equipment used in servicing the building
- Insurance
- Taxes
- Maintenance, replacement, resurfacing, or repaving parking areas
- Landscaping
- Capital improvements

This list indicates the costs for which the landlord will look to the tenant for reimbursement.

Tenant-sought Exclusions

The tenant, on the other hand, will seek to limit the costs that are included in this definition. You may remember that in Chapter 4, the representatives of Leaning Towers (owned by Mr. Galileo) was attempting to arrange a lease with an accounting firm, GOOF. Notwithstanding the unassuming acronym, let's hypothesize that GOOF has been building its practice at a rapid pace and requires additional space. Leaning Towers is conveniently located across the street from a major regional racetrack, providing diversion for the partners of the firm, who nostalgically remember how they got their start in the accounting business.

Accordingly, GOOF has entered into negotiations with representatives of Leaning Towers. At the time that we come upon their negotiations they are discussing the operating costs provisions. The senior partner of

GOOF is Willie B. Partright, noted rooter of columns and son-in-law of founder Frank Feckless. Mr. Partright, in reviewing the definition of operating costs along the lines previously described, has some objections. He notes, for example, the following issues, which he is anxious to discuss in more detail:

1. He will require additional utility services when his people are working seven days and nights a week during tax season. Will there be an additional charge?

2. What if some heavy user of utilities or other services becomes a tenant in the building? Will he have to pick up a pro rata share of the excessive charges? Businesses such as 24/7 multimedia and Internet companies, advertising agencies, and law firms are notorious for following the modern-day trend of all work and little play.

3. He has noted that legal fees and accounting fees are included, but expresses little desire to incur any share of expenses for legal fees that result from new lease negotiations or procedures to evict defaulting tenants from the building, or, for that matter, any expense that results from the actions of one tenant or are for the benefit of one tenant.

4. Mr. Partright has expressed reluctance to contribute to the costs of reconstructing Mr. Galileo's building. (See discussion in Chapter 9, Maintenance.)

5. Finally, Mr. Partright advises the landlord that one of its principal clients is the largest janitorial firm in the metropolitan area, Undocumented Workers of the Americas, Inc., known as (Undocs). GOOF knows that it can have janitorial services performed by its client for steeply reduced rates. This is a little favor that Undocs will do for people who know too much. GOOF has requested that the landlord permit it to do its own janitorial service and receive a credit against its pro rata share of the operating costs that would otherwise be charged a tenant of its size.

How shall Mr. Galileo respond to these pithy remarks?

First, Mr. Galileo will observe that he has a 90,000 square foot building, of which GOOF is going to occupy 10,000 square feet, or 11 percent of the building. Moreover, although 11 percent of the building certainly represents a large tenant, Mr. Galileo anticipates having 25 or

30 tenants in total. Further, Mr. Galileo, an energetic man, owns eight other buildings, some of which are larger. In the aggregate, he has under management (and under the same accounting and billing system) more than 500 tenants. He says to Mr. Partright, "If I were to make exceptions for each tenant it would be impossible for me to efficiently manage the buildings I own." He then launches into a heartrending tale concerning the fairness of his operating costs definition, after which Mr. Partright is barely able to restrain an impulse to give Mr. Galileo a small gratuity to assuage his pain.

However, there are a few agreements that Mr. Galileo might consider making without threatening the integrity of his accounting and billing system. Here are a few possibilities.

1. There can be a standard rate schedule for additional charges for the use of the HVAC in off hours. The rate schedule will be attached to the lease, subject to revision from time to time by the landlord (much as rules and regulations are treated).

2. The landlord may agree that legal or accounting charges incurred in a new lease negotiation or for the termination of a tenant for default will be excluded from operating costs.

3. Although landlords are frequently reluctant to make exceptions to capital expenditures, a few concessions might be possible.

   • Redefining capital expenditures to include only those costs that would not recur more frequently than every five years (or seven years, or ten years) in the operation of similar buildings in the area.

   • Once having adopted such a definition of capital costs, restrict it further by having it pertain to only those capital costs incurred as a result of a governmental requirement or for the purpose of reducing other costs (e.g., a more modern HVAC system) and include capital costs only to the extent of current amortization. (See Chapter 7, Maintenance).

   • The landlord may refuse outright any request by the tenant to perform its own services as being too complex an administrative problem, thus denying GOOF the use of Undocs. However, there are situations in which a landlord agrees to modify its definition of operating costs to allow for such a contingency by stating that costs will not be included to the extent supplied by one tenant for its own use, and in such case, the pro rata share of the remaining costs will be altered to exclude that tenant.

For example, if GOOF provides its own janitorial service, the pro rata share allocable to the balance of the building is 89 percent (remember that GOOF occupies 11 percent of the building). Therefore, if another tenant in the building occupies five percent of the building, as its pro rata share, it will pay 5/89 or 5.6 percent of janitorial costs instead of five percent because the janitorial costs in which the other tenant will share do not include the normally expectable costs that would have been incurred for cleaning the space occupied by GOOF had GOOF not provided its own services. I caution that this is a negotiated solution that is possible, but fraught with danger, because it invites each tenant to see if it can get some building operations work done at less expense than the landlord will charge. This could create quite a headache for the landlord, even if it was adamant in its refusal to permit any other party from doing so.

The mischief that can be caused by claims of favoritism for a particular tenant or shoddy work performed by the tenant who is doing its own work is obvious. The landlord should agree to such a provision only under the most exigent marketing circumstances in which the deal could not be made without such a concession to a major tenant.

Services

HVAC Standards

The performance standards to be met by the HVAC system should be specified either in the lease or in the construction exhibit. There are three principal methods of specifying such performance in a lease.

1. Provide a comfortable atmosphere in the tenant's offices during working hours;

2. To maintain a constant temperature of 72 degrees in the tenant's premises during normal working hours; and

3. To maintain a temperature of 72 degrees in the tenant's premises, but in no event less than 20 degrees below the outside temperature (i.e., if the outside temperature is 100 degrees, the system need only provide an inside temperature of 80 degrees).

As you can see, there is a vast difference between these three alternatives. The first is vague because it relates to a subjective standard of "comfort."

The second standard is absolute. The landlord is obligated to deliver 72 degrees during business hours, no matter what the ambient temperature. In the desert areas of the Southwest, where ambient temperatures rise to 120 degrees in the summer, a 72-degree inside temperature represents 48 degrees below ambient levels. This is a lot of work for the HVAC system.

The final offering provides the landlord with an opportunity to buy a less expensive system in areas where temperatures can rise to those levels. For an appropriate price break the tenant may be willing to accept this if it is unusual for the temperature to rise to such levels (more than 92 degrees) more than once or twice each year.

Other Services

The lease may contain a provision requiring the landlord to maintain the premises in a manner comparable to those of other first-class buildings in the area.

Landlord Responsibility

Repair vs. Maintenance

The landlord will be sure to point out that there is a distinction between repair and maintenance. Under the provisions of a full-service lease, the landlord will agree to maintain the premises by regular cleaning and janitorial services. However, the landlord will demand that the tenant *repair* any damage to any portion of the interior of its premises (excluding the structure, as a rule). This includes the interior partitions and walls, fixtures, and all tenant improvements. Further, it will include electrical and telephone outlets, special mechanical and electrical equipment installed for the lessee, and the like. Thus, if the tenant damages the landlord's property, or its own property installed on the premises is damaged or wears out, the lessee will be responsible. This, at least, is what the landlord will seek.

Careless Tenants

GOOF is proud that all of its employees have been brought up well by their mothers. Their desks are clean at night (this assists in the security of their clients' accounting information as well as pleasing the mothers of the employees), all coffee cups are in the kitchen, and the premises are generally in an orderly condition. The janitorial staff comes in to dust, vacuum, turn on the dishwasher and empty the ashtrays. The work is done in just a few minutes. However, GOOF's next floor neighbor, the State Lottery Oversight Board (SLOB), is not blessed with such tidy employees. Moreover, they all have tenure. The premises at the end of the day are strewn with slips of paper, files have to be lifted to dust furniture, coffee cups are strewn about every desk and partition, and coffee spills are common. In general, it looks more like a kindergarten classroom at the end of a day when the teacher was absent. For this reason, the janitorial staff takes three times the amount of time to cover half the space that is occupied by GOOF. GOOF will not be pleased at paying the additional costs to service SLOB.

It is not unusual, therefore, for language to be included in a lease that causes an additional charge to be assessed against a tenant who accumulates more rubbish than is ordinarily accumulated in the daily routine of a customary business office occupancy (whatever that means) or for the clearing and cleaning of eating utensils and facilities. If such specification is made in a lease by a landlord, it will have a method of protecting itself and its other tenants from abusive tenants such as SLOB.

Frequency and Availability

The parties will want to specify how often the janitorial service will be provided. A good landlord's lease will state that the landlord will provide the service from time to time on weekdays. The tenant will want it more specifically stated as being provided on every weekday after business hours.

Additional Services for Additional Charges

If the tenant requires additional services, as SLOB certainly will, the landlord will bill the cost of that additional service on some hourly rate basis. Similarly, rates should be adopted for additional charges that will be incurred by tenants who make use of the facilities after business hours, as GOOF will do during tax season and as law firms do all year round. Such additional charges would accrue for elevator service and air-conditioning.

The tenant will not want to forget to include provisions in the lease specifying the hours that the elevators will be in service. This should include the right to use the elevators during off hours without additional charge.

Overload

It is important for the landlord to include language specifying that the tenant will be responsible for any charges for overloading the electrical system, including payment for installation of additional power panels or power lines to service the tenant's special demands.

Interruption of Service

Landlords will insist on being absolved from any responsibility for losses caused by an interruption in utility service. This is simply a transfer of the risk that the utility company will be unable to supply the premises adequately (brownouts/blackouts and the like). The tenant will insist that the landlord bear that risk. If it is customary in the area at all, it would not be unusual for such an assignment of risk to occur. However, if the interruption in utility service arises out of some flaw in the building, or is the result of negligence on the part of the landlord's staff, an altogether different issue is presented.

The real argument will take place over how much risk the tenant is willing to bear. The tenant will take the position that if the interruption exceeds a certain length of time (5, 10, 15, 20, 45 days), it should have the right to terminate its lease and move out because it is unable to operate without utilities. The landlord's argument will be that the tenant should obtain business interruption insurance to provide for losses the tenant may suffer, including provision of temporary quarters. The argument gets even more interesting when the risk is split between extended delays caused by the utility or an extended delay caused by the landlord's negligence. In the latter case, the tenant may insist on a right to terminate and collect damages. In the former case the argument is more closely negotiated. However, one cannot lose sight of the fact that the tenant cannot terminate its business operations, no matter what the reason, without drastic effect. Whatever may have caused an unexpected cessation of operations, the tenant is not going to simply close up shop. It must make alternative arrangements in order to conduct its business. In fact, it is as if a casualty has occurred to the premises. (See Chapter 13, Destruction and Condemnation.)

Allocation of Costs

This discussion closely parallels the discussions found in Chapters 6, Taxes, and 9, Common Areas. The issues are identical: base amounts, caps or ceilings, occupancy levels in the entire complex, and estimated payments.

We make particular note, however, of the circumstance in which the tenant is able to bargain for a ceiling on costs. For example, "Tenant's pro rata share of operating costs will not exceed five dollars ($5) per square foot in the first operating year of the term, nor shall the operating costs be permitted to increase by more than five percent (5%) per annum thereafter for purposes of calculating tenant's pro rata share thereof. All such operating costs in excess of the amounts specified in the preceding sentence shall be borne by the landlord."

Under such a provision the landlord has a more compelling argument for including everything, without exception. The landlord will take the position that the tenant is amply protected by the caps and that, therefore, there is no necessity to limit what is to be included in operating costs. The landlord's position is that the tenant should simply budget the full amount of its capped cost-sharing arrangement.

Porter Wage Scam

In some areas of the country, most notably New York City, it is not unusual for the standard form of office or industrial lease to call for the tenant to agree to pay for increases in operating costs based not on actual expenses but, rather, on the change in some labor index, such as the wage rates negotiated by the Real Estate Board with the Porter's Union. With mechanization, outside contracting, and other developments, the number of porters working in the building management industry has declined dramatically over the past 40 years. This has not dampened the ardor of New York landlords for this rent escalation device, and one can see why. Because building owners have relatively few porters (or those represented by the Porter's Union) on the payroll and have leases in which increases in porters' wages are a direct generator of rental increases, it stands to reason that the higher the porters' wages are, the more profit the building owner will earn. In fact, under this system, the landlord is not looking for cost reimbursement at all. It is looking to make a profit. It is not at all unusual for this clause to be found in New York buildings in which there are no Porter's Union employees! One can see where building owners might be tempted to wish for astronomic increases in porters' wage rates.

CHAPTER 11
Assignment and Subletting

The assignment and subletting paragraph is one of the most crucial to any lease negotiation. It is perhaps the single most important clause in the lease after rent and premises. More blood is spilled on this battleground than on any other.

The rent paragraphs generally do not represent a contentious issue because rent is customarily the first thing the parties agree upon. And premises, other than the few odds and ends described in Chapter 2, rarely represents a contentious issue except for construction problems. Assignment and subletting, however, is almost always contentious.

For the landlord, the assignment and subletting clause represents the battle for control of its property. For the tenant, it was once the search for an exit from an unfortunate selection of a location. Lately, it has become important in creating asset value for the tenant company.

Although it is not my objective to spend much time in this book discussing purely legal issues, I will make one brief exception here.

There is a legal difference between an assignment and a sublet. An *assignment* constitutes a transfer of all of the assignor's (tenant's) interest. A *sublet* constitutes a transfer of less than all of the interest (less than all the property, less than all the term, less than all the rights). Frequently, from a business standpoint the distinction is not important.

Other legal issues concerning the distinction between assignment and subletting relate to which party is to be primarily responsible to the landlord under the lease. However, I am not going to discuss either of these issues in this chapter. Why deprive your lawyers of such a good time? For purposes of our discussion, I am going to eliminate the distinction between assignment and subletting and simply refer to both as a *transfer*, or simply use the terms assignment and subletting interchangeably.

Objectives

Landlord

The landlord wants to maintain strict control of its property. The landlord will feel that it has entered into a transaction with a particular tenant. It may have selected the tenant with care. The landlord may, in fact, have checked with her mother-in-law or her sister to be sure that this is the right type of tenant to which to entrust the family's property. The landlord will not want to cede this right of selection to the tenant by granting a blanket transfer right. Thus, the first issue of concern to the landlord is *control*.

Bear in mind that unlike the sale of an automobile, the lease of property involves a reversion. Reversion is the legal term for the landlord's right to reenter and take possession of the property on expiration of the lease term. Thus, the landlord should care very much about the parties in possession of its property.

The landlord might have difficulty obtaining the rent it wishes from a subsequent occupant if the premises have been occupied for five years by a notorious topless shoe store. Moreover, if the landlord has bargained for a financially qualified tenant, it will not want the rent obligation transferred to one whose financial incapacity will result in irregular monthly checks from the bankruptcy trustee. Examples of how a lease can be transferred to a party in a manner wholly foreign to the original contemplation of the landlord are limitless. All of these reasons for the landlord's objections are legitimate.

However, beneath the surface of these legitimate reasons for the landlord wishing to control the space is the landlord's underlying desire to capture all of the real estate profit. In the days of escalating rents, landlords learned to their consternation that tenants developed real assets in leases that were entered into when rental rates were one-half or one-third of current market rates.

Such situations posed a dilemma for some tenants. Was there more virtue in transferring their lease to a transferee who would pay them market rent or should they continue to operate their business in the same space? The question arose as to which would be more profitable. Let's suppose that a tenant has rented 5,000 square feet at $1 a square foot. The space has risen in rental value to $2.25 per square foot, and 10 years remain in the term. One can see without much effort that the gross differential between the value of the contract rent and the undiscounted value of the market rent over 10 years is $750,000.

$$5,000 \times \$1 \times 120 = \$600,000$$
$$5,000 \times \$2.25 \times 120 = \$1,350,000$$

$$\$1,350,000 - \$600,000 = \$750,000$$

This has a present value, if discounted at eight percent interest, of $502,500, as follows:

$750,000 divided by 10 years = $75,000 per year.

$75,000 per year for 10 years discounted at 8% per year has a present value of $502,500.

That's a lot of money. A landlord may have entered into a long-term lease with a tenant only to find inflation and supply and demand have pushed the market value of the space to two or three times the original value. That landlord will be chagrined indeed to find the tenant making huge profits in the real estate business on the landlord's real estate! This is the true crux of the transfer issue.

In summary, the historic interest of the landlord in controlling the transfer is to maintain control of its property to protect its reversionary interest. However, with the advent of rapidly escalating rental rates in the 1970s and early 1980s, the quest for the real estate profit became the true issue.

Tenant

One of the primary rules of negotiation — indeed, a rule of business practice in general — is not to enter into any transaction from which one cannot extricate oneself in event of unexpected circumstances. Business people who place themselves in situations from which they have no escape, are asking for trouble. Thus, the historic rationale for the tenant's insistence on a right of transfer was to reserve for the tenant the opportunity to transfer the lease obligation to someone else in the event the tenant ran into financial difficulty or otherwise found the location unsuitable for its needs.

For example, what if the tenant rented 5,000 square feet for five years only to find its business growth far exceeded its expectations? Only two years later it had a need for 15,000 square feet. The tenant had to move. If it did not have a suitable right to transfer its premises, it would have had to pay rent on the new 15,000 square foot space as well as on the old 5,000 square foot space. If this had been the case, the original lease would indeed have been a box from which there was no exit. So we can see that the historic objective of the tenant in negotiating a right of transfer of its lease obligation was to have an available alternative in the event a change in circumstances required that it vacate the premises.

Having said that, we come again to the new issue described in our discussion of the landlord's objectives: Tenants have found in recent years that rapidly escalating rental rates have created assets they never contemplated before. Leases used to be thought of as contingent liabilities to be footnoted on the balance sheet. In the 1980s, with the advent of leveraged buyouts, tenants found a cache of secret resources as they sat on long-term flat rent leases in rapidly escalating rental markets.

In the situation we described above, the small tenant who took that 5,000 square foot space found itself with a lease having a present value about $500,000. This value could far exceed the value of the business as a going enterprise. When one extrapolates this into larger spaces and longer terms (particularly when including option periods) one can see that enormous values can be created that yield huge profits to the tenant. This is the normal case for larger tenants with leases running 30 to 50 years, including options.

In summary, the historic objective of the tenant was to preserve a way to dispose of a lease obligation in the event of changed circumstances. The modern objective is to attempt to build asset value in the lease.

The Court Steps In

A Brief History

Historically, leases stated that the tenant had no right to transfer its lease for the premises without the consent of the landlord. At common law this meant that the landlord had the absolute, arbitrary right to grant or withhold its consent in its sole discretion. In the late 1970s and early 1980s, courts around the country slowly started turning toward the modern view, which holds that in cases in which a standard of reasonableness is not set forth, the landlord is obligated to act in good faith and reasonably. What this means in plain English is that the landlord cannot withhold its consent in order to obtain the transfer profit. To do so, said the courts, is an act of bad faith.

Profit making as bad faith is a uniquely modern principal that could only have arisen in an affluent society. Many states still adhere to a traditional common law view, Texas being a leading example. However, the number of states moving toward the modern view is growing as each day passes and now includes many of the most commercially active states in the country (Florida, California, Illinois, and New York among them). In these jurisdictions, unless the parties expressly agree that the landlord can be arbitrary and capricious, the landlord must be reasonable. To be reasonable means that the tenant gets the profit unless the lease expressly states otherwise. At least that is what the courts say.

Landlord's Approach to the Modern Legal View

The landlord can take the following steps to protect itself against a tenant transfer:

1. Draft language in the lease reserving to the landlord the right to the profit on transfer.

2. Insert in the lease specific standards that must be met by any transferee, such as:

   Financial adequacy;

   Experience and reputation;

   Use of the premises (see Chapter 3, Use); and

   Use of the common facilities to be controlled so that the transferee's use won't inconvenience the other tenants in the complex, including increases in the cost of operating the common areas because of heavy usage.

3. Agree that in the event there is a transfer, the terms of the lease are changed — for example, that the options not be transferable in any lease transfer; that the lease rent changes to fair market value or to the highest rent payable in the previous three years by the original tenant; that percentage rent previously paid be included in minimum rent; or that rent is to be increased by CPI.

4. Institute procedures for a transfer. Be sure the tenant, in seeking the landlord's consent, supplies adequate information on which the landlord can base a decision as if it were a new lease — for example, financial statements of the transferee, bank references, a resume of business experience, a business plan for the operation to be conducted in the premises, a statement of the use to which the premises is to be put, how many employees, and the like.

Let us say, for example, that we have a supermarket chain called Junk Bond Stores (we'll call them Junkies), which has hundreds of stores throughout the western United States. Junkies has just been taken over in a leveraged buyout by Luvem, Leevem & Breakemup (whom we'll call LLB), whose previous food retailing experience consisted of buying liquor at the local convenience store for all-night parties at college. LLB sees lots of lettuce in Junkies' leases. By illustration, the Junkies store in Gawnbust, Colorado, in the heart of energy country, has not been doing well. An offer has been received from a theater chain to take over the former Junkies' space to install a six-plex in the shopping center where Junkies is located. This is the largest shopping center in Gawnbust. However, it is a small town and the shopping center consists of a supermarket (Junkies), a drugstore, and 30,000 to 40,000 square feet of other space. Unless the landlord has protected itself (an unlikely situation against a strong chain in a small market), it is easy to see that devastation is about to come to the balance of the merchants in the center.

In the first place, movie theaters are dense users of the common facilities, particularly on weekends when the other merchants are doing their best business. In the second place, the other merchants are looking to do business by attracting the customers of the supermarket chain. These are customers who come to shop several times a week. This traffic supports the small shops in the center. People who go to theaters tend not to be shopping at the same time. Thus, the other tenants in the center will suffer both an increase in their common area costs from the heavier usage by the theater and a decrease in shopping traffic. If the lease did not contain restrictions on transfer, on use, and on use of the common facilities, or if it did not allow the landlord to use its reasonable judgment as to the proposed transfer, then LLB will realize a handsome profit on its lease; the movie theater will probably be thrilled to open in the new location; the landlord is about to suffer severe vacancies in the balance of this center as merchants leave for other, more attractive locations; and the merchants will be devastated. All of this will be of little interest to Luvem, Leevem & Breakemup, who have decided on the fate of the Gawnbust location while having lunch at the Harvard Club in New York.

Tenant's Response

The tenant, in the ideal tenant's world, will bargain, as did Junkies above, for an absolute right of transfer. However, absent overwhelming negotiating strength, it is unlikely to be able to obtain all of what it wishes. The next best solution is to bargain for the right to transfer with the landlord's reasonable consent.

Reasonable Consent

What constitutes reasonable consent is a matter of judgment on the part of an objective third party — a jury, for example! However, once the tenant requests an amendment to the lease (i.e., a change in the terms of the lease), the landlord has no obligation to act reasonably toward such a request. The landlord is perfectly within its rights to stand on the precise terms of the lease. If the tenant has failed to bargain for the right to change the use, then it will find itself in the anomalous position of trying to find a tenant with the same use it has had under circumstances in which it has been unsuccessful. Why would another supermarket feel that it could profit where Junkies has not been successful? Such a possibility, of course, exists. However, one can see that it could cause some difficulty for the Junkies in marketing the space.

The tenant should ensure that the landlord is obligated to respond in a timely fashion. If the landlord does not respond after some agreed time, such as 10, 20, or 30 days, the transfer should be deemed automatically approved. But bear in mind that the time period should not start until the landlord has received adequate information on which to form a judgment.

If the use clause states that the premises is to be used exclusively for a food store and for no other use, then an amendment will be required to permit movie theater use. In this case, the landlord will have all of the cards. It is entitled, at least under California law, to ask for more rent once a lease amendment is requested. A clause one could include in the use provision of the lease, if the tenant has to be restricted at all, would be one in which the tenant agreed to use the premises as stated in the use clause and for no other use "except in connection with an assignment or subletting, in which event any change in use required by the transferee shall be subject to the prior written consent of the landlord, which consent shall not be unreasonably withheld or delayed." In this manner, a lease amendment is not required and the landlord would have to act reasonably.

The next question would be whether the landlord is reasonable in declining to approve a movie theater where a food store once existed. From the scene I painted for you, you can see that at the very least the landlord has the framework of a considerable argument.

Corporate Transfers

Landlord's Perspective

The landlord fears that the tenant will strip the company of all meaningful assets. Unless specific language is placed in the lease declaring that the sale of stock in a corporate tenant or a merger, consolidation, or sale of assets constitutes a transfer subject to the landlord's consent, then the landlord's consent will not be required under the law of many states. This may even be true (and is true in California) in cases in which the lease states that transfers by operation of law will be subject to the landlord's consent.

One can readily see that the landlord could end up with a lot less than it thought it had under such circumstances. We can envision a situation in which our mythical supermarket chain, Junkies, had a net worth at the time of the execution of the lease of, let's say, $200 million. Several years later when LLB did its takeover, supported by management, junk bonds were issued to finance the leveraged buyout in the amount of $175 million. In this manner, the buyout was accomplished with $25 million in cash. This now constitutes the equity of the company. This is a materially different tenant from the standpoint of financial prowess than that with whom our landlord started.

One can also see that without the protection a landlord gains when it has the right to consent to a change in control of the company, that landlord's careful screening of its tenants might go for naught. Junkies may have been carefully selected as a high-quality market chain bringing the type of customer suitable for the balance of the merchants in the shopping center. Several years later, Junkies may sell its stock to Cans and Splinters, a "right out of the crate" low-end discounter, which brings an altogether different customer to the shopping center.

For these reasons, the landlord will want to be sure to include language in its lease giving it a right of consent to any merger, sale of assets, sale of stock, or other transfer of control of its tenant.

Tenant's Perspective

The tenant wants to be certain that it has investment control of its own company. If Junkies is a chain of 250 stores, it is not difficult to foresee the problems it will have in selling the company if it has to obtain the consent of each of 250 landlords to such a change in control. Each landlord, acting in its own interest, might demand different concessions in return for its consent. The idea that investors in a retailing or other company could be held hostage by a multitude of landlords from whom individual premises are leased is frightening to contemplate. Therefore, tenants will insist on the right to dispose of the corporation as a whole in their sole business judgment.

Some tenants will not compromise on this issue, demanding at all times that the corporate control of a multiunit tenant should rest with its board of directors, not its landlords. However, the fewer leased premises a tenant has, the less compelling this argument becomes. If a company consists of only one retail location, it is difficult to distinguish the sale of the company from the sale of the lease.

In cases in which the subject is a legitimate issue of negotiation, the landlord might insist on a net worth and other financial tests for the surviving entity, such as a minimum net worth, earnings, earnings history or, even better for the landlord, a net worth and financial performance not less than the entity responsible prior to the change in control. Further, the landlord will insist that to qualify for a change of control not requiring landlord's consent, substantially all of the locations must be involved in the transaction. Otherwise several locations can be cut out like the old and ailing from a herd of deer by a hunting lion, leaving the landlords of those locations exposed while the bulk of the company is retained in operation by what used to be the landlord's original tenant.

Compromises

The Profit Split

Once the issues of control (for the landlord) and potential escape from liability (for the tenant) are resolved through negotiation of standards and procedures, the parties can get down to the real subject of negotiation: real estate profit.

The landlord will claim with passion and conviction that the tenant has no right to earn profits from the landlord's property. The landlord will steadfastly protest its earnest wish that Junkies rake in quantum cartfuls of money selling milk, eggs, and kiwi fruit. Further, the landlord will wish for reciprocity, i.e., that the landlord earn its full measure of profit as an owner of real property.

This view, however, does not mirror that of the tenant. The tenant will take the position that having signed a 10, 15, or 20 year firm lease (ignoring options), from which obligations it cannot escape; it deserves to make any profit that accrues to it for taking the lease risk because it is obliged, no matter what the economic circumstances, to pay the rent as contracted, good times or bad times. The tenant will understandably take the view that it has taken a risk from which it should profit — if profit there be. The landlord will counter that profits are there to be made by the tenant's selling lettuce, not leases.

That is the setting for and substantial content of the argument. How it is settled is a matter of negotiating talent and strength. If the landlord successfully holds out for 100 percent of the profit, it may indeed be a Pyrrhic victory. The tenant, when it does come time to sublease, will simply want to have its obligations covered, no matter how great a bargain it is giving to its subtenant, because any sums it collects in excess of its own obligation to the landlord go to the landlord. The tenant will be unattracted by the proposition of seeking to obtain a higher rent solely for the benefit of the landlord. Wise landlords, for this reason, will leave some percentage of the profit for the benefit of the tenant, even if they are in a commanding negotiating position, so as to give the tenant an incentive to expend the effort to locate a subtenant at higher subrents.

Forms of Consideration

One must bear in mind that there are many ways a transferee can compensate a transferor of a leasehold. This can take the shape not only of subrent but also of a lump sum payment for assignment, inventory, goodwill, and fixtures (any of which can be in excess of true value), thereby avoiding any limited claim to excess rents that might be made by the landlord. Landlords would be wise to defend themselves by including all forms of consideration in respect of the business at the location. This raises the counterargument from the tenant that, in fact, it is selling other assets at the location for valuable consideration, in which the landlord has no interest, including the value of the operating business. Approaches must be developed, particularly in the case of a tenant with a single location, to protect the landlord from a scheming tenant and to protect the tenant from an overreaching landlord. One way, of course, is simply to value the space to be transferred based on its current fair market rent as if unencumbered by the lease. Any consideration in excess of that can be deemed to be consideration for the tenant's business.

Once having decided on what percentage of profit is to accrue to the landlord and what will accrue to the tenant, the tenant will want to be sure to include language stating that it will first receive its costs for subleasing the premises before there is any division of excess proceeds. The tenant doubtless will be spending money for real estate commissions, and perhaps even for architecture, engineering, and tenant improvements. Any expenses it incurs in obtaining a subtenant, the profit from whom is to be shared by the parties, should be taken from the gross consideration received from the transferee before the profit is split. In other words, off the top. A question then arises as to whether such expenses should be amortized over the term of the sublease, or over the remaining term of the lease if it is an assignment, or should come from the first excess rents received.

For example, let's use the hypothetical example we described early in this chapter in which we posited a tenant with a 5,000 square foot space, the value of which had increased from $1 per square foot to $2.25. Our tenant subleases to a transferee (let's call the transferee Sub) for that price. However, the present tenant has to spend $3 per square foot to improve the space and $1 per square foot for brokerage commissions. Presumably, the landlord and the tenant will have decided to share the $1.25 excess rent per month ($2.25-$1=$1.25). However, how is the tenant to get back the $4 per square foot it has spent putting Sub in possession? Does it get the first $4 (that's $20,000 total) of excess rent to reimburse itself or is the $4 to be amortized over the 120-month term and reimbursed at the rate of 3.33 cents per square foot per month, or $167 per month? There is a rather large difference.

We will leave the parties to decide this issue.

Termination

The landlord has listened with interest to Junkies' appeal that it has obligated itself to the risk of the lease and should, therefore, garner the profit for itself. Listening attentively, the landlord's representatives respond, "Risk? Obligation? Fie, fie, fie. If we elect to take the profit, we will relieve you of your obligation." My mother used to call this giving away ice in the winter. What the landlord is really saying is that once it can divine that additional real estate profits can be made from recapturing the leasehold, it will opt for taking the profits and release the tenant of the so-called liability. The problem with its reasoning, however, is that the lease is no longer a liability — it is, in fact, an asset.

However, as we have discussed previously, a good many tenants are focused more on having an escape hatch from the obligations of the lease than on real estate profits. Junkies' founders, for example, were doubtless far more attuned to the opportunities for profit in the food retailing business than they were in speculating in leasehold interests. For this reason, even LLB might very well be willing to forgo the real estate profits in return for release of the contingent liability on its books. There are a number of ways in which this issue can be handled.

Offer Notice

If there is to be a termination (Let's call it *recapture* because, in fact, that is what is happening: The landlord is recapturing the space for itself.), the most favorable method for Junkies is to be able to give the landlord advance notice of its desire to *offer* the premises for transfer before it has actually sought a subtenant, and certainly before it has caught the interest of one. At that point, the landlord has a specified period of time (30, 60, 90 days) in which to elect whether it wishes to terminate the lease and recapture the space. During this period, the landlord, theoretically attuned to the marketplace, will analyze whether it would be profitable to take the space back and attempt to find a substitute tenant. If market rates are higher, then the landlord is likely to do so. If the market rates are the same as or lower than Junkies has agreed to pay in its lease, or if the market is sluggish and the waiting time to obtain a new tenant might be too long, then, in those events, the landlord is likely to forgo the opportunity to terminate. Once its termination period has expired, Junkies is free to seek to obtain a transferee for the space. When it has done so, it then submits that transferee for approval by the landlord in the normal processes. However, the landlord, at that point, will no longer have a right of termination.

Deal Notice

Under this scheme, the tenant must first go out and find a transferee. Having done so, and having entered into a transaction (or at least written a letter outlining the basic terms of a proposed transaction), it then submits the transaction for the landlord's consent under the usual procedures. The landlord would then have the right to terminate or to approve or to deny consent, based on standards previously established (i.e., reasonableness, sole discretion, or any of a multitude of variables). If the proposed transferee is creditworthy and is paying a higher rent, then doubtless the landlord will terminate and redo the transaction directly with the proposed transferee. If not, the landlord may elect to leave the tenant in place, acting as a sublessor, or, if it has the right to refuse to accept the subtenant, it may elect to do so.

Clearly, this is a less desirable (even undesirable) alternative for the tenant because the landlord has, in effect, a right of first refusal. No busy potential transferee will want to spend a great deal of time negotiating the terms of a proposed sublease when the landlord is sitting there with the possibility of terminating its negotiations at will or refusing to let the tenant proceed with the transaction. No tenant with any negotiating strength would agree to such an arrangement.

The landlord may answer this argument by suggesting that if it does elect to terminate the lease, it will agree to do so only by accepting the proposed transferee on the same terms and conditions as those negotiated by its present tenant. In this manner, it is possible to attract prospective transferees because they know that even if the lease with the tenant is canceled, its proposed transaction will nonetheless survive. The proposed transferee, in all likelihood, doesn't care whether its landlord is the tenant or the landlord. The tenant, however, has many problems with this, not the least of which is that it finds itself acting as a procurer or broker for the landlord. This is adding insult to the injury of a failed location.

CHAPTER 12

Insurance and Indemnity

Insurance provisions evoke a yawn in the average lease negotiation. Neither lawyers nor principles wish to spend much time on the subject. It is not unusual for one of the parties to defer any comments to his or her insurance agent. I have found that this frequently presents an opportunity to an astute negotiator because the insurance agents I have met are loath to make any changes to the existing structure of their clients' coverage. As a result, they rarely agree to make alterations, revisions, or amendments to current coverages to meet the requirements of the deal. What they very often say is, "No, we can't do what you ask." Their clients, with astonishing frequency, simply agree. This is an opportunity for a canny negotiator to gain a concession at little cost. **When the other side says that what you request is impossible and that "impossible" item has relatively little cost, it is an opportunity to trade for something of value.**

For example, I have heard insurance agents say that:

1. They will not agree to obtain a contractual liability endorsement to insure their clients' indemnity obligation under a lease; or

2. That their clients will not agree to bear the cost of any waiver of subrogation endorsement; or

3. That they will not agree to indemnify a landlord against the landlord's own negligence.

This is a very brief recitation of a very long list of provisions that insurance agents, from time to time, have advised their clients not to agree to in a lease negotiation. It is advantageous to act aghast, while at the same time stating that perhaps something could be arranged, at great sacrifice to your side, of course, if they would concede that little issue on assignment or sublet about which there has been so much difficulty. The other side has been placed in the position by its insurance agent of simply not being able to deliver on the small insurance question, because insurance is an arcane issue that everyone is afraid to touch lest the heavens be made to open. Consequently, they will frequently concede a much more major point that is within their discretion. For this reason it may be profitable to know more about insurance provisions than the other side does, if for no other reason than to bluff your way into conceding five cents' worth of insurance provisions in return for fifty dollars' worth of some other negotiating provision over which there had been an impasse.

Landlord Insurance

Form of Coverage

Many sagacious landlords include insurance provisions in which they are not *required* to carry any property insurance. Tenants will often miss this obvious omission. They assume that the landlord will carry property insurance. This is a violation of one of the first rules of survival in an irrational world: Don't assume anything.

Good landlords' insurance clauses simply state that the premium cost for the insurance the landlord carries, whatever it is, will be allocated among the tenants; that any tenant causing an increase in the cost of the policy will pay for the full portion of it; and that the landlord has the right to collect estimated payments. One might think that tenants would be inclined not to require the landlord to carry insurance to save themselves the cost of the premium. However, wise tenants would rather have an insurance policy in place for which they pay a portion of the cost so they can be assured that the premises will be rebuilt if a casualty occurs.

When tenants make a demand that landlords agree in writing to carry adequate insurance, landlords may state that they will carry a fire insurance policy with extended coverage endorsement (ECE). The ECE perils are *named* perils. That is, the risks that are covered are risks *specifically listed* in the policy. Typically, these are windstorm, hail, explosion, riot attending a strike or civil commotion, aircraft, vehicles, and smoke. Excluded are earthquake, flood, explosion from steam boiler and pipes, damage from malicious mischief and vandalism, plate glass, and nuclear explosion.

In recent years, the *all risk policy* (now called the *special form*) has come into favor. This policy insures against all perils except those specifically and expressly excluded. Exclusions include costs of reconstruction arising from building code changes, earthquake, earth movement, flood, water damage, mysterious disappearance, and collapse. It is clearly more favorable to carry a special form policy rather than an ECE policy.

The Lease Negotiation

In the course of the lease negotiation, if the landlord is compelled to agree that it will carry a certain type of policy, it may bargain for a number of other rights, such as:

Blanket Policy

In cases in which a landlord owns many buildings, it may have one policy covering all of them, a proposition that can involve material savings. It costs more money to buy five insurance policies on five buildings than it does to buy one insurance policy for five buildings for the same aggregate face amount.

Self-Insurance

The parties may bargain to self-insure a given risk. If the self-insuring party (whether landlord or tenant) is a sufficiently large company, this might be agreeable to the other party. There is a substantial difference, however, between self-insurance and a large deductible. In a technical sense, to be a self-insurer, a party should behave like an insurance company and do such things as setting up reserves for losses. Some of the larger companies indeed have some self-insurance programs. A large deductible, on the other hand, involves no reserves but simply specifies that the party obligated to carry the insurance policy will simply pay the first $x amount of the loss.

Umbrella Coverage

Another possibility for savings would be the use of excess liability coverage (umbrella coverage). This generally pertains to liability coverage rather than property damage. The coverage of the umbrella policy is triggered after the primary policy or underlying coverage is exhausted. For example, if the primary policy is in the amount of $1 million and the umbrella policy is $3 million, a loss in the amount of $1.5 million would be covered as follows: $1 million from the proceeds of the primary policy and $500,000 from the proceeds of the excess liability coverage.

Primary and excess liability policies have annual aggregate limitations and frequently cover many locations. However, such policies may be endorsed at the option of the carrier so that the limits apply separately to each location.

Endorsements

Replacement Value

One of the consequences of inflation, particularly in the construction business, is the necessity for keeping one's policy limits current and sufficient to reconstruct in event of a loss. To further this objective, a replacement cost endorsement is available.

Difference in Conditions

This coverage pays for additional perils not customarily covered by the standard form of special form policy and, even more important, accounts for the additional expense required to meet different code regulations that may have been enacted after the original construction and that must be complied with on reconstruction.

Contractual Liability

The contractual liability endorsement assures each party that the other will be capable of meeting the indemnity obligations that it has undertaken under the lease. This endorsement assures the landlord that the tenant will be able to meet its obligation to indemnify the landlord for injury that occurs on its premises, and vice versa.

Rental Income Insurance

This is coverage carried by a landlord to insure against interruption of the rental income stream derived from the lease as a result of a casualty that has abated the tenant's rent obligation.

Landlord Protective Policy

This policy covers the landlord when it leases substantially all of a building to one tenant who is responsible for operation of the building.

Allocations

The typical landlord lease will allocate, according to size, all operating costs. (See discussion in Chapters 6, Taxes, and 10, Operating Costs.) However, a shrewd tenant who is conducting an unexceptional business operation as far as insurance peril is concerned will want to be sure that it isn't paying a portion of a premium that has been calculated, or rated, by the insurance carrier based on the hazardous business of some other tenant in the complex. For example, the apparel store will not want to pay the additional premiums caused by the conduct of a charcoal broiler hamburger operation next door or the dry cleaner two doors down, both of which are high fire hazard operations.

Similarly, the tenant operating a computer software firm in a business park will not want to pay the additional premium required of the chemical testing laboratory next door.

While the proposition of refusing to pay for somebody else's risk seems justified, the landlord will argue that the administrative difficulty of allocating the premium among tenants based on their varying uses far outweighs the cost savings. Just imagine, the landlord's manager may have to spend as much as two or three hours a year in the calculation. This is, in the end, a matter that will have to be dealt with by the insurance carrier, the only one who can do the risk allocation. The negotiation may come down to probabilities. If one is located in a shopping center, what is the probability that there will be a sufficient number of hazardous uses to cause the premium to rise by a significant amount?

One solution a clever tenant might advocate is that it pays a premium based on the value of its premises, rated (valued for premium purposes) as if it were a freestanding building for its use. In other words, the landlord would have to get a quote from its insurance carrier for the insurance premium on the entire complex as if it were operated as, say, an apparel store. Or just let your imagination wander to a 250,000 square foot hamburger operation. The tenant would then pay its pro rata share of *that* number, no matter what the actual premium was. There is no advantage for the landlord in going through this contortion, except to please the tenant. The landlord can counter that it will agree to do this exercise; however, it then will not give the tenant the benefit of the reduction in premiums effected by the landlord's blanket policy. At this point the tenant has to weigh whether it is worth all the trouble to trade one saving against another.

All of the other issues of allocation are the same as previously discussed in this book in the chapters devoted to taxes, common areas, and operating costs.

Whose Improvements?

The landlord will want to restrict the coverage of its insurance policy to the improvements that it has constructed or that it owns during the lease term. Typically this means the shell. The shell generally means the structure of the space. That is, the roof and walls, with utilities to the space. It often includes the slab floor, but not always. If the landlord gives the tenant a tenant improvement construction allowance, the improvements constructed with the allowance funds would also be included in the landlord's insurance coverage because the landlord should own what it pays for.

The tenant will take the view that the landlord's policy should cover all real property, including the so-called tenant improvements that constitute the leased premises. Tenant improvements are typically defined as everything in the leased premises that are realty but are in addition to the shell.

Tenant Insurance

Personal Property

Landlords will require that the tenant insure its personal property for an amount sufficient to avoid co-insurance provisions, that is, that the tenant will carry insurance to cover at least 80 percent of insurable value so that at least the first 80 percent of the value of the tenant's property is 100 percent covered by insurance.

The tenant will argue that it is none of the landlord's business whether it carries insurance or not, because the landlord will still have a lease obligation from the tenant even if the tenant does suffer damage in its premises. However, the landlord's objective is simply to be sure that there are sufficient proceeds available to the tenant to insure that the tenant has sufficient funds to rebuild and restock its premises and continue in business. A tenant who hasn't got enough money to do that isn't going to be a very valuable tenant to the landlord. The lease will be valueless if the tenant is bankrupt. The provision for requiring that tenant's property be insured is one that can typically be negotiated out of the deal by a strong tenant, but not by a weak tenant. Because almost all tenants, strong or weak, insure their personal property, the only saving for the larger tenant is in avoiding the landlord's review of the tenant's insurance program, including deductibles and self-insurance.

Commercial General Liability

The landlord will be most insistent that the tenant carry a commercial general liability policy, just as the tenant will insist that the landlord carry a similar policy for the common areas. The policy will contain the contractual liability provision previously discussed and, if the landlord is to be a named insured, a cross-liability endorsement as well. Two principal issues are to be negotiated with respect to tenant's liability insurance coverage:

1. Additional vs. named insured, and

2. Policy limits

Additional vs. Named Insured

There is a difference between being named as an *additional insured* and as a *named insured* on a policy. A named insured is covered for its own acts and is not disqualified from coverage by the act of any other named insured (so long as there is a cross-liability endorsement). An additional insured is insured only against liability for the acts of the named party, in this case the tenant, although the benefit of that protection will go to the landlord. The difference may seem a bit abstruse; however, the difference in premium is substantial. If the landlord is to be a named insured, the insurance carrier will want to value the risk record of the landlord as well as that of the tenant. It is like writing two policies. The premiums will be higher. If the landlord carries its own liability policy, the landlord may be willing to make a concession in return for a concession elsewhere in the lease because it will be without cost.

Policy Limits

The landlord will naturally want the policy limits to be as high as possible to keep everybody protected against large claims. The tenant will weigh the protection afforded by the large policy limits against the additional cost of such high limits. The landlord may ask for $3 million single limit coverage. The tenant might come back with an offer that includes a two-tier structure. The tenant may offer $500,000 in primary coverage to keep its primary policy premiums low, but add $3-$5 million additional in umbrella coverage, which is typically much cheaper than primary coverage because of the huge deductible. The landlord may find this acceptable once it weighs the number of locations that the tenant has covered with its policy.

Indemnity

For reasons having more to do with the ego of negotiators than with business economics, the indemnity provisions of a lease seem to take more time to negotiate, relative to their value, than any other provision.

The landlord will take the position that the tenant is responsible for everything that happens on the premises because the tenant has possessor control over the premises and is also responsible, indirectly, for everything that happens in the common area through its payment of common area insurance premiums.

The tenant will take the position that it will be responsible for its negligence and the landlord should be responsible for the landlord's negligence. A simple solution to this problem is simply to convert the lease, as to indemnity, to no fault. The resistance to this proposition, as efficacious as it sounds, is nearly universal. Some day I hope to have the reasons explained to me.

No Fault Provisions

The theory of the no fault indemnity provision is simple: The risk of loss for any given damage or claim of damage falls on the party who is obligated to carry the insurance for such a loss under the terms of the lease.

For example, if the landlord is obligated to carry the special form policy for the building, as discussed above, then it doesn't matter *why* the building burns down. Except for certain exclusions we will examine, the landlord is declared to be the responsible party. The underlying reason is that because the landlord has paid the insurance premiums to the insurance company, the insurance company who collected those premiums should be obligated to step up to the line and pay the claim when it occurs, no matter who is at fault.

If, on the other hand, an innocent party trips and falls in the tenant premises, thereby injuring himself or herself, and files a claim, then the tenant will be responsible, even though the trip and fall may have occurred because of a leak in the roof that was the maintenance responsibility of the landlord. The reason is that the tenant, under the terms of a customary lease, is obligated to carry the liability policy covering incidents occurring within the premises. Thus the provisions for indemnity are "no fault." That is, regardless of fault, the party obligated to carry the insurance is deemed to be the responsible party so its insurance carrier can cover the loss. The other party — the tenant in the case of the burning down of the building, the landlord in the case of the trip and fall — is indemnified by the party carrying the insurance policy, as required by the lease, and is held harmless from any claims, including costs of defense.

It's all very simple. The indemnity and insurance distinction is geographic. If it's within the leased premises, the tenant must carry the insurance policy and must indemnify the landlord. If it's outside the premises (excluding other tenant space) but within the building complex, it is the responsibility of the landlord.

No fault has clear advantages to a landlord because most of the insurance obligations rest with the tenant. That is, liability insurance, personal property insurance, and, generally, insurance for tenant improvements installed by the tenant are all the obligation of the tenant. The landlord is obligated to carry the property insurance for the building and will be obligated to indemnify the tenant from any claims arising out of damage to the building. The common areas, however, are a different story. The tenant will insist that the landlord, under the no fault provision, indemnify the tenant against claims for occurrences in the common area. The tenant will state that the landlord constructed those areas and controls the areas by virtue of its management. Moreover, the landlord will be purchasing the insurance for the common areas, although the cost will be passed through to the tenants. This will be an argument because the landlord will claim that the tenant or tenant's customers and suppliers are the ones using the common areas.

Exclusions from No Fault

Generally, there are a number of exclusions from no fault coverage. Courts in some states will forbid a party from being indemnified against its own active negligence. Insurance companies will almost universally balk at the idea of indemnifying a party against its own gross negligence or willful acts. *Gross negligence* is the degree of negligence that represents a willful or wanton disregard of the consequences of one's acts. It borders on criminal activity. Similarly insurance companies will balk at indemnifying anyone against their own willful acts. If the landlord enters the tenant's premises and hits one of the tenant's customers over the head with a baseball bat, the tenant's insurance company will not indemnify the landlord, nor should the tenant, notwithstanding that there may be a no fault provision in its lease.

Fall Back Positions from No Fault

The following describes several fall back positions from no fault that can be taken in a lease negotiation.

1. The no fault provision establishes the position that the insured party indemnifies and holds the noninsuring party harmless from any claims arising as a result of the insured loss, including losses that arise from the negligence of the noninsuring party or its breach of the lease. In the example we used earlier in the chapter, the landlord may have had the obligation to maintain the roof. It failed to do so, a roof leak resulted, water fell on the floor of the tenant's premises, and one of the tenant's customers injured herself as a result. This is a damage that arises out of a breach of the lease by the landlord, if the landlord had, in fact, been notified

of the roof difficulty. In many states, including California, one can be indemnified against one's negligence or breaches if it is expressly stated in the indemnity. A distinction is made between a general and explicit indemnity in the law. But this is not a law book, leave it to your attorney. In some states, it may not be possible to indemnify against either one's own negligence or some form of one's own negligence.

2. The indemnity shall apply to all acts of the noninsuring party, excluding sole negligence. Sole negligence is what it sounds like. The injury or damage was caused by the negligence of the landlord alone in the trip-and-fall example we used. That is to say, there was no contributory negligence by the tenant, even to a small degree. If the water had been lying on the tenant's floor for two days without the tenant's taking the trouble to clean up the wet spot, that would be contributory negligence.

3. The noninsuring party is not indemnified against its own active negligence. Active negligence results from an affirmative act by the uninsured party — for example, if the tenant, in building out the tenant improvements to the premises, left exposed wires in the wall that ignited a fire. This can be contrasted with passive negligence, which may arise, for example, when the landlord neglects to sweep the sidewalk in the common areas. However, some courts have held that such an omission may also be considered to be active, if flagrant enough and if done knowingly.

4. The noninsuring party is not indemnified against its own negligence. Here we do away with all distinctions with respect to negligence, including gross, sole, active, and passive. Any negligent act, however arising, is not indemnified against. This effectively negates the no fault provision, reverting to the simplest form of indemnity: Each party is responsible for its own negligence, notwithstanding the existence of insurance.

Arguments Against No Fault

The most typical argument against no fault insurance is that the insured party is paying premiums to its carrier that are based on its own loss record. It may have a very fine loss prevention system in its organization that has resulted in an enviable loss record and low insurance premiums. However, by switching to no fault, it takes on the obligation of paying for losses that are not its fault but rather the fault of its landlord (or its tenant, as the case may be). This is a more persuasive argument for a large tenant, which, in fact, may have its premiums directly tied to its loss record, than it is for a small tenant or landlord whose rates are more standardized. One way to combat such an argument is with proof by the other party of its exemplary loss record.

Fault Provisions

If there is to be a provision in which the party at fault is to indemnify the party who is not at fault (the opposite of a no fault provision), then there are a number of issues the parties may want to include in the lease negotiation. The fault provisions generally favor the tenant because, as previously mentioned, the tenant, rather than the landlord, is generally saddled with the obligation for insurance coverage. A good tenant's provision will state the following elements: The tenant's obligation to indemnify is restricted to losses arising out of its use or occupancy of the premises, and only to the extent that such losses arise out of the acts or omissions of the tenant or its agents. The landlord will want to include *invitees*. An *invitee* is simply any person on the premises with the permission of the tenant. The tenant will resist this because any number of people can enter its premises with permission — people over whom the tenant has no control whatsoever. In a store, for example, this would include customers.

The landlord, in such a provision, should be responsible for maintenance of the premises (remember our roof leak), as well as for the design, maintenance, and operation of the complex, including the common areas. This places the burden on the landlord for any damage or claims arising out of latent or patent defects in the construction of the real property or for any damages occurring in the common areas over which the landlord has management control and for which, presumably, it has purchased insurance.

It will take a strong tenant, indeed, to saddle the landlord with these strictures. Landlords are very insistent about their passive role and generally will agree to be responsible only when they are obliged to carry insurance and only to the extent that it is a cost that will be passed through to the tenants.

Waiver of Subrogation

This issue usually is not heavily negotiated. Waiver of subrogation is a form of no fault for the benefit of the tenant. In this provision the parties agree that the noninsuring party shall not be responsible for losses suffered by the insuring party or for claims for damages caused by a peril for which one of the parties has insurance. The provision will go on to state that the parties will have their insurance policies endorsed to reflect this agreement. This is called a waiver of subrogation endorsement.

For example, let's assume that the landlord carries a property insurance fire policy and that an employee of the tenant accidentally throws a lit match into the trashbasket, an act that burns down the premises. The landlord's insurance carrier will cover the loss and, absent the waiver of subrogation provision, will be subrogated to the landlord's rights against the tenant (that is to say, the insurance carrier will step into the shoes of the landlord) and will take the landlord's claim against the tenant for the tenant's negligence. However, if the parties have waived subrogation, in effect the insurance company has waived its right to sue the tenant for this negligent act. This is *true* no fault. It used to be that this endorsement was easy to obtain without cost. With the changes in the insurance business in the past five years, today there occasionally is some charge for this endorsement. However, it still rarely represents an issue of contest in negotiations between the parties.

Waiver of Claims

All landlords will require some waiver of claim by the tenant for damage suffered by the tenant to its property as a result of the landlord's negligence. This is different from indemnity because indemnity generally applies to the issue of damage suffered by a third party. The waiver of claims provision addresses claims filed by the landlord against the tenant or by the tenant against the landlord. A waiver of claims most specifically deals with claims that would otherwise be filed by the tenant against the landlord for the landlord's negligence. Let's take that roof leak. Let's say the roof leak develops right over the tenant's mainframe computer and results in the obliteration of thousands of records. The cost to reconstruct these records is substantial. With a waiver of claims provision, the tenant will have to look to its own insurance coverage for the cost of reconstruction. The landlord's rationale is that it has no way of knowing from one day to the next what the value of the tenant's property is. Accordingly, it has no way to purchase insurance if it doesn't know how much it should buy, and it is up to the tenant to carry its own insurance and not look to the landlord for indemnity.

CHAPTER 13
Destruction and Condemnation

There are three critical issues to bear in mind when negotiating destruction and condemnation clauses:

1. Rent abatement

2. Termination rights

3. Use of proceeds

In this chapter we illustrate these three issues with a hypothetical restaurant tenant, coincidentally called The Embers, which has leased space in a shopping center from Opportunity Knocks Again, whom we will refer to as OKAY. OKAY purchased the shopping center from the original developer. The shopping center was built approximately seven years ago, when rental rates were not nearly what they are today. The Embers has been doing adequate business to earn a fair profit for the owners. However, it has not paid material percentage rent. The business profits earned by the owners of the restaurant are augmented by the favorable rent arising under their seven-year-old lease, which has three years remaining plus a five-year option to extend. At this time, the chef in charge of the charbroiler seeks to assist the flame with a vigorous squirt of charcoal lighter that results in the destruction of half of the restaurant (in terms of reconstruction costs) but, fortunately, no injury to humans.

Abatement of Rent

When Does Rent Abate?
Landlords frequently take the position that rent should not abate for a casualty because the tenant can purchase rent insurance. The cost of this insurance, however, is substantially higher than the cost of purchasing a rental income endorsement to be appended to the landlord's property insurance policy. If the tenant is successful in

convincing the landlord that the rental income insurance will cover the landlord's losses, then the parties can generally agree that rent will abate from the date of the casualty (i.e., when the insurance claim becomes valid).

Tenant Negligence

The landlord will often insist that the rental loss coverage — and, concomitantly, the rental abatement — not be effective in the case of tenant negligence. This position creates two problems for the tenant. First, because the tenant is the occupant of the premises, and because fires rarely occur without *someone* being negligent, it is likely that any fire that arises will be caused by the negligence of the tenant, its guests, or employees. In our case, for example, the chef's action would surely have disqualified him in the competition for a Rhodes scholarship. Thus, in almost all cases of fire, someone operating under the tenant (or under another tenant in the building complex) will likely have been negligent. The result is that under such a provision, the tenant will rarely have rental abatement. If this is the case, why pay for rental loss insurance, the cost for which is surely a pass-through under the lease.

Second, if the lease states that rent does not abate in event of tenant's negligence, then rental loss insurance will not pertain; therefore, any premiums paid for this endorsement are wasted. If there is no rental loss, there will be no valid rental loss claim. Thus, it is a Catch-22 situation for the tenant: The landlord says the tenant can have rent abatement if the landlord is covered for rental loss; there is no coverage for rental loss if there is no abatement under the lease; there is no abatement under the lease if the loss is caused by tenant's negligence. In effect, the tenant will receive no benefits at all from the rental loss endorsement for which it is surely paying. For this reason the parties should decide whether the rental loss is to be covered by landlord's rental loss insurance or by tenant's rent insurance. If the former, then the rent should abate, notwithstanding the tenant's negligence. If the latter, then the rental should not abate under any casualty circumstances.

What Is the Abatement Period?

Most often the parties will simply agree that the rental will abate until the landlord reconstructs (assuming it is the landlord's obligation to do so) and redelivers the premises, reconstructed, to the tenant. Many tenants, however, insist that they have the same fixturing period that they had at commencement of the term. For example, in those cases in which a tenant has a substantial amount of tenant improvement work to do, as is surely the case with a restaurant such as Embers, which must repurchase and reinstall all kinds of restaurant equipment (stools, booths, counters and the like), the tenant insists that the rent should not start until after this fixturization period. A landlord should check carefully with its insurance carrier to be sure it can continue to collect rental loss insurance after the date on which all of its construction obligations are complete. Customarily, insurance carriers will pay rental loss claims only until repairs are completed. For rental loss coverage to continue beyond such a date may require a special and costly endorsement. Landlords beware.

How Much?

The most typical lease arrangement provides that the rent shall abate in proportion to that percentage of the premises rendered unusable by the casualty. In this case, we hypothesized that 50 percent of the premises had been damaged. Thus, half the rent is abated. The problem is immediately apparent. With 50 percent of the premises damaged, the tenant is unable to operate. With no operations and no revenue, it still is obligated for one half of the rent and other charges. Some businesses may be able to operate in a portion of their space by conducting a reduced business operation. Others, in which the space is compartmentalized into integral units, cannot operate unless all integral units are in operation. A restaurant has a kitchen and a serving area that are separate. If the kitchen is destroyed, then, obviously, the serving area is not of much use, there being nothing to serve.

For this reason, tenants usually insist on some vague language to the effect that rent is to abate to the extent of the interference with tenant's normal business operations. If this last concept is agreed to, the parties should be specific about how to decide about the degree of interference. Arbitration provisions can be useful in this circumstance. Larger tenants will insist that they make the decision as to when and in how much space they should operate. Such tenants do not abide instructions as to how to conduct their businesses.

Termination Rights

This is the true battleground in the original lease negotiation. OKAY may have purchased the shopping center in part because it saw that some of the tenant leases were at rents that were below market, and thus the intrinsic value of the space was greater than the contract rents being received. It had purchased the center with an eye to increasing these below market rents at the first opportunity. Where do you think they got their name?

Embers presents a perfect example of why they bought, and a wonderful opportunity. Embers is operating under its seven-year-old lease, and it hasn't been paying much in percentage rent. OKAY now will look at this space with an eye toward termination and renegotiation of the lease with Embers or finding somebody else if it has the chance to do so under the original lease. The tenant, on the other hand, now considers the lease to be an asset because its contract rent is less than the fair market rental value of its space (see the discussion in Chapter 11). It is clear to see that the landlord's objective and the tenant's objective are diametrically opposed.

Landlord's Objective

OKAY will seek to maximize the opportunity. Its objective will be governed in large part by the degree of control that its lender has and the reliance that the lender has placed on the tenant's lease in arranging the financing. If Embers were a credit tenant and the lender had relied on the stream of income from that lease to service its debt, the lender will be very reluctant to allow OKAY to terminate Embers' lease. If, however, this is a relatively small lease from a noncredit tenant, and that surely is our case, the lender may allow the landlord free rein to deal with the situation. In such a situation, a number of considerations will cause the landlord to want to negotiate a right to terminate in event of a substantial casualty. There are two principal factors.

The first motive for the landlord, and the least defensible, is that the landlord simply wants to take this occasion to increase its rent or obtain a better tenant. This reason cannot be expressed to any tenant in the course of the original lease negotiations when the parties are thinking about making love, not getting a divorce. However, be assured that the landlord is first and foremost thinking about trying to improve its position.

The landlord may see the situation as an opportunity to reconfigure the building. A seven-year-old shopping center presents an opportunity for remodeling and refurbishing, particularly when insurance proceeds are available. Thus, the landlord may be thinking that if it must reconstruct the premises, with only three years remaining in Embers' lease, it will not reconstruct it in the original manner. It may not, in fact, want a restaurant there at all. The landlord may have learned from experience that the use is not suitable for the shopping center the way it has finally matured. If the shopping center has become an upscale specialty type center as it evolved over seven years, the landlord may not think that the charcoal-broiled hamburger operation is suitable any longer, particularly when one thinks of the odors that are emitted from any restaurant, let alone one with an open kitchen. The landlord may now feel that the use no longer represents the highest and best use of the space. Not only does the landlord prefer a different use, but that different use may produce a higher rent.

For these reasons, the landlord may take the view that it is not interested in spending its insurance proceeds to reconstruct anew that which is no longer suitable. You recall there are three years left in the term, with a five-year option. It is frequently negotiated among landlords and tenants that if some minimum initial term remains, with an option (say one, two, or three years remaining in the initial term at the time of the casualty), that the tenant may be terminated by the landlord unless the tenant at the time of the casualty exercises its option to extend the term. The tenant's argument is that the insurance proceeds are not being used to construct obsolete space because there is a minimum of eight years remaining in the term (that is, three years remaining in the original term plus the five years of the option). This will not solve the landlord's primary objectives of changing the use and increasing the rents. However, if the tenant exercises its option at the time of the casualty, it does provide a solution to the problem of using construction funds to build a specialized facility that will only be used for a relatively short additional period.

Tenant's Objective

The tenant will take the position that under no circumstances should the landlord have a right to terminate its lease as a result of a casualty. The tenant will argue with fervor that the landlord should not take opportunistic advantage of an unforeseeable chance occurrence to damage the tenant's business rights. The tenant will argue that the landlord has undertaken a ten-year obligation (with an option to extend) that should not be erased by the accidental happening of a casualty such as a fire. Random occurrences should not give the landlord, (argues the tenant) the right to redo the transaction.

The tenant wants to protect its lease for a number of reasons.

Having invested seven years in developing a clientele at this location, it will not want to have this goodwill eradicated without trace by an accidental event.

To duplicate the location, recognizing the escalating rents of the past few years, the tenant may have to pay considerably more money than its contract rent under the existing lease. Therefore, the lease has developed into an asset, as we explained in Chapter 11, Assignment and Subletting. The tenant does not think this asset should be expunged by a chance event, although such a loss may be covered by purchase of a Leasehold Insurance Policy.

For these reasons, the tenant will want to negotiate to obligate the landlord to rebuild the premises in event of a casualty. Moreover, the tenant may with a straight face argue that it should have a termination right that it may elect to exercise if the location has been unprofitable, at the same time insisting that the landlord should not have a termination right in the event of a casualty. If the tenant raises such an argument, it will be hard pressed to counter a landlord's reciprocal demand.

However, this will not stop the tenant's arguing that it should have a right to terminate in the event the landlord does not reconstruct the premises in a timely fashion. Embers' argument is that there is only a limited amount of time that it can stay out of business before the goodwill it has developed over the years disappears as its customers and clients go to competitors to slake their voracious appetites for burnt hamburgers (or stylish lingerie, or bifocal lenses, or any other product). No retailer likes to close down a profitable location for any reason. Anyone who has been associated with retailers knows that closure is anathema. Once a casualty occurs, all hands are on deck to get the store open as soon as possible. The tenant will want the landlord to cooperate in a similar vein.

This sword, as almost all swords, has multiple edges. First, before the landlord will agree to give the tenant a termination right, it will insist that its lender first approve. If the lender has relied on this lease in making its loan, it will not want that lease terminated, lest the source for repayment of its loan be affected. Further, if the tenant obligates the landlord to reconstruct and yet reserves the right to terminate if the construction is not completed in a timely fashion, the landlord could find itself in the uncomfortable position of having reconstructed space especially for the existing tenant only to find that the tenant cancels when the landlord is delayed and cannot complete the space on time. In such a circumstance, the landlord will want to take unto itself protections against the occurrence of such an unfortunate event. You can picture OKAY's displeasure when, having reconstructed the charcoal broiler restaurant in space it does not consider suitable for that use, it finds that because it was one month delayed, for reasons it couldn't control, it is stuck with the restaurant, but is no longer reciprocally benefited with the tenant. For this reason, parties frequently negotiate language obligating the landlord to be diligent and providing extra time if the reconstruction is delayed as a result of causes not reasonably within the control of the landlord. This is commonly referred to as *force majeure*.

Uninsured Casualty

One principal exception to the rules governing termination rights and reconstruction pertains to uninsured casualty. An uninsured casualty is typically a casualty that is not a named peril under a standard form of "special form" property insurance policy. Frequently parties don't negotiate specific language. Rather, lease provisions simply discuss *uninsured casualty*. In that case, sloppiness will lead to treating large deductibles as uninsured, because they are, in fact, simply an amount of risk for which insurance was not purchased. It is better to include a definition along the lines that I have outlined above. Landlords take the adamant position, with some justice, that they will not obligate themselves to reconstruct a premise out of pocket when no insurance proceeds are available.

The tenant, for its part, will argue that the landlord is going to rebuild something after the casualty, thus, why not rebuild the tenant's premises? The landlord will take the position that what it elects to do over a period of time is none of the tenant's business. This is not an endearing argument. Endearment is not an objective of either party, however.

It is unlikely that the landlord will simply allow its property to lie fallow and undeveloped. Some development is likely to occur when the landlord arranges to finance it. But the landlord will argue that if it must reconstruct from scratch with its own funds, it should have the right to decide on the use and the terms of any lease with any lessee, just as if it were constructing a brand-new project without the burden of leases.

The tenant may counter with the following arguments:

There should be some minimum amount of uninsured casualty that the landlord should be obligated to reconstruct ($50,000, $100,000, or 5 percent or 10 percent of the reconstruction value of the premises).

If the cost of repairing an uninsured casualty exceeds this floor amount, then the landlord could simply elect not to pay any excess. If the landlord makes this "negative" election, the tenant could then elect to either terminate or pay the difference itself.

If the landlord insists on an absolute right to terminate the lease in the event of an uninsured casualty, the tenant may insist that the landlord have no such right unless it terminates all other tenants similarly situated. That is to say, if three or four premises were damaged by an uninsured casualty, the tenant will request that the landlord not be discriminatory as to which tenant it terminates and which it keeps.

Compromise Solutions to Termination Demands

If the landlord successfully presses its requirement that it have a right to terminate the lease in event of a casualty, then a tenant may want to mitigate this right. This mitigation can take a number of forms, which we will list here without preference.

The landlord may terminate the tenant if it terminates all other tenants in the shopping center. In this manner, the tenant can be assured that the landlord's objective is to reconstruct for a different use or in a different configuration, and that the landlord will not simply use the excuse of the casualty to discriminate among its tenants when reviewing its leases to see which tenants it wants to keep and which it would wish to discard.

Alternatively, if the landlord terminates the tenant, it must terminate all other tenants within a given area of the shopping center. For example, if the shopping center has three or four separate buildings or wings, then the tenant may not be able to argue for termination of every tenant in every wing but, rather, only those in its wing or all tenants within 500 feet or other similar geographic designation. The landlord may be willing to review this fall-back position because at least it has the logical consistency of proposing that only other tenants in a similar position are terminated.

If the tenant is terminated, landlord will give the tenant a right of first refusal for the space it reconstructs on the site of the original premises. As we explained in Chapter 2, a right of first refusal has no virtue to a landlord because it obligates the landlord to seek and find another prospect before the tenant makes any decision. Other disadvantages to the landlord also have been previously discussed.

The tenant will be granted a right of first offer for the space constructed on the site of the original premises. This may be a little more palatable to the landlord if it wants to retain the tenant at all.

Use of Insurance Policy Proceeds

Landlord's Objective

In negotiating provisions in a lease concerning the use of insurance proceeds, the landlord has the following objectives:

The landlord will want to be sure that any obligation it has to its tenant is subject to the landlord's obligations to its lender. The lender always comes first. The landlord cannot promise to do certain things with the proceeds when it may have an obligation to assign those proceeds to its lender. I will not discuss here the law concerning the lender's rights, or lack of rights, to commandeer the proceeds to pay down the loan. I will only observe that in many states the lender does not have the right to require application of the insurance proceeds to the loan unless its security has been impaired. In many states, however, the contrary is true; the lender has the free right to appropriate the money.

The landlord will further want to insist that its obligation for construction be restricted to the amount of proceeds available to it. This is the out-of-pocket theory that I described in discussing uninsured casualty above. No self-respecting landlord will obligate itself to spend new funds of its own for the purpose of reconstructing a tenant's space. The tenant's counterargument is that the landlord should carry insurance to cover 100 percent of the replacement value; therefore, this should not present a problem if the landlord complies with its lease obligations. Further discussion of this issue revolves around what constitutes tenant improvements that are to be insured by the tenant and what constitutes shell or structural improvements that are to be reconstructed and insured by the landlord. This is a question that should be dealt with under the insurance provisions, rather than under the destruction provisions, of the lease.

Tenant's Objectives

The tenant will want to focus on three primary objectives with regard to proceeds.

1. All funds should be used in reconstructing the premises, at least to the extent required.

2. If the damage is substantial, an independent third party, such as the lender or other financial institution, should act as a stakeholder for the insurance proceeds to be sure that the funds are used in reconstruction.

3. If the landlord does not judiciously undertake its obligations for repair, the tenant has the right to undertake that repair on the landlord's behalf to get its premises back in operation. In such a case, the tenant will want the right to use the insurance proceeds.

Tenants should not fool themselves that the positions outlined above in this chapter are easily available in a lease negotiation. They are not. Only the most tenacious and desirable tenants will be able to get the benefit of most of these alternatives. **But there is a rule of salesmanship that pertains with equal force to any negotiation: Ask for the order. If you don't ask for it, you have my personal guarantee that you won't get it. If you ask, who knows what might happen. Someone might even say "yes.")**

Condemnation

Condemnation and casualty issues are substantially the same. The identical concepts that pertain to rent abatement, termination rights, and the use of proceeds will apply. However, there are several material differences that must be considered.

Premises

After a condemnation, the premises are not the same. Unlike a casualty, in which one rebuilds the building, after a condemnation some portion of the premises or the common areas will be gone. From the tenant's perspective, this isn't the same deal that it entered into originally. There is a question as to whether the tenant would have made the same transaction if it had known that some portion of its premises would be taken or that the access to the parking lot was going to be reconfigured to be at a position 500 feet instead of 50 feet from its premises. If the tenant leased 5,000 square feet and 1,000 square feet are taken in a condemnation, the question is whether the tenant, in the initial instance, would have leased a 4,000 square foot premises. If not, why should it have to take a 4,000 square foot premises after the condemnation? Thus a tenant will often insist that it have the right to terminate for any taking because the transaction will have changed, involuntarily.

The landlord will argue that the tenant should not have a right of termination unless the taking materially interferes with the conduct of its business. Conceptually this is a sound argument. However, carrying it out involves a substantial amount of subjective judgment.

The Award

The primary issue of negotiation with respect to condemnation clauses usually revolves around the distribution of the condemnation award. Landlords will insist that they be paid for the entire value of their real property before the tenant gets any award.

The tenant, on the other hand, will insist that it be paid for all of its property — such as tenant improvements, moving expenses, and the bonus value of the leasehold.

The bonus value of the leasehold is the difference between the contract rent stated in the lease and the fair market value of the space. Stated another way, it's the difference between what the tenant is obligated to pay under the lease and what another tenant would pay for the space if it were available for lease. A landlord justifiably takes the position, as stated in the discussion of assignment and subletting, that it does not want the tenant to be making a profit on the real estate. It will insist that all proceeds from the real estate of which the leasehold bonus value is a part are the property of the landlord. The tenant will argue that its asset value in the lease should not be terminated by a fortuitous event that neither party could have foreseen at commencement of the term. Further, argues the tenant, it will now have to lease other space and pay higher rent. It will be obligated to pay more than it had contracted to pay under its existing lease to replace its premises elsewhere. The cost of doing this, when it was otherwise entitled to an additional three years on the term, should be paid by the condemning authority. In fact, the condemning authority is paying it, but it is called the bonus value of the leasehold.

This sets the terms of the argument. It will have to be a strong tenant indeed who will prevail.

CHAPTER 14

Default and Other Provisions

A s a rule, default provisions (those provisions set forth to remedy any violation of the terms of the lease) are not intensely negotiated. I know a landlord, a man partial to aphoristic simplification, who states that, "A tenant in default has no rights." Although this phrase contains the hyperbole one might expect of a successful developer, it is indicative of the principle that a party that has not lived up to its obligations under the lease is not going to be the object of much sympathy. Nonetheless, the parties do want to include certain protective elements in the default clause to prevent disproportionate consequences for technical or minimal breaches. Moreover, as we shall see, the landlord is not wholly without interest: it wants to protect its own flanks in the event it goes into default.

Tenant Default

Tenant Concerns

Notice and Opportunity to Cure

The tenant will bargain for adequate notice of its breach and a sufficient period in which to correct it. Almost all state statutes provide for some "grace" period, even for a failure to pay rent. A large corporation has just as great a bureaucratic problem as a government has, and it needs to be told that a check hasn't been mailed or that the computer has taken further nourishment in the form of a mouthful of chewed-up rent checks. For this reason, the tenant will ask that it not be declared in default for failure to pay rent or other sums of money until it has received written notice from the landlord. The tenant's argument is that it should be able to avoid a default that arises out of an inadvertency, a technical or mechanical error, such as our hungry computer, a dilatory post office, or an accounts payable clerk who took a one-week lunch hour.

Landlords, while they are often sympathetic to the principle addressed in the tenant's argument, see themselves at risk of becoming a form of lender to the tenant each month for the period of the required notice. The landlord foresees sending out a written notice every month, then waiting five or ten days for receipt of its rent check. One must bear in mind, as the landlord surely will, that mortgage payments are generally due on the first of the month, not on the tenth. The landlord will want to restrict the applicability of this notice provision to avoid becoming an involuntary financier of the rent obligation. One or two inadvertencies a year is one thing, every month is another. The landlord does not want to agree to become a type of outside reminder service for the tenant and may say that it will deliver this written notice twice in any single year, after which it is not obligated to do so. This argument will meet with vigorous resistance from the tenant who does not want to forfeit a valuable lease no matter how many inadvertencies it commits. In the last resort, the tenant may have to rely on the protection of the unlawful detainer statutes in the state in which the property is located.

The Cure Period

The period allowed to cure or remedy a default may range according to the type of default, from just a few days for a monetary default to a longer period for situations that require more substantial action than writing a check.

Monetary Default — The landlord will not want to grant the tenant much time to cure a monetary default. If a payment of money is due, it is one thing for the tenant to argue that it was an inadvertency or mechanical error and another thing to argue that it needs time to come up with the money. The latter argument will evoke no sympathy from the landlord. The cure period for a monetary default will be very brief — several days, perhaps.

Nonmonetary Default — The breach of some other obligation in the lease, such as failure to build according to plans, failure to properly maintain the air-conditioning system, or any one of hundreds of other possibilities for breach within a lease document, presents a different problem. A monetary default is curable by writing a check, whereas a nonmonetary default may require some preparatory action, such as advance ordering of materials, locating a particular product or service, getting a government permit, obtaining insurance proceeds, or any number of other acts that depend for performance on third parties. For this reason, the tenant is given additional time to cure, even in a standard form of lease. But even several weeks may not be sufficient if the tenant is being delayed by causes it cannot control. For this reason it is not unusual to include a lease provision stating that the tenant will not be deemed to be in default so long as it has commenced measures to cure the default within the cure period stated in the lease and in good faith diligently pursues those measures until the default is remedied.

Remedies for Tenant Default

I have found that the clause concerning remedies for tenant default is rarely negotiated, and I have tried not to discuss infrequently negotiated clauses in this book. However, an observation may be helpful. The most favorable tenant lease would state that the landlord's remedy for default by the tenant is to terminate the lease. In effect, the tenant has the right to end its obligations simply by defaulting.

Under common law, the landlord also has the right simply to collect (or sue for) the monthly rent each month as it becomes due. Finally, also under common law, the landlord has the right to retake possession of the premises in the name of the tenant and attempt to sublease on behalf of the tenant.

Many states in the past 30 or 40 years or so have enacted *present value* remedies for the landlord. Under these provisions, when a tenant defaults, the landlord may terminate the lease, and the tenant then becomes responsible for a lump sum payment to the landlord in the amount of the present value of the rental stream for the balance of the term less the reasonable rental value of the premises. In this manner, the tenant is faced with a potential sizable lump sum money obligation. The greater the expense to the landlord to lease the premises and the higher the contract rent relative to fair market value, the greater the obligation. Thus, if the rental value of the premises has declined since the lease was originally entered into, the tenant could be facing a sizable penalty payment. If the rental rates for the space have substantially increased, the tenant will simply lose the bonus value of the leasehold interest but will not be out of pocket.

Landlord Concerns

Statutory Remedies

The landlord wants to be sure it has the benefit of all statutory remedies. In some states, the statutes providing remedies have, within the language of the statutes, provisions that declare that certain remedies are only available if specifically referenced in the lease. So the landlord's first concern is to reference all of its legal remedies in the lease, specifically enumerating those that have to be expressly described.

Multiple or Recurring Defaults

Landlords may want to build into the lease protection from the types of recurring defaults described below.

Nonmonetary Multiple Defaults — Do you remember Plain Pipe Rex, our tenant in Chapter 6? You may recall that Rex occupies one building in a complex within a business park. The business park has a specific proscription against storing merchandise, goods, equipment, even garbage, in the front yard. The landlord/developer is interested in keeping its park looking like the first-class development that it intended, with nothing but manicured lawns and architecturally controlled buildings.

Rex has taken to storing unused dress racks and bins of P-traps from its plumbing supply business in the front yard because its success has been so dramatic that it fully utilizes all of its interior space. The lease states that the tenant has 20 days to cure a nonmonetary default. The landlord sends the 20-day notice. On the 19th day Rex removes the unsightly property from the front yard, and the default now is cured. On the 22nd day, the offending debris is again out in the front yard, and the landlord proceeds to send another notice.

You can see the circle that the landlord gets itself into: The tenant is in breach of the lease 90 percent of the time. For this reason, some landlords include a multiple default remedy that states, in effect, that if the tenant breaches the lease in the same manner more than a certain number of times in a limited period (e.g., twice in one year, three times in eighteen months, and so on), the default becomes noncurable. It may not be legal to create a noncurable default, but at least the landlord will be able to get the cure period down to the statutory cure period for the payment of rent.

Monetary Multiple Defaults — Let's assume that the landlord has agreed to give a tenant written notice of a failure to receive the tenant's rent check. Let's further assume that this now is happening on a regular basis and that the landlord has become unhappy about it. The landlord could have provided for such a contingency in advance if it had inserted into its lease a provision stating that if the tenant is late more than x number of times in a given period, then:

- The tenant must thereafter pay the rent quarterly in advance; or

- The tenant must deliver to the landlord 12 postdated checks on the first day of each succeeding year of the term (just try to enforce this beauty!); or

- Any of many other possible remedies.

My own preference would be for quarterly payments if I were a landlord, because postdated checks aren't much good if there's nothing in the bank and you can't enforce such a provision anyway.

Miscellaneous Landlord Protections

There are some additional protective features the landlord may want to consider including in its lease. For example: A lien on personal property (but you'd better be fast on your feet if you want to catch a fleeing, defaulting tenant).

The provision of late charges for failure by the tenant to pay the rent on time. The landlord should be careful not to state the late charge in such a manner as to constitute a penalty, because courts don't like to enforce penalties. The better way to assess late charges is by way of liquidated damages. The tenant, on the other hand, will try to be sure that the late charge is not assessable until after the default notice period expires.

Landlord Default

In case of landlord default, the tenant will want to accomplish several things.

- Give the landlord a brief amount of notice. If the problem is not taken care of within that time, then the tenant should have the right to cure the problem itself, but for the account of the landlord (for example, fixing the roof, repairing the parking lot, carrying the appropriate amount of insurance on the building).

- Be able to deduct from the rent the cost of effecting a cure of the landlord's breach.

Exculpation

The landlord — if an individual, or an entity such as a partnership, in which there is individual responsibility — will want a specific provision exculpating them personally from any damages suffered by the tenant as a result of a landlord breach, thereby limiting the tenant's remedy to the value of the individual owners' interest in the property that is leased.

Rationale for Exculpation

At one time the landlord's purpose in limiting the tenant's source of relief had a rational basis. Most businesses incorporate; the tenant is incorporated the vast majority of the time. The prime attraction of incorporation is limited liability. That is, the principals of the corporation are liable only to the extent of the investment they have made in the corporation.

Until the 1986 revisions to the Tax Code, the availability of tax benefits from owning real estate dictated that in most cases corporate ownership was not appropriate because losses could not be passed through to the shareholders. For this reason, real estate was invariably owned in individual or partnership names so that losses could be passed through to the individual owners.

The owners then took these losses to offset other income. Landlords came to realize that they were trading off tax benefits for unlimited liability. To have the best of both worlds, exculpation provisions were placed in the leases. In effect, these clauses provided that for liability purposes under the lease, the ownership would be treated as if it were a single asset corporation, that asset being the property in which leased premises are located. There is actually a certain amount of logic to this position.

But landlords are a group of perfectionists. They have perfected the exculpation clause to the point where it is now included in leases in which there are corporate as well as individual property owners because, in most cases, the tenant does not have sufficient negotiating strength or sufficient interest by the time it gets to the last two pages of the negotiated lease to argue away the exculpation provisions. Essentially, the argument in favor of exculpation is applicable only to individual real property owners. The rationale is gone when there is a corporate owner. As we have stated elsewhere in this book, however, in negotiating a contract, choose power over reason all the time.

Alternatives for the Tenant

If the tenant has sufficient negotiating strength to contest the exculpation provision, there are a number of variants on a pure exculpation that the parties may be willing to settle for. The following constitute four possibilities of compromise:

1. The exculpation provision applies to the landlord only to the extent that there is liability for individuals. That is to say, the provision will apply only so long as the landlord is an individual,

a group of individuals, a partnership or a limited partnership in which there is individual personal liability. The protection would not, in this case, extend to a corporation.

2. The tenant agrees to limit its remedy to a lien on the property so long as the landlord has some minimum equity in the property. For example, the tenant will not subordinate its lease to liens that exceed 70 percent, 75 percent, or 80 percent of the value of the property. This is an attempt to prevent the landlord from borrowing out the full amount of its equity, leaving the tenant with no substantial source to repay any damage the tenant suffers as a result of the landlord's breach. Thus the tenant will not agree to recognize any lender or subordinate itself to any lender's security instruments if the loan, when aggregated with all other loans, exceeds a certain ratio of loan amount to appraised value.

3. The landlord agrees that it is personally liable under the terms of the lease, subject to a ceiling of an agreed-on amount. Thus the parties stipulate that personal liability is limited to a specific dollar sum.

4. The exculpation applies to the landlord so long as the obligations are guaranteed by a corporate guarantor with a net worth of some minimum amount. Many investors take title in individual names for tax reasons but, in fact, have corporate entities with substantial net worth that manage their properties. These corporations could act as corporate guarantors for their landlords/principals.

Odds and Ends

Now we will discuss briefly some items often referred to as "boilerplate" but that are worth paying some attention to from a business standpoint.

Security Deposit

Landlord's Interest

The landlord's interest in a security deposit is obvious. If the tenant defaults, it may take months to get such a deadbeat tenant out of the premises, even with the summary remedies that are available in an unlawful detainer action. During this period of time, there is almost no chance that the landlord will be collecting rent or any other charges. The standard one-month security deposit is almost always inadequate in the face of a defaulting tenant.

Tenant's Interest

No tenant likes to see its money sitting idle. It is no challenge to calculate the value of leaving a security deposit in the amount of one (or two or three) month's rent in the landlord's hands, earning no return for the tenant for the entire term of the lease. Bear in mind that most tenants feel sure that they will be earning on their working capital substantially more than they would earn if the money were simply invested in a bank or government instrument. If they didn't think that, they wouldn't be in business. For this reason, the tenant is not going to be willing to accept an offer by the landlord to pay interest on the security deposit, even in the unlikely event that the landlord made such an offer.

This problem is further aggravated for any company with multiple locations. Take that one-month security deposit and multiply it by the number of lease locations. Obviously, the cost in working capital that could otherwise be used for inventory and other profitable purposes is something that a tenant would be loath to incur. Most multiple location tenants take the position that they refuse to place a security deposit to secure their performance under the lease for exactly those reasons.

Alternatives

If the landlord and the tenant are at loggerheads over this issue, there are a number of solutions. However, these solutions do not usually pertain to chain stores, which will take a very hard position that no security deposit is to be included in the lease provisions.

Right of Early Return — Some parties will negotiate for the right of the tenant to have its security deposit returned on the expiration of a period that is less than the lease term. Thus, for example, if the term of the lease is five years, the tenant may bargain for the right to have the security deposit returned to it after only one or two years of the term have expired without breach of the lease by the tenant: If the tenant has been a good boy or girl, the money is returned. Another alternative would be to make a percentage of the security deposit returnable at regular intervals — for example, 20 percent returned for each year of the term, provided tenant does not breach any of the provisions of the lease.

Noncash Security — A tenant who is compelled to come up with a security deposit naturally would prefer to use something other than cash. It is not unusual for letters of credit to be used. The difficulty with letters of credit is that they are rarely issued for longer than one year. In the case of a small tenant, they would probably never be issued for longer than one year. Thus language would have to be incorporated to require that the letter of credit be renewed one month prior to expiration or the tenant would be presumed to be in default.

A promissory note would be the alternative device least desirable to the landlord because the landlord already has one lawsuit, in unlawful detainer, that it must contend with. However, a smart landlord may agree to take the promissory note if it is for a far greater sum than one month's rent and is due on written demand of landlord. In this manner, if the tenant defaults, the landlord will either get the cash or sue on the note, based on the fact that it was due on demand, regardless of the outcome of the unlawful detainer action.

Personal Guarantees — Finally, the landlord might agree to waive the security deposit if the lease has an adequate personal or corporate guarantee. This is the least desirable solution for the tenant guarantor, who would be exposed for the lease liability. However, the tenant can soften this burden by simply limiting the applicability of the guarantee to what would have been the security deposit, i.e., one month's rent. The landlord, justifiably, will also look on the guarantee with much suspicion, because collection on a guarantee is an undertaking fraught with peril. Cash is always better.

Estoppels

An *estoppel certificate* is a document in which either the tenant or the landlord acknowledges to a third party (usually the landlord's lender or the purchaser of the landlord's interest) that the lease is in existence, that there is no default, and that certain terms and conditions are included. The purpose of the estoppel certificate is to show a prospective investor that there have been no changes in the lease or that there are no defaults that haven't been revealed. Tenants similarly can require the landlord to provide an estoppel certificate if it is the kind of lease that the tenant might try to finance. The critical element for the tenant is that it have sufficient time to respond to the landlord's request. The tenant doesn't want to be in breach of its lease just because the lease says it will respond to a request for the estoppel certificate within 10 days when, in fact, it may take 10 days to get to the right person within the tenant's organization.

Moreover, not as a drafting matter but just as something for the tenant to bear in mind when faced with the execution of an estoppel certificate, the tenant should read the certificate carefully to be sure that it doesn't include provisions that aren't in the lease. This can be a clever way for a landlord or lender to, in effect, amend the lease. One simple way to avoid this is to attach to the lease, as an exhibit, the form of estoppel certificate that the parties will be obligated to execute. The landlord will want to be sure that the tenant knows how much trouble can be caused if the estoppel certificate is not signed in a timely manner. A landlord who requests an estoppel certificate is usually faced with the prospect of the impending closing of a loan or a sale of its building or shopping center. If the tenant fails to execute and submit the estoppel certificate in a timely fashion, it is possible that the deal may be threatened. Landlords frequently deal with this by stating that the tenant will be subject to consequential damages, which is a legal term meaning any damages that might arise out of the breach, whether or not those damages were foreseeable at the time of the original lease execution.

Remember that the default clause gives the tenant a certain number of days to cure a nonmonetary breach. If the lease provides an estoppel certificate provision that allows the tenant 10 or 20 or 30 days in which to execute and return the document, then the tenant simply breaches the lease if it doesn't do so in a timely fashion. Now the landlord may have to give the tenant the additional notice of default before the tenant is actually in breach. Landlords should take care not to grant the tenant the benefit of this *double notice*. One way to avoid this would be to include language in the default provision stating that a default under the estoppel certificate paragraph is a default subject to the notice provision of a monetary breach (usually three days), rather than to that of a nonmonetary breach (usually 10 to 30 days).

Subordination

Landlord's Interest

Most form leases provide for the tenant to subordinate its leasehold interest to that of the lender. If unqualified, this means that if the lender forecloses on the property, the tenant's lease may be terminated. However, subordination is important in order to obtain financing. There is a genuine question whether an agreement to subordinate to a future financing is enforceable against the tenant when the terms of the loan to which the tenant will be subordinating are unknown. But landlords must obtain this subordination right or risk not being able to obtain beneficial financing.

Tenant's Interest

The tenant, for its part, generally will cooperate with the landlord, provided it has bargained for and gotten a nondisturbance agreement. Under the terms of a nondisturbance agreement, the tenant agrees to subordinate its interest to that of the lender in return for the lender's promise not to disturb the tenant in its possession of the premises under the terms of the lease unless the tenant goes into default. Lenders customarily grant this request.

Tenants often try to obtain the same subordination right *from* the landlord with respect to their personal property and fixtures. That is, if the tenant intends to finance its fixtures with a bank or other lender, that lender may insist that the landlord subordinate any contingent interest it may have in the property on the premises to that of the lender. Unless the tenant bargains for this right in advance, it is likely to have some difficulty with the landlord if it asks for this favor at a later date.

Mortgagee Protection

On behalf of its lender, the landlord needs to include in the lease the right to additional notice in the event of the landlord's default if the lease is going to be an important element of the security given the lender for a loan made to the landlord. That is, if the lender is relying on the income stream from the lease in making its loan, then the lender will want to be sure that the tenant will not terminate the lease for the landlord's default without the lender's having an adequate period of time in which to cure the default and maintain the security of the income stream. Provisions are frequently included in the lease declaring that the lender has some period of time (60 days is typical) beyond the period of time given to the landlord to cure a landlord breach following notice from the tenant. Tenants will object to this provision on the grounds that there is no reason why they should have to give *additional* notice to the lender. Tenants should agree as a matter of course to give the lender notice at the same time as they give the landlord notice, but a strong tenant will not want to provide additional notice while it suffers the consequences of the landlord's failure to repair or other breach. This is obviously a negotiable issue.

TENANT CLAUSES

The following lease clauses have been excerpted from various forms of shopping center leases. They are for illustration purposes only and should not be used without a lawyer's advice. Because they are illustrative, the language may not pertain to particular situations, all of which are different from deal to deal. Like human beings, no two lease deals are alike. Moreover, because these clauses have been excerpted without editing, references may be confusing or misleading. These clauses do not include extensive definitional language, which is essential for drafting purposes, but not necessary for purposes of illustrating the negotiating positions. **Therefore, *do not use these clauses without the benefit of legal counsel.* This is not a complete lease. Many provisions have been excluded.**

Chapter 2 – Premises

A. <u>Demising.</u> Landlord hereby leases the Store to Tenant, together with all easements, rights and privileges appurtenant thereto. Tenant has entered into this Lease in reliance upon representations by Landlord that the Shopping Center is and will remain retail in character, and, further, no part of which shall be used as a theater, auditorium, meeting hall, school, church or other place of public assembly, "flea market," gymnasium, health club, dance hall, billiard or pool hall, massage parlor, video game arcade, bowling alley, skating rink, car wash, facility for the sale, leasing or repair of motor vehicles, night club or adult book or adult video tape store (which are defined as stores at least ten percent (10%) of the inventory of which is not available for sale or rental to children under 15 years old because such inventory explicitly deals with or depicts human sexuality). No restaurant shall be permitted in the Shopping Center within five hundred (500) feet of the Store. No restaurant shall be permitted in any other location in the Shopping Center without the prior written consent of Tenant.

B. <u>Dimensions.</u> Immediately following the substantial completion of Landlord's Construction Obligations, Landlord shall cause the Store to be measured and shall deliver to Tenant an architect's certificate stating the Leasable Floor Area thereof. In the event that the Leasable Floor Area of the Store is less than the size specified in Section____, Minimum Rent and other charges shall be proportionately reduced, but this shall not be construed as permitting a material variance in dimensions or area.

C. <u>Site Plan.</u> Landlord warrants that the Site Plan depicts the Shopping Center and that the boundaries thereof are accurately delineated thereon. The buildings depicted thereon contain no more than one (1) story (but mezzanines having Leasable Floor Area not in excess of one third (1/3) of the occupant's ground floor Leasable Floor Area, when not used for selling purposes, shall be permitted) and do not exceed thirty (30) feet in height. The Site Plan is a material consideration for Tenant entering into this Lease, and no significant change, alteration, or addition shall be made to the Site Plan, including but not limited to the configuration of the Common Areas, methods of ingress and egress, direction of traffic, lighting, curbing, building heights and stories, without the express written consent of Tenant.

D. <u>Construction Activity.</u> No construction shall be permitted in the Shopping Center, except for emergency repairs diligently pursued, during the period from October 1 to December 31 of any year, without the prior written consent of Tenant, which consent may include conditions designed to eliminate interference with the operation of the Shopping Center or the effect of such construction upon Tenant's business.

Chapter 3 – Use

A. <u>Type.</u> The Store is intended to be used principally for the sale of _____ and such other items as are sold in Tenant's similarly merchandised stores; provided, however, in no event shall any substantial portion of the Store be put to a nonretail use without Landlord's written consent.

B. <u>No Implied Covenant of Operation.</u> Notwithstanding any provision in this Lease to the contrary, it is expressly acknowledged by Landlord that this Lease contains no implied or express covenant for Tenant to conduct business in the Store, continuously or otherwise, or (when conducting business in the Store) to operate during any particular hours or to conduct its business in any particular manner. Tenant has the sole right in its unrestricted discretion to decide whether or not to operate in the Store and in what manner to conduct operations, if any.

Chapter 4 – Term

Construction and Acceptance

A. <u>Construction Obligations.</u> Landlord, at its own expense and cost, shall construct or remodel, with reasonable diligence, the buildings and Common Areas and the Off Site Improvements as shown on the Site Plan; the Store shall be constructed strictly in accordance with the scope of work as specified in Exhibit "C" to this Lease. Landlord shall hold Tenant harmless from all costs and liabilities arising out of such construction, remodeling, alteration or other work.

B. <u>Construction Commencement.</u> Landlord must commence construction, under the terms of Section A hereof, prior to the date specified in Section __ ("Commencement of Construction"). If Landlord has not, then at any time thereafter, but prior to commencement thereof, Tenant shall have the right to terminate this Lease by notifying Landlord in writing. To commence construction means to pour the foundation for the Store.

C. <u>Completion of Construction.</u> Landlord shall use its best efforts to complete Landlord's Construction Obligations and deliver possession of the Store to Tenant prior to the Promised Delivery Date.

D. <u>Construction Completion Notice.</u>

1. The requirements of this Section D shall apply in all cases in which the cost to perform Landlord's Construction Obligations can be reasonably anticipated to exceed one hundred thousand dollars ($100,000). The parties

acknowledge the necessity for Landlord to provide Tenant with the notice specified herein in order that Tenant have adequate time to, among other things, hire personnel, arrange promotion, purchase and arrange for delivery of merchandise, perform Tenant's improvements and fixturization to the Store and enter into other commitments required to timely occupy and conduct business within the Store.

2. At least one hundred (100) calendar days (but not more than one hundred fifty (150) days) prior to the Promised Delivery Date, Landlord must notify Tenant as to whether the Delivery Date will, in fact, occur on or before the Promised Delivery Date (the "Construction Completion Notice"). In the event Landlord fails to timely notify Tenant in accordance herewith, or notifies Tenant properly but does not timely deliver the Store as stated in such notice, or otherwise breaches the terms of this Section D, the parties acknowledge that Tenant will suffer damage arising from Tenant's need for adequate, proper, advance notice of the Delivery Date in order to properly stock the Store, arrange advertising and promotion, hire personnel, and the like. Landlord shall be responsible for such consequential damage, in addition to and cumulative with any other remedies available to Tenant at law, or in equity, or under the provisions of this Lease.

3. Landlord will be in breach of its obligations under this Section D if:

   a. It fails to timely deliver the Construction Completion Notice to Tenant notwithstanding the actual Delivery Date;

   b. It timely notifies Tenant it will not deliver the Store on or before the Promised Delivery Date, but does in fact tender delivery by such date; or

   c. It timely notifies Tenant that it will deliver by the Promised Delivery Date but does not do so.

E. Rollover. Notwithstanding the provisions of the above subparagraph D (3) (c), the breach denominated as (3)(b) above shall be subject exclusively to Tenant's right not to occupy the

Store nor commence payment of rent until the next permissible period as described in Section ___ ("Rollover").

F. <u>No Landlord Construction.</u> In the event there is no construction to be performed by Landlord, or the cost to perform Landlord's Construction Obligations are to be less than one hundred thousand dollars ($100,000) and the Delivery Date does not occur prior to the Promised Delivery Date, then the Rollover remedy as stated in Section E above shall apply in addition to all other remedies at law, or in equity, or under the terms of this Lease for Landlord's breach of this Lease.

G. <u>Right to Cancel.</u> If for any reason Landlord has not completed Landlord's Construction Obligations, or the Store is not delivered to Tenant prior to the date specified in Section ___, ("Right to Cancel Date"), Tenant may, at its sole option, cancel this Lease.

H. <u>Automatic Termination.</u> This Lease shall be automatically terminated if the Store, completed in accordance with Exhibit "C," is not delivered by the date specified in Section ___ ("Automatic Termination Date").

I. <u>Pre-Term Entry.</u> Tenant shall have the right, without an obligation to pay rent or other charge, to enter the Store for any purpose while Landlord's work is in progress. Tenant agrees that prior to the Delivery Date it shall not materially interfere with the progress of Landlord's work by such entry. No such entry by Tenant shall be deemed an acceptance of the Store. Tenant may use such utilities as are available during the course of such pre-term possession.

J. <u>Acceptance.</u> Tenant's occupancy of the Store shall not constitute acceptance thereof, but within thirty (30) days of occupancy of the Store by Tenant, Tenant shall provide Landlord with a list of items still to be completed by Landlord (hereinafter referred to as "punchlist"). Provision of the punchlist shall constitute notice under the terms of Section [Default] hereof. Landlord shall immediately commence to complete or correct the punchlist items which at all events must be completed within thirty (30) days thereafter or Landlord shall be in default of its Lease obligations. A sum equal to the minimum rent for one full month may be withheld by Tenant pending completion by Landlord of the punchlist items described above. Tenant shall accept the Store upon completion of the punchlist but not before commencement of the Term hereof.

K. <u>Completion of Common Area.</u> Notwithstanding any other provisions of this Lease, the Delivery Date shall not occur nor shall Tenant be deemed to have accepted the Store under any circumstances before the time that Landlord has completed all of the Common Area and Off Site Improvements, installed permanent power to the Store, and secured the Store from unauthorized entry by those without a key. An adjacent store without a store front or store rear or which has any unlocked opening in its exterior walls shall be deemed to render the Store insecure.

Lease Term

L. <u>Term.</u> The Term of this Lease shall commence on the Commencement Date and shall expire as specified in Section ___.

M. <u>Permitted Delivery Periods.</u> Notwithstanding the provisions of Section ___ or any other provision of this Lease with respect to delivery, Tenant is not obligated to accept delivery, commence the Term, or commence the payment of rent, unless the Store has been delivered in accordance with Landlord's obligations hereunder during one of the following periods:

1. February 1 through March 1

2. June 1 through July 1

3. September 1 through October 1

In the event the Delivery Date does not occur within any period specified above, then delivery shall not be deemed to have occurred under the provisions hereof until the next ensuing permissible period.

N. <u>Acknowledgment of Commencement.</u> After delivery of the Store to Tenant, Tenant shall execute a written acknowledgment of the date of commencement of the Term in the form attached hereto as Exhibit "E" and by this reference it shall be incorporated herein.

Option Periods

O. <u>Exercise.</u> Tenant shall have the right to extend the Term of this Lease (an "Option") for the number of separate, consecutive additional periods ("Option Periods") which are specified in Section_____ the terms and conditions set forth herein, except that the number of Option Periods remaining to be exercised shall, in each case, be reduced by one. If Tenant elects to exercise an Option, Tenant shall notify Landlord in writing at least ninety (90) days prior to the expiration of the Term, or the then current Option Period, as the case may be. If Tenant neglects to timely exercise any Option, Tenant's right to exercise shall not expire or lapse unless Tenant fails to exercise such Option within fifteen (15) days after notice from Landlord of Tenant's failure to timely exercise the Option. If Landlord does so notify Tenant, Tenant shall have the right at any time within fifteen (15) days after such notice to notify Landlord in writing of either Tenant's unqualified and irrevocable exercise of its Option, or Tenant's unqualified and irrevocable waiver of its Option. If Tenant fails to respond within such fifteen (15) day period, Tenant shall conclusively be deemed to have waived its Option and this Lease shall terminate on the then expiration date of the Term.

Chapter 5 – Rent

Minimum Rent

A. <u>Payment and Amount.</u> During the Term of this Lease, Tenant shall pay Minimum Rent to Landlord as specified in Section __. This rental shall be payable in advance on or before the tenth (10th) day of each calendar month during the Term. If the Lease commences other than on the first day of a calendar month, the first month's Minimum Rent shall be prorated accordingly and paid with the Minimum Rent for the first full month. All rent and other payments to be made by Tenant to Landlord shall be sent to the place to which notices are required to be sent, unless otherwise directed by Landlord in writing.

B. <u>Cotenancy.</u>

1. Landlord covenants and represents to Tenant that the

cotenants named in Section ___ shall be open in the Shopping Center at commencement of the Term, operating in at least the amount of square footage specified in Section ___, and shall continuously throughout the Term operate in such premises. Further, Landlord covenants and represents to Tenant that at commencement of the Term and thereafter throughout the Term at least seventy percent (70%) of the Leasable Floor Area of the Shopping Center (the Store shall be excluded from the numerator and denominator of the fraction used to calculate such percentage) shall be leased to bona fide lessees operating under leases of a minimum of three (3) years' duration open and conducting retail business within the Shopping Center. Anytime at commencement or during the Term when the above-referenced standards in this Section are not met is hereinafter referred to as a "Reduced Occupancy Period."

2. If a Reduced Occupancy Period occurs or is in effect at commencement of the Term, no Minimum Rent shall be due or payable whatsoever; if a Reduced Occupancy Period occurs at any time following commencement of the Term, Tenant's total obligation for Minimum Rent and Percentage Rent shall be to pay within fifteen (15) days after the close of each calendar month the lesser of (a) Minimum Rent as provided in Section A hereof, or (b) Percentage Rent as follows: within fifteen (15) days following the end of each calendar month thereof, Tenant shall be obligated for a monthly payment of Percentage Rent or Minimum Monthly Rent, as the case may be, upon the terms and conditions stated in Section ___ and ___ hereof (percentage rent paragraphs), adjusted on an annual basis, except that any rent paid which is applicable to the Reduced Occupancy Period shall be classified as "Minimum Rent" for purposes of computing the sum of Percentage Rent due in any given Lease Year under the provisions of Section ___. If the Reduced Occupancy Period continues for a period of sixty (60) consecutive calendar days, Tenant may, at its option, terminate this Lease upon thirty (30) days' notice to Landlord.

Percentage Rent

    C. <u>Amount and Calculation.</u>

        1. Tenant shall pay to Landlord as additional rent for each Lease Year during the Term which contains twelve (12) full calendar months, a sum equal to the amount by which two percent (2%) of Tenant's Gross Sales made during each Lease Year exceeds the aggregate total of the Minimum Rent paid for such year, the amount expended by Tenant for real property taxes and assessments (including the Store, the land under the Store and the Common Areas) and payment by Tenant under the provisions of Articles 11 and 18 hereof during said Lease Year; the amount of such excess is hereinafter referred to as "Percentage Rent."

        2. The Percentage Rent for any Lease Year having less than twelve (12) full months shall be based upon Gross Sales for the twelve (12) months immediately succeeding the Commencement Date (as to the first Lease Year) and for the twelve (12) month period immediately preceding the expiration or earlier termination of the Lease (as to the final Lease Year). The Percentage Rent due for such period shall be established by multiplying the Percentage Rent which would have been due for such twelve (12) month period by a fraction, the numerator of which is the number of days in such Lease Year and the denominator of which is 365.

    D. <u>Gross Sales Statement.</u> Within seventy-five (75) days after the close of each Lease Year, Tenant shall submit to Landlord a statement indicating the amount of its Gross Sales for the previous Lease Year and the amount expended for the above-mentioned expenses which are to be deducted and which relate to the Lease Year in question. Tenant shall accompany such statement with a payment of the Percentage Rent due, if any, after all deductions and offsets. Landlord covenants to keep such information confidential.

    E. <u>Maintenance of Records.</u> Tenant shall maintain adequate records for a period of one (1) year after the close of each Lease Year for the purpose of allowing Landlord to verify the reported Gross Sales for such year. At any time within said one (1) year, Landlord or its agents may inspect such records at Tenant's main office specified in Section _____ hereinabove during normal business hours and in the event an inaccuracy is disclosed, an adjustment shall thereupon be made. In the event the required adjustment arises from an understatement of Gross Sales in excess of three percent (3%), Tenant shall reimburse Landlord for Landlord's reasonable expense incurred in establishing the inaccuracy.

F. <u>Additional Consideration.</u> The Minimum Rent provided for in this Lease is acknowledged by the parties to be adequate consideration for the leasehold granted hereby, and the percentage rental specified herein is in addition to such adequate consideration.

G. <u>Gross Sales.</u> Definition of gross sales: The revenue received by Tenant from the selling price of all merchandise or services sold in or from the Store by Tenant, its subtenants, licensees and concessionaires, whether for cash or for credit, excluding, how-ever, the following: (1) the sales price of all merchandise returned and accepted for full credit or the amount of the cash refund or allowance made thereon; (2) the sums and credits received in settlement of claims for loss or damage to merchandise; (3) the consideration received in connection with a sale of inventory which occurs other than in the ordinary course of Tenant's business; (4) sales taxes, so called luxury taxes, excise taxes, gross receipt taxes, and other taxes now or hereafter imposed upon the sale or value of merchandise or services, whether added separately to the selling price of the merchandise or services and collected from customers or included in the retail selling price; (5) receipts from public telephones, vending machines, sales of money orders, and the collection of public utility bills; (6) bankcard discounts (e.g., Visa, MasterCard, etc.), interest, carrying charges, or other finance charges in respect of sales made on credit; (7) sales of fixtures, trade fixtures, or personal property that are not merchandise held for sale at retail; (8) sales to employees at discount; (9) revenue received from alterations, delivery or other services performed on a non-profit basis for the benefit of customers; (10) Tenant's accounts receivable, not to exceed two percent (2%) of Gross Sales, which have been determined to be uncollectible for federal income tax purposes during the Lease Year, provided, however, that if such accounts are actually collected in a later Lease Year, the amount shall be included in the Gross Sales for such later Lease Year; and (11) rents, subrents or other consideration received in connection with an assignment, sublease, license, concession or other transfer of any portion of the store (however, Gross Sales of any such transferee shall be included).

Chapter 6 – Taxes

A. <u>Obligation to Pay.</u> Landlord shall pay, on or before the delinquency date, all real property taxes and general assessments ("Tax" or "Taxes") levied against the Shopping Center.

B. <u>Tenant's Share.</u>

1. In addition to the Minimum Rent herein reserved, Tenant shall pay to Landlord its pro rata share, as defined in Section B (2), of the Taxes for each tax year or part thereof which falls within the Term within thirty (30) days after receipt by Tenant of a true copy of Landlord's Tax bill and a statement in writing from Landlord setting forth the amount of Tenant's pro rata share. Tenant's schedule of payments shall be concurrent with and proportionate to Landlord's obligations (annual or semi-annual) for payment to the taxing authority, but no sooner than twenty (20) days prior to the delinquency date for payment of Taxes. Within thirty (30) days after the delinquency date for payment of taxes Landlord shall provide Tenant with written evidence satisfactory to Tenant of Landlord's payment of Taxes, and in the event Landlord fails to provide Tenant with such evidence within thirty (30) days, Tenant may deduct from Minimum Rent and the other charges coming due under this Lease an amount equal to the sum paid by Tenant for Taxes, which sum shall be repaid to Landlord upon Landlord's delivery to Tenant of the required evidence of Landlord's payment of Taxes. In the event of assessments which may be paid in installments by reason of bonding or otherwise, Landlord shall elect to make payment under the installment plan. In any event, Tenant's payment obligations under this Article shall be as if Landlord made payment over

the longest period of time permitted by the assessment and Tenant shall bear no liability as to installments due following the expiration or earlier termination of this Lease. Tenant shall not be responsible for any interest, late charge or other penalty resulting from Landlord's late payment or non-payment of taxes, nor any administrative or other charge which may be claimed by Landlord.

2. Tenant's pro rata share is defined as that fraction in which the numerator is the Leasable Floor Area in the Store and the denominator is the Leasable Floor Area in the entire Shopping Center; provided, however, that in no event shall the denominator of said fraction be less than the maximum Leasable Floor Area as shown on the site plan attached hereto as Exhibit "B". Such computation shall be made separately for each tax year and shall be set forth in reasonable detail as a part of Landlord's statement to Tenant pursuant to Section A.

3. Should Tenant be in occupancy during only a portion of the first or final tax year, Tenant shall be responsible to Landlord for a pro rata portion of its Tax obligation as described herein, based on the portion of such tax year included in the Term of this Lease.

4. In connection with performing an audit of Common Area Charges as specified in Section ___ Tenant shall also have the right to audit Landlord's or Landlord's agent's records pertaining to Taxes.

C. Tax Limitation.

1. Tenant's payment in respect of real estate taxes for the first full Tax Year following commencement shall not exceed the sum specified in Section __ hereof. Any amount of Tenant's pro rata share in excess of such sum shall be borne by Landlord. "Tax Year" as used herein means the twelve (12) month period for which the taxing authority in question assesses the Shopping Center or Property of which the Store forms a part. The limitation of this Section is hereinafter referred to as the "Tax Limitation."

2. Tenant's payment in respect of real estate taxes for any Tax Year subsequent to the first Tax Year may not be greater

than the product derived by multiplying the Tax Limitation of Section C (1) by a percentage equal to the sum of one hundred per cent (100%) plus the product of multiplying the number of full Tax Years expired after commencement by three percent (3%).

D. Exclusions. There shall be excluded from the Taxes to which Tenant contributes (1) any increase in Taxes caused by construction in the Shopping Center commenced subsequent to occupancy by Tenant hereunder until such time as such newly constructed space constitutes Leasable Floor Area; (2) any increase in taxes caused by a "change of ownership" as defined in Sections 60 et seq. of the California Revenue and Taxation Code or any other law, regulation, ruling, or decision under which a reassessment or tax increase results from a transfer of all or a portion of any estate or interest in the Shopping Center, except that of Tenant; (3) income, excess profits, estate, single business, inheritance, succession, transfer, franchise, capital or other tax or assessment upon Landlord or the rentals payable under this Lease; (4) assessments relating to the initial construction of the Shopping Center or capital improvements (but not replacements) subsequently constructed therein or with respect thereto, and (5) Taxes on the Store or any other part of the Shopping Center which are payable pursuant to a separate assessment as described in Section _____.

E. Rebates. Any rebates, refunds, or abatements of real estate taxes received by Landlord subsequent to payment of taxes by Tenant shall be refunded to Tenant on a pro rata basis within ten (10) days of receipt thereof by Landlord. Any such rebate, refund or abatement realized by Landlord prior to payment by Tenant shall result in an immediate reduction in Tenant's pro rata share of Taxes then due to Landlord.

F. Contest. Tenant shall have such rights to contest the validity or amount of real estate taxes as are permitted by law, either in its own name or in the name of Landlord, in either case with Landlord's full cooperation. Any resultant refund, rebate or reduction shall be used first to repay the expenses of obtaining such relief. Landlord shall provide Tenant with government notices of assessment (or reassessment) in time sufficient to reasonably permit Tenant, at Tenant's election, to make contest;

and if Landlord fails to do so, then there shall be excluded from the tax bill to which Tenant contributes, any increased taxes resulting from such assessment (or reassessment). The term "contest" as used in this Section means contest, appeal, abatement or other proceeding prescribed by applicable law to obtain tax reduction or tax refund, howsoever denominated.

G. <u>Separate Assessment.</u> Notwithstanding Section ___, Tenant may at its option apply for a separate Tax assessment on the Store and shall have the right to pay the Taxes thereon directly to the Tax Collector in lieu of payment pursuant to Section ___. If no such separate assessment can be obtained then at Tenant's option, Tenant's Tax obligation with respect to the Store shall be determined by reference to the county assessor's work sheets or other appraisal information in the assessor's office reflecting the assessed value of the Store. In either event Tenant shall pay its pro rata share of Taxes on the Common Areas to Landlord pursuant to Section b. except as to any part of the Common Area separately assessed to Tenant or any other occupant. Landlord shall make a fair and reasonable allocation of Taxes between the Common Area and the remainder of the Shopping Center, using any data available from the county assessor's office or other pertinent information in the absence thereof.

If any other tenant or occupant of the Shopping Center pays Taxes pursuant to a separate assessment (which may include a part of the Taxes attributable to the Common Area) then Landlord shall exclude the amount thereof from Tenant's Tax bill and shall set forth the method of exclusion in reasonable detail. Landlord shall, in such case, also exclude the Leasable Floor Area occupied by said party from the calculation of Tenant's pro rata share; provided, however, that in no such case shall Tenant's total obligation in respect of all Taxes on the Shopping Center exceed its pro rata share of the same calculated pursuant to Section ___.

Chapter 7 – Maintenance

Maintenance and Repair by Tenant

A. Subject to Article (Casualty), Tenant shall maintain the interior of the Store (except for Landlord's interior maintenance obligations under Article next hereof), in good repair and condition, reasonable wear and tear and damage by casualty excepted, and will so deliver the Store to Landlord at the termination of this Lease. Tenant shall be responsible for a normal maintenance schedule for the servicing of the heating, ventilating, and air conditioning system (the "HVAC") in accordance with the terms of a customary air conditioning service contract as performed by reputable service companies in the area of the Store. However, any repairs to the HVAC beyond regular maintenance and servicing shall be the specific responsibility of Landlord. Tenant's repair obligations above are contingent upon receipt by Tenant prior to commencement of the Term of a valid assignment in form satisfactory to Tenant's counsel, of all warranties which are available from subcontractors, suppliers, manufacturers, and materialmen for construction of that portion of the Store which is Landlord's responsibility under Exhibit "C" but which will be Tenant's maintenance responsibility. Further, Tenant shall have no obligation to repair any damage or defects caused by the negligence of Landlord, its agents or contractors, and any such repairs effected by Tenant shall be promptly reimbursed by Landlord within five (5) days following billing from Tenant.

Maintenance and Repair by Landlord

B. Landlord agrees that it will make all repairs and all alterations required by any laws, ordinances or regulations of any public authorities, to bring the Store in conformity with all governmental codes prior to commencement of the Term. Landlord shall, at its sole cost and expense, maintain and repair the foundation, floor slab, roof, roofing (including the interior ceiling damaged from leaking), exterior walls, storefronts (including front doors), structural portions of the Store, perform repairs to the HVAC as provided in Article (Tenant Maintenance Obligations) hereof, sprinkler system, gutters and downspouts, concealed wiring and plumbing, pipes, conduits and other utilities, plus all Common Areas of the Shopping Center and building exteriors, in good and sightly condition consistent with first class shopping center facilities in the county in which the Shopping Center is located. Landlord shall repair any damage or defects caused by the negligence of Landlord, its agents or contractors, or by any previous Landlord work done improperly. Tenant shall give Landlord notice of such repairs as may be required under the terms of this Article, and Landlord shall proceed forthwith to effect the same with reasonable diligence, but in no event later than thirty (30) days after having received notice. In event of an emergency Tenant shall be empowered to undertake immediate repairs of such nature as would normally be Landlord's responsibility, and notify Landlord promptly after such repairs have been undertaken. If Landlord fails to repair or maintain the Store within the thirty (30) day period imposed herein, or in the case of an emergency as above stated, Tenant may perform the repairs or maintenance and deduct the cost thereof from the rental or rentals next coming due.

Repairs Required by Governmental Authorities

C. Store. After completion of Landlord's Construction Obligations, any repairs, alterations or other improvements to the Store required by governmental authority or insurance rating bureau having jurisdiction because of the particular type of retail use of the Store by Tenant shall be performed by Tenant at its sole cost and expense. Any such work, however, which is required to the Shopping Center in general, or to all similar buildings or uses in the area of the Shopping Center, shall be done at the sole cost and expense of Landlord.

D. Shopping Center. Landlord warrants that the construction and the proposed use of the Shopping Center's Common Areas and buildings, including the Store, for retail purposes shall comply with all laws, ordinances, regulations and standards of public authorities and insurance rating bureaus having jurisdiction, including, without limitation, Environmental Regulations, as hereinafter defined, and zoning and building codes (all of the foregoing being hereinafter collectively referred to as the "Requirements").

E. Non-Compliance. Landlord agrees that if, at any time on or after the Delivery Date, any public authorities or insurance rating bureau having jurisdiction shall determine that the Store or the Shopping Center was constructed, or is being operated, in violation of, any Requirement and shall request compliance, with any Requirement or, absent such a request from the government authority, if the Store or the Shopping Center is otherwise not in compliance with or is in violation of any Requirement, and if failure to comply shall in any way adversely affect the use of the Store by Tenant or adversely affect any other rights of Tenant under this Lease or impose any obligation upon Tenant not contained in this Lease or shall increase the obligation of Tenant (such as, by way of example, increased insurance costs), Landlord shall, upon receipt of notice thereof, at Landlord's sole cost and expense, cause such repairs, alterations or other work to be done or action to be taken so as to bring about the compliance, or to effect the Requirement requested. If by reason of such failure of compliance or by reason of such repairs, alterations or other work done by Landlord, Tenant shall be deprived of the use or enjoyment of the whole or any part of the Store or the Common Areas, Rent shall abate and in lieu thereof Tenant shall pay Substitute Rent on a per diem basis until compliance with the Requirement is completed.

F. Zoning. If at any time the applicable zoning shall not permit the retail sale of all the types of merchandise customarily sold in Tenant's other stores, Tenant may, without waiving any other rights Tenant may have on account thereof, terminate this Lease by giving notice thereof to Landlord. Tenant's termination notice shall include a written specification of the Unamortized Cost of any improvements made to the Store by Tenant. Landlord shall pay such Unamortized Cost to Tenant, within thirty (30) days following the date of termination.

Chapter 8 – Alterations

A. Permitted Alterations. Tenant may make non-structural alterations or improvements to the interior of the Store, in a good and workmanlike manner, in conformity with all laws, ordinances and regulations of public authorities having jurisdiction. Tenant shall not make any alterations to the foundation, roof, or any structural portions of the Store without first obtaining the written approval of Landlord, except as specified in Section B. Such approval may not be unreasonably withheld and shall be deemed granted if Tenant is not notified in writing of a reasonable basis for withholding such approval within ten (10) days of notifying Landlord thereof. It is further agreed that upon termination of this Lease, Tenant may remove its furniture, fixtures and equipment and Landlord will accept the Store as altered without any obligation upon Tenant to restore the Store to its former condition.

B. Communications Equipment. Tenant shall have the right to place upon the Store a so-called "satellite dish" or other similar device, such as antenna, for the purpose of receiving and sending radio, television, computer, telephone, or other communication signals. In such event Tenant shall advise Landlord at least ten (10) days in advance of the planned installation of such device and shall comply with any reasonable request of Landlord with respect to the installation of such device. Tenant shall be responsible for any damage to the Store caused by installing such a device.

Chapter 9 – Common Areas

A. Right of Use. Tenant, as well as its agents, employees and customers (collectively, "Customers"), shall have and is granted complete, nonexclusive and undisturbed access to, and use of all Common Areas. Landlord shall use its best efforts to prevent (1) Common Area use by other than Shopping Center occupants and their Customers and (2) other Shopping Center occupants and their employees and officers from parking within two hundred fifty (250) feet of Tenant's front doors. In no event shall Customer use of Common Area be conditioned upon payment of parking or other charge by Tenant or Tenant's customers. Landlord shall maintain all Common Areas in first class condition, repair and cleanliness, including ice and snow removal, and free of any impediments to easy and safe movement within the Common Areas, including having the areas well lighted during and for sixty (60) minutes following the end of Tenant's business hours.

B. Tenant's Pro Rata Share. Subject to Sections C and E and provided Landlord maintains the Common Areas as specified in Section A, Tenant shall pay its pro rata share of the Common Area Charges, as defined for purposes hereof in Section E.

Tenant's pro rata share is defined as that fraction of Common Area Charges the numerator of which is the Leasable Floor Area in the Store and denominator of which is the greater of the Leasable Floor Area in the Shopping Center or larger parcel having the use of the Common Areas.

C. CAM Limitation.

1. Tenant's payment in respect of Common Area Charges shall not exceed the amount specified in Section __ for the first full calendar year following commencement (the "CAM Limitation"). Any amount of Tenant's pro rata share of Common Area Charges in excess of the CAM Limitation for the first full calendar year following commencement shall be borne by Landlord.

2. Tenant's payment in respect of Common Area Charges for any calendar year subsequent to the first full calendar year may not be greater than the product derived by multiplying the CAM Limitation of Section ___ by a percentage equal to the sum of one hundred percent (100%) plus the product of multiplying the number of full calendar years expired since commencement by three percent (3%).

3. Tenant's payment obligation under Section B as limited by this Section C is hereinafter referred to as Tenant's "Payment Obligation."

D. Payments. Tenant's payment under the provisions of Section B and C shall be due and payable not sooner than thirty (30) days following receipt by Tenant of an itemized billing from Landlord, which billing shall be no more frequently than monthly, nor less frequently than annually during the Term, and which billing shall be accompanied by copies of all billings, invoices and other evidence of costs incurred by Landlord with respect to Common Area Charges. Tenant shall not be responsible for any interest, late charge or other penalty on Common Area Charges resulting from Landlord's late payment or non-payment of its accounts payable. After the first full calendar year of Shopping Center operation, Landlord shall have the right once a year to estimate Common Area Charges, and Tenant's share thereof, based on the previous year's actual expenditures and Landlord's reasonable projections for the current year and so inform Tenant in writing along with the Annual Statement referred to below. Any increase in excess of five percent (5%) over the previous year's expenditures must be justified by itemization or shall be disregarded.

Beginning with the first full calendar month following thirty (30) days after Tenant's receipt of Landlord's written estimate, Tenant shall include one-twelfth (1/12th) of its annual obligation in accordance with Landlord's estimate with each payment of Minimum Rent for the next twelve (12) months thereafter. Within thirty (30) days following the close of each calendar year, Landlord shall calculate actual expenditures for Common Area Charges for such calendar year and Tenant's pro rata share thereof and provide such accounting to Tenant together with copies of all billings, invoices and other evidence of costs incurred by Landlord with respect to Common Area Charges not previously submitted (the "Annual Statement"). The Annual Statement shall be prepared, signed and certified by Landlord to be correct. In the event Landlord fails to provide such Annual Statement within thirty (30) days following the close of the calendar year for which the Annual Statement is due, Tenant may thereupon cease making any payments in respect of Common Area Charges until such time as the Annual Statement is received by Tenant and any requisite adjustments are made. Any sums accruing to Landlord as a result of such adjustment shall be paid to Landlord upon Landlord's delivery to Tenant of the Annual Statement, unless Tenant is auditing Landlord's records, in which event adjustment (if required) and payment shall be made upon conclusion of such audit at the time hereinafter specified.

If the Annual Statement shows that Tenant's payments of estimated Common Area Charges exceeded Tenant's total obligation in respect of such calendar year, Landlord shall accompany said Annual Statement with a payment to Tenant of the amount of such excess. If the Annual Statement shows that Tenant's payments of estimated Common Area Charges were less than its total obligation in respect of such calendar year, Tenant shall pay said difference to Landlord within thirty (30) days of Tenant's receipt of the Annual Statement.

Tenant shall have the right, not more frequently than once in any calendar year, to audit all of Landlord's or Landlord's agent's records pertaining to Common Area Charges, Taxes and insurance with a representative of Tenant's choice. Any overbilling discovered in the course of such audit shall be refunded to Tenant within thirty (30) days of Landlord's receipt of a copy of the audit. In event the overstatement of charges exceeds three percent (3%) of the sum previously billed to Tenant by Landlord, Landlord shall reimburse Tenant for all expenses of such audit. Landlord shall retain its records regarding Common Area Charges for a period of at least two (2) years following the final billing for the calendar year in question. At any time during such two (2) year period, upon notice to Landlord, Tenant may conduct its audit.

E. <u>Common Area Charges</u> are those costs reasonably incurred for maintenance and repair of the Common Areas and supervision thereof (but in no event shall the charge for such supervision exceed eight percent (8%) of all other Common Area Charges exclusive of taxes and insurance), repairing the parking area (subject to the exclusion of Capital Expenditures as provided below), repainting and restriping the parking areas, cleaning, sweeping and other janitorial services, liability insurance carried pursuant to Section ___, sanitation, maintenance of refuse receptacles, planting and replanting existing landscaping, directional signs and other markers, upkeep of lighting and other utilities.

In no event shall the term "Common Area Charges" as defined herein, include any Capital Expenditures. "Capital Expenditures" means those expenditures which, in accordance with federal income tax regulations, are not fully chargeable to current account in the year the expenditure is incurred. For purposes of allocating Tenant's pro rata share of Common Area Charges as specified in Section B, there shall be deducted from Common Area Charges, the pro rata share thereof properly allocable to any fast food restaurant or other restaurant in the Shopping Center which permits prepared food to be removed for off-premises consumption ("Take Out Restaurant"). Any Take Out Restaurant located within the Shopping Center shall pay a minimum of one hundred fifty percent (150%) of its pro rata share (as that term is defined in Section B of Common Area Charges (the "Take Out Share"). The Take Out Share, whether collected or not, shall be applied to reduce the Common Area Charges used for computation of Tenant's pro rata share thereof.

"Common Areas" are those portions of, and facilities within, the Shopping Center or greater land area of which the Store forms a part, which are intended for the common use of the occupants, their customers, agents and employees (and no others) including, without limitation, parking areas, driveways, walkways, common loading zones and landscaping. Enclosed malls are not includable for purposes of Common Area Charges hereof unless the Store has a direct customer door opening onto such mall, and Landlord keeps the mall open to customer access during all of Tenant's operating hours.

Chapter 10 – Operating Costs

For Tenant biased form, use the Common Area paragraphs above as a guide. Generally speaking tenant forms of office lease are rare.

Chapter 11 – Assignment and Subletting

Assignment

A. <u>Tenant Assignment.</u> Tenant may assign this Lease, or sublet the Store, or any portion thereof, without Landlord's consent.

B. <u>Tenant Notice.</u> Landlord, when giving notice to any assignee of this Lease in respect of any default hereunder shall also simultaneously give notice thereof to Tenant, who may cure said default at any time during the notice period; and in the event that Tenant shall cure the default, Tenant shall be subrogated to all rights and remedies of Landlord as against the assignee in respect of the default and shall have the right at its election to recover possession of the Leased Premises from the defaulting assignee, to cancel and revoke the assignment, and to be restored by Landlord to its leasehold estate hereunder.

Or

C. <u>General.</u> Tenant shall not assign this Lease, or sublet the Store, or any portion thereof, without the prior written consent of the Landlord, or the waiver thereof as hereinafter stated, which consent shall not be unreasonably withheld. Failure of the

Landlord to respond to Tenant's request for consent within ten (10) business days following receipt of a written request, including a description of the assignment or sublease transaction, with a written specification of the precise reasons for Landlord's refusal to consent, shall constitute a waiver of Landlord's right to deny consent hereunder.

D. <u>Corporate.</u> Notwithstanding anything to the contrary contained in this Lease, Tenant shall have the right, without Landlord's consent, to assign this Lease or sublet the Store, to a corporation with which it may merge or consolidate, or in connection with the sale of all or a portion of its assets, or to any parent or subsidiary of Tenant, or a subsidiary of Tenant's parent. The sale of stock by Tenant or by any shareholder of it shall not constitute an assignment under the terms of this Lease. Any provisions of this Lease which purport to grant to Landlord certain rights to take effect precedent to, or in event of assignment or subletting shall not apply to an assignment or sublet within the scope of this Section. Tenant shall have the right to operate departments within the Store without Landlord's consent by means of subleases, licenses or concession agreements provided that such departments shall not be separated by demising walls from the balance of Tenant's operations in the Store.

Chapter 12 – Insuarnce and Indemnity

Fire Insurance

A. <u>Landlord Insurance.</u> Landlord will maintain at all times during the Term an All Risk Policy insuring against damage to any portion of the Shopping Center. Such insurance shall be in the amount of the full replacement cost, including demolition cost, but excluding foundations, and shall provide that the proceeds of any loss shall be payable in the manner provided for in this Lease. Landlord shall, at least ten (10) days prior to the commencement date of this the Term, and thereafter upon request of Tenant, provide Tenant with a certification of such insurance coverage from an insurer licensed to do business within the state in which the Store is located, and which insurer is rated A+ and XII or better in Best's Insurance Guide, which certificate shall indicate, among other things, that Tenant is a named insured along with Landlord and that the Store and all the improvements and Landlord's fixtures appurtenant thereto, have been insured as required herein.

B. <u>Tenant Insurance.</u> In lieu of Landlord performing the obligation specified in Section A above, subject to Tenant's reimbursement, all as described in Sections A and C hereof, Tenant may, at its option, elect to carry such insurance on the Store including such other endorsements as Tenant in its judgment deems prudent under the circumstances, all at Tenant's sole cost and expense in which event Tenant shall not be responsible for reimbursement under Section C.

C. <u>Tenant's Share.</u> If Tenant does not exercise its rights under Section B, Tenant shall be responsible to reimburse Landlord for Tenant's pro rata share of the premium for the insurance described in Section A above within thirty (30) days after receipt from Landlord of billing therefor, together with a statement, certified by an agent of Landlord to be true, indicating the total cost of the premium applicable to the improved structure covered by the insurance policy which includes the Store. Tenant's pro rata share for purposes of this Article shall be that fraction the numerator of which is the Leasable Floor Area of the Store and the denominator of which is the Leasable Floor Area in the entire Shopping Center, or improved structure, covered by the insurance policy which is the subject of the premium; provided, however, at Tenant's election, Tenant's pro rata share shall be based on the rate applicable to the Store and the Tenant, and not a higher rate caused by other tenants. Such pro rata share shall not include any management fees or charges whatsoever, such share consisting solely of a fraction of the insurance premium. Said statement shall be accompanied by a copy of the premium billing from Landlord's insurer. Tenant's schedule of payments for reimbursement shall be established in the same manner as described in [the tax article of the lease]. Tenant shall not be responsible for any interest, late charge or other penalty resulting from Landlord's late payment or nonpayment of the insurance premium. If Landlord covers the Store with an insurance policy which includes premises other than the Shopping Center, the Landlord shall provide a breakdown indicating the premium portion attributable to the Shopping Center.

In no case shall Tenant's payment to Landlord exceed that amount which Tenant would have paid had it obtained the same coverage from its own carrier pursuant to Section B.

Within thirty (30) days after the payment by Tenant of its pro rata share of Landlord's cost of the insurance premium as herein required, Landlord shall deliver to Tenant evidence (satisfactory to Tenant) of payment of the premium by Landlord, and in the event Landlord fails to provide such evidence of payment within said thirty (30) days, Tenant may deduct from the Minimum Rent and other charges coming due under this Lease an amount equal to the sum paid by Tenant under this Section C, which sum shall be repaid to Landlord upon Landlord's delivery to Tenant of the evidence herein required of Landlord's payment of such insurance premiums. In connection with performing an audit of Common Area Charges as specified in Section [Common Area charge payments], Tenant shall also have the right to audit Landlord's, or Landlord's agent's records pertaining to insurance maintained for the Shopping Center.

D. Insurance Limitation.

1. In no event shall Tenant's payment in respect of premium costs referred to in Section C above exceed the amount specified in Section ____ for the first full calendar year following commencement. The sum specified in Section __ is hereinafter referred to as the "Insurance Limitation." Any amount of Tenant's pro rata share in excess of the Insurance Limitation for the first full calendar year (January 1 to December 31) following commencement shall be borne by Landlord.

2. Tenant's payment in respect of premium costs for any calendar year subsequent to the first full calendar year may not be greater than the product derived by multiplying the Insurance Limitation by a percentage equal to the sum of one hundred per cent (100%) plus the product of multiplying the number of full calendar years expired since commencement by three percent (3%).

Liability Insurance

E. Tenant. Tenant shall at all times during the Term keep in force a policy or policies of public liability insurance, or an endorsement on a blanket liability insurance policy or policies, against any and all damages and liability on account of or arising out of injuries to or the death of any person in the Store, or for property damage arising out of or relating to Tenant's use of the Store in the minimum amount of ONE MILLION ($1,000,000) single limit. Said policy or policies shall name Landlord as an additional insured and shall contain Contractual Liability Insurance recognizing the liability assumed in Section __ [Indemnity] hereof.

F. <u>Landlord.</u> Landlord shall at all times during the Term keep in force a policy or policies of public liability insurance or an endorsement on a blanket liability insurance policy or policies which policy, policies or endorsement shall provide that Tenant is named as additional insured, against any and all damages and liability on account of, or arising out of injuries to persons or property or the death of any person or for property damage resulting from acts or omissions of Landlord, its agents or representatives, occurring in the Common Areas, in the amount of THREE MILLION DOLLARS ($3,000,000) single limit in any one accident. Said policy or policies shall include Contractual Liability Insurance recognizing the liability assumed in Section [Landlord Indemnity] hereof, and include a cross-liability endorsement providing that Landlord and Tenant although named insureds may recover on account of the negligence of the other, and shall be with an insurer with a policy holder's rating of at least A+ and a financial rating of not less than XII in Best's Insurance Reports.

G. <u>Evidence of Insurance.</u> Landlord and Tenant agree to deliver to the other certificates of insurance evidencing the existence in force of the policies of insurance described in this Article. Each of the certificates shall provide that such insurance shall not be cancelled or materially amended unless ten (10) days' prior written notice of such cancellation or amendment is given to the party designated on such certificate as the holder thereof.

Indemnification

H. <u>Tenant Indemnity.</u> With respect to its use and occupancy of the Store, Tenant agrees to save Landlord harmless from and indemnify and defend Landlord against any and all injury, loss, damage, liability (or any claims in respect of the foregoing), costs or expenses (including, without limitation, attorney's fees, reasonable investigative and discovery costs), of whatever nature, to any person or property caused or claimed to be caused by or resulting from any act, omission or negligence of Tenant or agent of Tenant, provided that Landlord shall, upon becoming aware of such claim or damage, promptly notify Tenant. Tenant's obligation hereunder shall be limited to the amount in excess of any insurance proceeds in event of casualty damage.

I. <u>Landlord Indemnity.</u> With respect to its maintenance of the Store, its operation and maintenance of the Common Areas, the manner of design and construction of the Shopping Center, and the manner of construction and design of the Common Areas, Landlord agrees at Tenant's option, to save Tenant harmless from and indemnify and defend Tenant against any and all injury, loss, damage, liability (or any claims in respect of the foregoing), costs or expenses (including, without limitation, attorney's fees, reasonable investigation and discovery costs), of whatever nature, to any person or property caused or claimed to be caused by or resulting from any act, omission or negligence of Landlord or its employees or agents, provided that Tenant, upon becoming aware of such claim or damage, shall promptly notify Landlord as soon as reasonably possible.

J. <u>Waiver of Subrogation.</u> The provisions of this Article as to property damage shall be subject to the provisions of Article __ regarding Waiver of Subrogation.

Chapter 13 – Destruction and Condemnation

Casualty

A. <u>Occurrence.</u> If the Store is damaged or destroyed by fire or other casualty ("Casualty") to the extent that rebuilding or repairs (collectively, the terms "rebuild" and "repair" and their various conjugations and declensions, whether used as verb or noun are referred to hereafter as "Repair" with its conjugations and declensions, whether used as verb or noun) cannot reasonably be completed within one hundred eighty (180) days from the date of Casualty, Tenant may, at its option, terminate this Lease as at the date of Casualty by notice to Landlord within forty-five (45) days of such date. If Tenant does not so terminate this Lease, or if the improvements are so damaged that Repairs may be completed within one hundred eighty (180) days from the date of Casualty, then this Lease shall not terminate. Landlord shall proceed forthwith to Repair such improvements to substantially the condition as existed immediately prior to the Casualty and shall diligently pursue such Repair to completion. If the Repair is not completed within one hundred eighty (180) days from the date of Casualty, Tenant may terminate by written notice to Landlord at any time prior to completion. For purposes hereof the term "completion" is the date upon which the Redelivery Date, as hereinafter defined, is achieved. All rent payable hereunder shall abate from the date of Casualty to the earlier of (1) sixty (60) days following the Redelivery Date but only if the Redelivery Date falls within the Permitted Delivery Period; (2) if the date described in (1) does not fall within a Permitted Delivery Period, the sixtieth (60th) day following the Redelivery Date, but in no event prior to the next ensuing Permitted Delivery Period; or (3) the date on which Tenant again opens for business in the Store; provided that if Tenant continues to do business in the Store during the period of Repair, Tenant's total obligation for Minimum Rent and Percentage Rent shall be adjusted as provided in this Section. During the period of Repair, Tenant's total obligation for Minimum Rent and Percentage Rent shall be the lesser of (a) Minimum Rent as provided in Section ____ hereof, or (b) Percentage Rent as follows: within fifteen (15) days following the end of each calendar month thereof, Tenant shall be obligated for a monthly payment of Percentage Rent or Minimum Rent as the case may be, upon the terms and conditions stated in Sections ____ [Percentage Rent paragraphs] hereof, adjusted on an annual basis, except that any Percentage Rent so paid which is applicable to said period shall be classified as Minimum Rent for purposes of computing the sum of Percentage Rent due in any given Lease Year in accordance with Section ___.

B. <u>End of Term Casualty.</u> Landlord shall not be required to Repair any Casualty occurring during the final eighteen (18) months of the Term if the cost of such Repair would exceed the product obtained when the Leasable Floor Area of the Store is multiplied by five dollars ($5.00) unless Tenant exercises in writing, within ten (10) days after receipt of Landlord's notice that it intends not to effect Repair, any option to extend given Tenant hereunder. If Tenant does not elect to extend, it shall so notify Landlord within ten (10) days of Landlord's notice of election not to Repair, and, thereupon, this Lease shall terminate effective as of the date of Casualty.

C. Shopping Center Casualty. If more than thirty percent (30%) of the Leasable Floor Area in the Shopping Center or building of which the Store forms a part, excluding the Store, or if any part of the Common Areas within five hundred (500) feet of the Store are damaged by Casualty, then all of the preceding terms of this Article shall be equally applicable excepting that the unadjusted Minimum Rent and Percentage Rent (if any) payable hereunder shall resume upon reoccupancy of the Repaired Leasable Floor Area by the occupants affected, in the one case, or the completion of the Repair of the Common Area improvements as certified by the architect or engineer in charge of the Repair, as well as approvals of all required governmental authorities, in the latter case.

D. Insurance Proceeds.

1. As used in this Section, the term "Lender" means the holder of indebtedness secured by a first lien upon the Shopping Center, whether the interest creating such lien be denominated as mortgage, deed of trust, security agreement, vendor's lien or otherwise, but only if Lender (a) is a financial institution, such as a bank, savings and loan, insurance company, or other entity regularly engaged in making loans secured by real property, and (b) has two hundred million dollars ($200,000,000) of such loans outstanding.

2. Insurance proceeds for damage or destruction to the Store ("Proceeds"), if under one dollar ($1.00) per square foot of Leasable Floor Area in the Store, shall be paid directly to Landlord. If in excess of such amount, the Proceeds shall be deposited with Lender provided Lender agrees to apply the Proceeds in the manner described herein. If Lender does not so agree, or there is no Lender, then the Proceeds shall be deposited with a bank, trust company, or title insurance

company (collectively with Lender referred to as "Stakeholder") designated by Tenant and approved by Landlord, for use as provided in this Article. Stakeholder shall disburse the same to the party performing restoration upon certification by the architect in charge of restoration that the amounts requested have been paid in connection with such restoration or shall be due to contractor, subcontractors, materialmen, architects or other persons who have rendered services or have furnished materials for such restoration and upon the completion of such restoration the remaining balance of any of such proceeds shall be paid to Landlord upon demand.

E. Tenant Repair. If Landlord is obligated to Repair the Store under the terms of this Article, but does not commence within fifteen (15) days of date of Casualty, and continue the Repair of the Store thereafter with reasonable dispatch Tenant shall have the right upon notice to Landlord, to Repair the Store at Landlord's sole cost and expense. If Tenant elects to Repair, Landlord shall promptly pay to Tenant any insurance proceeds in respect of the Casualty and shall assign to Tenant all Proceeds held by Stakeholder as provided in Section D. Further, Landlord shall reimburse Tenant upon demand for any cost or expense incurred by Tenant for such Repair (not including any amount by which the cost and expense of Repair is increased by any change or changes made by Tenant) in excess of Proceeds received by Tenant plus interest. Until Tenant has been fully reimbursed for such costs and expense plus interest, Tenant may deduct the same from any payments of rent or other charges due hereunder to Landlord. If at the expiration of the Term, Tenant has not been fully reimbursed, Tenant shall have the right to extend the Term for any period of time (but not in excess of twenty-one [21] years) selected by Tenant which is less than or equal to the period which shall enable Tenant to recover such cost and expense plus interest from rents or other charges due hereunder to Landlord. During such extension, rents shall be imputed as being those in effect, in the month immediately preceding such extension.

F. Waiver of Statute. The parties waive such rights of Lease termination as are granted to them under the laws of the state wherein the Store is located, it being their agreement that the rights of termination in the event of casualty, as set forth herein, shall be exclusive.

Condemnation

G. During the Term, if, as a result of a Taking, any portion of, or interest in, the Store, or twenty percent (20%) or more of the Common Areas, or twenty-five percent (25%) or more of the Leasable Floor Area of the Shopping Center (not including the Store in either the numerator or denominator of such calculation), is taken, or if parking therein or access thereto is permanently impaired, then within thirty (30) days following the date of such Taking, Tenant may terminate this Lease upon written notice to Landlord. A "Taking" means any governmental act, condemnation proceeding, moratorium, initiative, or referendum whereby Landlord or Tenant is divested of ownership or any of the incidents thereof, or any transfer in lieu thereof. In the event Tenant does not terminate this Lease, Landlord shall promptly and diligently restore the Store, Common Areas, or other space, as the case may be, to as near their condition as existed prior to such Taking as is reasonably possible, and, during the course of such restoration, Tenant's total obligation for Minimum Rent and Percentage Rent shall be adjusted as provided in Section ___. Minimum Rent shall thereafter be abated: (a) in the case of a Taking of any portion of the Store, in the amount of that fraction of Minimum Rent the numerator of which is the Leasable Floor Area taken, and the denominator of which is the Leasable Floor Area of the Store prior to the Taking; (b) in the case of a Taking of any portion of the Common Areas, to the amount of that fraction of Minimum Rent the numerator of which is the fair rental value of the Store following the Taking and the denominator of which is the fair market rental value of the Store prior to the Taking. The abatements provided for in (1) and (2) shall be cumulative. Further, if the parties are unable to agree as to the amount of abatement, within forty-five (45) days after the Taking the matter shall be submitted to arbitration under the rules of the American Arbitration Association.

H. Claims. Nothing herein contained shall prevent Landlord and Tenant from prosecuting claims in any condemnation proceedings or otherwise for the value of their respective interests.

I. <u>Waiver.</u> The parties waive such rights of Lease termination as may be granted them in the event of condemnation by the laws of the state wherein the Store is located, it being their agreement that the rights of termination set forth in this Lease shall be exclusive.

Chapter 14 – Default and Other Provisions

Tenant's Default

A. <u>Breach.</u> The occurrence of either of the following shall constitute a default by Tenant pursuant to this Lease: (1) a failure by Tenant to pay rent within ten (10) business days of Tenant's receipt of written notice from Landlord specifying such failure; or (2) a failure by Tenant to perform obligations pursuant to this Lease other than as specified in (1) above, within thirty (30) days of Tenant's receipt of written notice from Landlord specifying such failure or, if it reasonably would require more than thirty (30) days to cure such failure, within a time reasonably necessary to cure such failure after Tenant's receipt of such written notice. Upon Tenant's default, Landlord may, in addition to any other remedy available at law, upon written notice, terminate this Lease and retake possession of the Store and remove all persons and property therefrom.

B. <u>Insolvency.</u> It is expressly understood and agreed in the event Tenant makes an assignment for the benefit of creditors, or if any proceedings are commenced under the provisions of the Bankruptcy Act whereby Tenant seeks to be, or would be, discharged of its debts, or the payment of its debts are sought to be delayed, this Lease shall not become an asset in such proceedings, however, the commencement of such proceedings shall not affect this Lease or permit its termination so long as all covenants on the part of Tenant to be performed shall be performed by Tenant or a party claiming under Tenant.

C. <u>Personal Property Waiver.</u> Landlord waives such liens, if any, to which it may have a right with respect to the merchandise, furniture, trade fixtures and other personal property of Tenant located on or about the Store and shall from time to time execute such documents as Tenant may reasonably request to acknowledge such waiver.

Landlord's Default

D. If Landlord should be in default in the performance of any of its obligations under this Lease, which default continues for a period of more than thirty (30) days after receipt of written notice from Tenant specifying such default, or if such default is of a nature to require more than thirty (30) days for remedy and continues beyond the time reasonably necessary to cure (provided Landlord must have undertaken procedures to cure the default within such thirty (30) day period and diligently pursue such efforts to cure to completion), Tenant may, in addition to availing itself of any other remedies available at law and in equity, at its option, upon written notice, terminate this Lease, or may incur any expense necessary to perform the obligation of Landlord specified in such notice and deduct such expense from the rents or other charges next becoming due.

Nondisturbance and Subordination

E. <u>Existing Liens.</u> Landlord covenants to obtain from each lender the security for whose loan encumbers the Store or the Shopping Center (and each lessor whose interest in the Shopping Center is paramount to Landlord's ["Overlessor"]) at the time of execution hereof, or at any time prior to the recordation of the Memorandum of Lease specified in Article ___, an executed nondisturbance agreement assuring Tenant that notwithstanding any default by Landlord to the lender or Overlessor, or any foreclosure or deed in lieu thereof (or Overlessor's termination proceedings), Tenant's rights under this Lease shall continue in full force and effect and its possession of the Store shall remain undisturbed except in accordance with the provisions of this Lease so long as Tenant is not in default hereunder so as to permit Lease termination and that the proceeds of any insurance recovery or condemnation award shall be used for the purposes stated in this Lease. Such agreement(s) must be satisfactory in form and content to counsel for Tenant. If Landlord breaches its obligation(s) hereunder, Tenant may terminate this Lease by written notice to Landlord at any time prior to Tenant's receipt of all required nondisturbance agreements.

F. Future Liens. Tenant shall upon Landlord's request, subordinate this Lease in future to any first lien placed by Landlord upon the Store, or the Shopping Center or building of which the Store forms a part, with an insurance company, bank or any other institutional lender, provided that such lender executes a Nondisturbance Agreement providing that if Tenant is not then in default under this Lease, this Lease shall not terminate as a result of the foreclosure of such lien, or conveyance in lieu thereof, Tenant's rights under this Lease shall continue in full force and effect and its possession be undisturbed except in accordance with the provisions of this Lease, and that the proceeds of any insurance recovery or condemnation award shall be used for the purposes stated in this Lease. Tenant will, upon request of the lienholder, be a party to such an agreement, and will agree that if such lienholder succeeds to the interest of Landlord, Tenant will recognize said lienholder (or successor in interest of the lienholder) as its Landlord under the terms of this Lease. Such agreement must be satisfactory in form and content to counsel for Tenant.

LANDLORD CLAUSES

The following lease clauses have been excerpted from various leases. They are for illustration purposes only and should not be used without a lawyer's advice. Because they are illustrative, the language may not pertain to particular situations, all of which are different from deal to deal. Like human beings, no two lease deals are alike. Moreover, because these clauses have been excerpted without much editing, references may be confusing or misleading, and previously defined terms of a given lease may not have been included in the examples. **Therefore, *do not use these clauses without the benefit of legal counsel.* This is not a complete lease. Many provisions have been excluded.**

Chapter 2 – Premises

A. <u>Demising Clause.</u> Lessor hereby leases to Lessee, and Lessee hires from Lessor a portion of the Complex as hereinafter defined.

B. <u>Description.</u> The "Complex" is that parcel of real property, or parcels of real property in common ownership with, and contiguous to, the parcel of which the Leased Premises forms a part, which is described with particularity in Exhibit "A" attached hereto and made a part hereof by reference, and described generally in Section ____ hereof. The premises leased herein are described in Section____ and delineated on Exhibit "B," which is attached hereto and made a part hereof by reference, consisting of the approximate amount of square footage as specified in Section____ hereof. The term "Building" shall refer to the Building in which the Leased Premises are located. The portion leased herein to Lessee is hereinafter referred to as the "Leased Premises." Lessee acknowledges that Lessor may change the shape, size, location, number and extent of the improvements to any portion of the Complex without consent of Lessee and without affecting Lessee's obligations hereunder. Lessor reserves the area beneath and above the Building as well as the exterior thereof together with the right to install, maintain, use, repair and replace pipes, ducts, conduits, wires, and structural elements leading through the Leased Premises serving other parts of the Complex, so long as such items are concealed by walls, flooring or ceilings. Such reservation in no way affects the maintenance obligations imposed herein.

C. <u>Substituted Premises.</u> In the event the Leased Premises herein are less than 2500 square feet, Lessor reserves the right, upon sixty (60) days' prior written notice to Lessee, to relocate Lessee to another location in the Complex of approximately the same size as the original Leased Premises described herein ("Substituted Premises"). Any such relocation shall be at the sole cost and expense of Lessor. In the event Lessee declines such a move, it shall inform Lessor within thirty (30) days of receipt of the above described written notice. Lessor shall thereupon have the election either to terminate this Lease upon thirty (30) days written notice to Lessee, which notice shall be given within thirty (30) days after receipt of Lessee's notice that it declines the proposed move, or in the alternative, Lessor may withdraw its notice of relocation.

D. <u>Covenants, Conditions and Restrictions.</u> The parties agree that this Lease is subject to the effect of (a) any covenants, conditions, restrictions, easements, mortgages or deeds of trust, ground leases, rights of way of record, and any other matters or documents of record; (b) any zoning laws of the city, county and state where the Complex is situated; and (c) general and special taxes not delinquent. Lessee agrees that as to its leasehold estate, Lessee and all persons in possession or holding under Lessee, will conform to and will not violate the terms of any covenants, conditions or restrictions of record which may now or hereafter encumber the property (hereinafter the "restrictions"). This Lease is subordinate to the restrictions and any amendments or modifications thereto.

E. <u>Declaration of Restrictions.</u> The Leased Premises are subject to a Declaration of Restrictions as referenced in Section ____ hereof.

Chapter 3 – Use

A. <u>Permitted Use.</u> As an express and material consideration to Lessor for entering into this Lease, the Leased Premises shall be used solely for the purposes specified in Section __ hereof and for no other purpose. Lessee shall not use, or permit the Leased Premises, or any part thereof, to be used, for any purpose or purposes other than the purpose or purposes stated hereinabove. Lessee shall not conduct or permit to be conducted any sale by auction on the Leased Premises.

B. <u>Hazardous Uses.</u> Should any of the above uses of the Leased Premises, or any acts done in conjunction therewith, increase the rate of insurance above that for the least hazardous retail use in the Complex, said increased premium costs shall be borne exclusively by Lessee. Lessee shall not engage in any activities or permit to be kept, used, or sold in or about the Leased Premises, any article that may be prohibited by the standard form of fire insurance policy. Lessee shall, at its sole cost and expense, comply with any and all requirements of any insurance organization or company, pertaining to the Leased Premises, necessary for the maintenance of reasonable fire and public liability insurance covering the Building and appurtenances.

Shopping Centers Only

C. <u>Non-Selling Areas.</u> In no event shall more than 15% of the square footage in the Leased Premises be used for other than selling purposes. Non-selling areas shall include storage, bathrooms, offices, and other areas not directly used for the display and sale of merchandise to retail customers in the ordinary course of business.

Offices Only

D. <u>Safes, Heavy Equipment.</u> Lessee shall not place a load upon any floor of the Leased Premises that exceeds fifty (50) pounds per square foot live load. Lessor reserves the right to prescribe the weight and position of all safes and heavy installations which Lessee wishes to place in the Leased Premises so as properly to distribute the weight thereof, or to require plans prepared by a qualified structural engineer at Lessee's sole cost and expense for such heavy objects. Notwithstanding the foregoing, Lessor shall have no liability for any damage caused by the installation of such heavy equipment or safes.

E. <u>Machinery.</u> Business machines and mechanical equipment belonging to Lessee which cause noise and/or vibration that may be transmitted to the structure of the Building or to any other leased space to such a degree as to be objectionable to Lessor or to any Lessees in the Complex shall be placed and maintained by the party possessing the machines or equipment, at such party's expense, in settings of cork, rubber or spring type noise and/ or vibration eliminators, and Lessee shall take such other measures as needed to eliminate vibration and/or noise. If the noise or vibrations cannot be eliminated, Lessee must remove such equipment within ten (10) days following written notice from Lessor.

Chapter 4 – Term

A. <u>Commencement.</u> The term of this Lease shall commence the number of days after delivery of the Leased Premises to Lessee as specified in Section ____ hereof or when Lessee opens for business, whichever is the first to occur, and, unless sooner terminated as hereinafter provided, shall continue for the number of months specified in Section ____ hereof, plus any partial month at the commencement of the term. Lessor agrees to deliver possession of the Leased Premises to Lessee, and Lessee agrees to accept the same from Lessor upon notice from Lessor to Lessee that the portion of Lessor's work relating to the Leased Premises which is scheduled for completion prior to the commencement of Lessee's work has been substantially completed as specified in Exhibit "C" attached hereto and incorporated herein by reference. If despite Lessor's diligent efforts, the Leased Premises so improved shall not be delivered by the date specified in Section ____ hereof, any remaining work shall be completed by Lessor with reasonable dispatch, but not later than ninety (90) days thereafter, provided that said date shall be extended for a period equal to the time construction has been delayed due to causes beyond the reasonable control of Lessor, including, without limitation, strikes, lockouts, or other labor disturbances, governmental orders, regulations, or embargoes, shortages of materials, inclement weather, fire, flood or other casualty. Lessor's liability hereunder shall be restricted to abatement of rent for the period of any such delay.

B. Cancellation. If the term of this Lease has not commenced within eighteen (18) months from the date of execution hereof, either party may cancel this Lease at any time thereafter, by written notice to the other prior to the commencement date.

C. Termination. If the term of this Lease has not commenced within three (3) years from the date of execution hereof, it shall be automatically terminated.

D. Acknowledgement of Commencement. After delivery of the Leased Premises to Lessee, Lessee shall execute a written acknowledgment of the date of commencement in the form attached hereto as Exhibit "D" and by this reference it shall be incorporated herein.

Pre-Term Possession

E. Conditions of Entry. In the event the Leased Premises are to be constructed or remodeled by Lessor, Lessor may notify Lessee when the Leased Premises are ready for Lessee's fixturing or Lessee's work, which may be prior to substantial completion of the Leased Premises by Lessor. Lessee may thereupon enter the Leased Premises for such purposes at its own risk, to make such improvements as Lessee shall have the right to make, to install fixtures, supplies, inventory and other property. Lessee agrees that it shall not in any way interfere with the progress of Lessor's work by such entry. Should such entry prove an impediment to the progress of Lessor's work, in Lessor's judgment, Lessor may demand that Lessee forthwith vacate the Leased Premises until such time as Lessor's work is complete, and Lessee shall immediately comply with this demand.

During the course of any pre-term possession, whether such pre-term period arises because of an obligation of construction on the part of Lessor, or otherwise, all terms and conditions of this Lease, except for rent and commencement, shall apply, particularly with reference to indemnity by Lessee of Lessor under Article__ herein for all occurrences within or about the Leased Premises.

Options

F. <u>Exercise.</u> Lessee shall have the right to extend the initial term hereof for an additional period of ____ years ("the option period") upon the same terms and conditions as stated herein, except for the Minimum Monthly Rent and this paragraph. Lessee may exercise its right by written notification to Lessor not less than ____ days prior to the expiration of the original term hereof, provided that:

1. Lessee has not been in default of any of the provisions of this Lease during the original term, and

2. The options granted in this option to extend are personal to the original Lessee executing the Lease document, and notwithstanding anything to the contrary contained in the Lease, the rights contained in this Addendum are not assignable or transferable by such original Lessee, and

3. Lessor grants the rights contained herein to Lessee in consideration of Lessee's strict compliance with the provisions hereof, including without limitation, the manner of exercise of the option.

G. <u>Option Rent.</u> The Minimum Monthly Rent provided for herein shall be subject to increase at the end of the initial term hereof and at the end of each ( ) month of the option period thereafter ("the adjustment dates"), as follows:

1. The base for computing the increase is the Consumer Price Index, All Urban Consumers, All Items, _____ area, published by the United States Department of Labor, Bureau of Labor Statistics, (1982-84 = 100) ("Index"), which is published for the last month prior to the commencement of the original term hereof ("Beginning Index"). If the Index published for the month containing the adjustment date ("Extension Index") has changed from the Beginning Index, the Minimum Monthly Rent for the following _____ ( ) month (until the next rent adjustment date) shall be established by multiplying the Minimum Monthly Rent in effect immediately prior to the expiration of the original term hereof, by a fraction, the numerator of which is the Extension Index and the denominator of which is the Beginning Index. In no event,

however, shall the Minimum Monthly Rent established at the adjustment date be less than the Minimum Monthly Rent established at the previous adjustment date or in effect at the expiration of the original term of the Lease, whichever last occurred. Lessor shall notify Lessee of the amount of such adjustment, and Lessee shall acknowledge such adjustment within five (5) days of such notice from Lessor. On adjustment of the Minimum Monthly Rent as provided herein, the parties shall immediately execute an amendment to the Lease on request of either party stating the new Minimum Monthly Rent. In event the Extension Index has not been published at the Adjustment Date, the previous Minimum Monthly Rent shall remain in effect until publication thereof. On the first day of the first calendar month following publication of the Extension Index (the "Retroactive Date"), Lessee shall pay to Lessor the following as Minimum Monthly Rent (a) the Minimum Monthly Rent for the current month as adjusted to reflect the Extension Index; and (b) the monthly increase in the Minimum Monthly Rent resulting from the calculation upon publication of the new Extension Index multiplied by the number of months elapsed from the last Adjustment Date to the Retroactive Date so that the newly revised rent shall have been paid in full commencing with the Adjustment Date.

2. If the Index is changed so that the base year differs from that used as of the month immediately preceding the month in which the term commences, the Index shall be converted in accordance with the conversion factor published by the United States Department of Labor, Bureau of Labor Statistics. If the Index is discontinued or revised during the term, such other government index or computation with which is replaced shall be used in order to obtain substantially the same result as would be obtained if the Index had not been discontinued or revised.

Chapter 5 – Rent

A. <u>Payment.</u> Lessee shall pay to Lessor at the address specified in

Section ___, or at such other place as Lessor may otherwise designate, as "Minimum Monthly Rent" for the Leased Premises the amount specified in Section ___ hereof, payable in advance on the first day of each month during the Lease term. If the Lease term commences on other than the first day of a calendar month, the rent for the first partial month shall be prorated accordingly.

All payments of Minimum Monthly Rent (including sums defined as rent in the Default section of this Lease) shall be in lawful money of the United States, and payable without deduction, offset, counterclaim, prior notice or demand.

B. <u>Advance Rent.</u> The amount specified in Section ___ hereof is paid herewith to Lessor upon execution of this Lease as advance rent, receipt of which is hereby acknowledged, provided, however, that such amount shall be held by Lessor as a "Security Deposit" pursuant to Section ___ hereof until it is applied by Lessor to the first Minimum Monthly Rent due hereunder.

C. <u>Late Payment.</u> If during any twelve (12) month period Lessee fails on more than one occasion to make any payment of Minimum Monthly Rent to Lessor on the date when it is due, then Lessor may, by giving written notice to Lessee, require that Lessee pay the Minimum Monthly Rent to Lessor quarterly in advance.

Percentage Rental (Shopping Centers)

D. <u>Additional Rent.</u> In addition to the Minimum Monthly Rent hereinabove agreed to be paid by Lessee, Lessee will pay to Lessor at the times and in the manner herein specified, an additional rental in an amount equal to the percentage specified in Section ___ hereof multiplied by the amount of Lessee's gross sales made in, upon or from the Leased Premises during each calendar year of the term hereof less the aggregate amount of the Minimum Monthly Rent previously paid by Lessee for said calendar year.

E. <u>Gross Sales.</u> The term "gross sales" as used herein, shall include the entire gross receipts of every kind and nature from sales and services made in, upon or from the Leased Premises, whether upon credit or for cash, in every department operating in the Leased Premises, whether operated by Lessee, or by a sublessee or sublessees, or by a concessionaire or concessionaires, excepting therefrom any rebates and/or refunds to customers, and the amount of all sales tax or similar tax receipts which have to be accounted for by Lessee to any government or governmental agency. Sales upon credit shall be deemed cash sales, whether or not payment be actually made therefor.

F. Payment. Within twenty (20) days after the end of each calendar quarter of the term hereof, commencing with the twentieth day following the end of the first calendar quarter of the term hereof and ending with the twentieth day of the month next succeeding the last month of the Lease Term, Lessee shall furnish to Lessor a statement in writing, certified by Lessee to be correct, showing the total gross sales made in, upon or from the Leased Premises during the preceding calendar quarter, and shall accompany each such statement with a payment to Lessor equal to the percentage specified in Section ____ hereof of the total quarterly gross sales made in, upon or from the Leased Premises during each such calendar quarter, less the Minimum Monthly Rent for such calendar quarter, if previously paid. Said payments of Percentage Rental shall be adjusted annually as of December 31st of each year, so that the aggregate of Minimum Monthly Rent and Percentage Rent payable during each calendar year shall be the greater of either (1) the total Minimum Monthly Rent for said year or (2) the percentage specified in Section ____ hereof of gross sales during said year less the credits and deductions herein authorized.

G. Books and Records. Lessee shall keep full, complete and proper books, records and accounts of its daily gross sales, both for cash and on credit, of each separate department or concession at any time operated in the Leased Premises. Lessor and his agents and employees shall have the right at any and all times, during regular business hours, to examine and inspect all of the books and records of Lessee, pertaining to the business of Lessee conducted in, upon or from the Leased Premises which Lessee shall produce upon demand by Lessor or his agents for the purpose of investigating and verifying the accuracy of any statement of gross sales. Lessee shall submit to Lessor copies of all sales tax reports prepared for any governmental authority, within five (5) days of their due date. Lessee shall further submit to Lessor copies of any audit performed by a certified public accountant upon Lessee's books and records, within five (5) days following the date that such audit is completed by such CPA.

Lessor may once in any lease year cause an audit of the gross sales of Lessee to be made by an independent certified public accountant of Lessor's selection, and if the statement of gross sales previously made to Lessor by Lessee shall be found to understate Lessee's gross sales by two percent (2%) or more than the amount of Lessee's gross sales shown by such audit, Lessee shall immediately pay to Lessor the cost of such audit, as well as the additional rental shown to be payable by Lessee to Lessor; otherwise the cost of such audit shall be paid by Lessor.

H. <u>Acceptance of Payment.</u> The acceptance by Lessor of any moneys paid to Lessor by Lessee as additional rental for the Leased Premises as shown by any yearly statement furnished by Lessee shall not be an admission of the accuracy of the yearly statement or of any of the quarterly statements furnished by Lessee during the year reported therein, or of the sufficiency of the amount of such additional rental payment, but Lessor shall be entitled at any time within three (3) years after the receipt of any such additional rental payment to question the sufficiency of the amount thereof and/or the accuracy of the statement or statements furnished by Lessee to justify such amount. Lessee shall, for said period of three (3) years after submission to Lessor of any such statement, keep safe and intact all of Lessee's records, books, accounts and other data which in any way relate to or are required to establish in detail Lessee's gross sales and any authorized deductions therefrom as shown by any such statement, and shall upon request make the same available to Lessor, Lessor's auditor, representative or agent for examination at any time during said three (3) year period.

I. <u>No Partnership.</u> It is understood and agreed that nothing contained in this Lease nor in any act of the parties hereto shall be deemed to create any relationship between the parties hereto other than the relationship of Lessor and Lessee.

Operating Covenant

J. <u>Continuous Operation.</u> Lessee shall continuously during the entire term, conduct and carry on Lessee's business in the Leased Premises, and shall keep the Leased Premises open for business and cause Lessee's business to be conducted therein during the business hours of each and every business day as specified by

Lessor from time to time for the Complex, provided, however, that this provision shall not apply if Lessee's business shall be temporarily shut down on account of strikes, lockouts or causes beyond the control of Lessee (financial inability excepted). The business hours designated by Lessor at the commencement of the term shall be: 10:00 a.m. until 6:00 p.m. Monday through Thursday; 10:00 a.m. until 9:00 p.m. Friday and Saturday; noon until 5:00 p.m. Sunday. Lessee shall keep the Leased Premises adequately stocked with merchandise and with sufficient sales personnel to care for the patronage and conduct of said business in accordance with good business practices. In the event Lessee does not so operate its business as specified herein, then Lessee shall pay Lessor, as additional rent, one-thirtieth (1/30th) of the Minimum Monthly Rent for each day Lessee does not so operate. Such payment shall be in addition to the Minimum Monthly Rent herein provided and shall compensate Lessor for the loss of Percentage Rental caused by Lessee's failure to so operate as well as for other damage to Lessor caused by the creation of vacant or non-operating space in the Complex. The parties agree that this represents a fair and reasonable estimate of the damage Lessor shall suffer by reason of this breach and that the precise calculation is difficult to ascertain at this time. Lessee shall keep the display windows of the Leased Premises suitably illuminated on each and every day from 8:00 a.m. to midnight unless prohibited by law. Lessor reserves the right to change such hours of illumination from time to time.

Additional Rent (Office Buildings Only)

K. <u>Personal Property, Gross Receipts, Leasing Taxes.</u> This Section is intended to deal with impositions or taxes directly attributed to Lessee or this transaction, as distinct from taxes attributable to the Complex which are to be allocated among various tenants and others and which are included in Operating Costs. In addition to the Minimum Monthly Rent and additional charges to be paid by Lessee hereunder, Lessee shall reimburse Lessor upon demand for any and all taxes required to be paid by Lessor (excluding state, local or federal personal and corporate income taxes measured by the income of Lessor from all sources, and estate and inheritance taxes) whether or not now customary or within the contemplation of the parties hereto:

1. Upon, measured by, or reasonably attributable to the cost or value of Lessee's equipment, furniture, fixtures and other personal property located in the Leased Premises or by the cost or value of any Leasehold Improvements made in or to the Leased Premises by or for Lessee, other than Building Standard Work, regardless of whether title to such improvements shall be in Lessee or Lessor;

2. Upon or with respect to the possession, leasing, operation, management, maintenance, alteration, repair, use or occupancy by Lessee of the Leased Premises or any portion thereof to the extent such taxes are not included as Real Estate Taxes as defined in Section ___; and

3. Upon this transaction or any document to which Lessee is a party creating or transferring an interest or an estate in the Leased Premises.

   In the event that it shall not be lawful for Lessee so to reimburse Lessor, the Minimum Monthly Rent payable to Lessor under this Lease shall be increased to net Lessor (i.e. after payment of the Taxes for which Lessor may not receive reimbursement from Lessee) the amount of Minimum Monthly Rent plus reimbursement for Taxes which would have been receivable by Lessor if such tax had not been imposed. All taxes payable by Lessee under this Section shall be deemed to be, and shall be paid as, additional Rent.

L. Operating Costs.

1. If the Operating Costs for any Lease Year, calculated on the basis of the greater of (a) actual Operating Costs; or (b) as if the Complex were at least ninety percent (90%) occupied and operational for the whole of such Lease Year, are more than the Base Operating Cost, Lessee shall pay to Lessor its Proportionate Share of any such increase as additional Rent in accordance with Section K above.

2. If any Lease Year of less than twelve (12) months is included within the Term, the amount payable by Lessee for such period shall be prorated on a per diem basis (utilizing a three hundred sixty [360] day year).

M. Method of Payment. Any additional Rent payable by Lessee under Sections K and L above shall be paid as follows, unless otherwise provided:

1. During the Term, Lessee shall pay to Lessor monthly in advance with its payment of Minimum Monthly Rent, one-twelfth (l/12th) of the amount of such additional Rent as estimated by Lessor in advance, in good faith, to be due from Lessee.

2. Annually, as soon as is reasonably possible after the expiration of each Lease Year, Lessor shall prepare in good faith and deliver to Lessee a comparative statement, which statement shall be conclusive between the parties hereto, setting forth (a) the Operating Costs for such Lease Year, and (b) the amount of additional Rent as determined in accordance with the provisions of this Article.

3. If the aggregate amount of such estimated additional Rent payments made by Lessee in any Lease Year should be less than the additional Rent due for such year, then Lessee shall pay to Lessor as additional Rent upon demand the amount of such deficiency. If the aggregate amount of such additional Rent payments made by Lessee in any Lease Year of the Term should be greater than the additional Rent due for such year, then should Lessee not be otherwise in default hereunder, the amount of such excess will be applied by Lessor to the next succeeding installments of such additional Rent due hereunder; and if there is any such excess for the last year of the Term, the amount thereof will be refunded by Lessor to Lessee, provided Lessee is not otherwise in default under the terms of this Lease.

Chapter 6 – Taxes

A. Definition. In this Article the terms "Real Property Taxes" and "Taxes" are used interchangeably. "Real Property Taxes" as used in this Lease shall include all Real Property Taxes on the Building, the Complex, the land on which the Building is situated, and the various estates in the Building and the land, including this Lease, as well as all personal property taxes levied on the property used in the operation of the Building or land, whether or not now customary or within the contemplation of the parties to this Lease. "Taxes" also shall include the reasonable cost to Lessor of contesting the amount, validity, or applicability of any Taxes mentioned in this Section. Further included in the definition of Taxes herein shall be general and special assessments, fees of every kind and nature, commercial rental tax, levy, penalty or tax (other than inheritance or estate taxes) imposed by any authority having the direct or indirect power to tax, as against any legal or equitable interest of Lessor in the Leased Premises or in the real property of which the Leased Premises are a part, as against Lessor's right to rent or other income therefrom, or as against Lessor's business of leasing the Leased Premises, any tax, fee, or charge with respect to the possession, leasing, transfer of interest, operation, management, maintenance, alteration, repair, use, or occupancy by Lessee, of the Leased Premises or any portion thereof, the Building, or the Complex, or any tax imposed in substitution, partially or totally, for any tax previously included within the definition of Taxes herein, or any additional tax, the nature of which may or may not have been previously included within the definition of Taxes. The term "Real Property Taxes" or "Taxes" shall not include any tax which may be levied upon or against the net income or profits of Lessor or its successors or assigns.

B. <u>Assessments.</u> With respect to any general or special assessments which may be levied upon or against the Leased Premises, the Building, the Complex, or the underlying realty, or which may be evidenced by improvement or other bonds, and which may be paid in annual or semi-annual installments, only the current amount of such installment, pro rated for any partial year, and statutory interest, shall be included within the computation of Taxes for which Lessee is responsible hereunder.

C. <u>Separate Assessment.</u> If the Leased Premises are assessed separately by the county assessor or other taxing agency, Lessee shall pay to such agency at least ten (10) days prior to the date when such Taxes would be delinquent, all Real Property Taxes as hereinabove defined applicable to the Leased Premises or arising under Section ____ above. In the event the Leased Premises share parking and Common Areas with other premises, the provisions of Section ____ below shall apply to Taxes thereon.

D. <u>Pro-ration.</u> If the Leased Premises are not separately assessed as an individual tax unit as described in the previous Section, Lessee shall pay, as additional rent, to Lessor, within ten (10) days after receipt of billing, its pro rata share of all Real Property Taxes stated in the tax bill in which the Leased Premises are included, including the parking and Common Areas, as well as the improvements on all of said land, or otherwise arising under the provisions of this Article. Pro rata share is defined as that fraction the numerator of which is the square footage in the Leased Premises and the denominator of which is that portion of the Leasable Floor Area of the Shopping Center which is leased and occupied (the "Occupied Floor Area") and which is included in the property covered by the Tax bill. "Leasable Floor Area" shall mean all areas available, or held for the exclusive use and occupancy of occupants or future occupants of the Shopping Center, measured from the exterior surface of exterior walls (and from extensions thereof in the case of openings) and from the center of interior demising partitions.

E. <u>Estimated Payments.</u> Lessor may, at its option, estimate the amount of Taxes next due and collect from Lessee on a monthly or quarterly basis, at Lessor's option, the amount of Lessee's estimated tax obligation. On or before March 1 of each year during the term, Lessor shall provide Lessee with a reconciliation of Lessee's account with respect to such estimated tax payments. In event it is established upon such reconciliation that Lessee has not paid sufficient amount in estimated tax payments to cover its pro rata share for the year in question, Lessee shall pay to Lessor the full amount of any such shortage within ten (10) days of date of billing. If it is established that Lessee has made an overpayment of its tax obligation upon such reconciliation, Lessee shall receive, at Lessor's option, either a credit applicable to the next ensuing estimated tax payments, or a credit to a tax reserve account to be held by Lessor for application to sums due in respect of reassessment or escape assessments applicable to the period in question, but yet to be billed.

F. <u>Personal Property Taxes.</u> Lessee shall pay prior to delinquency all Taxes assessed against and levied upon trade fixtures, furnishings, equipment and all other personal property of Lessee contained in the Leased Premises or elsewhere. When possible, Lessee shall cause such trade fixtures, furnishings, equipment and all other personal property to be assessed and billed separately from the real property of Lessor. If any of Lessee's said personal property shall be assessed with Lessor's real property, Lessee shall pay Lessor Taxes attributable to Lessee within ten (10) days after receipt of a written statement setting forth the Taxes applicable to Lessee's property.

Chapter 7 – Maintenance

A. <u>Obligations of Lessor and Lessee.</u> Lessee shall, at its sole cost and expense, keep and maintain the Leased Premises and appurtenances, and every part thereof in good and sanitary order, condition and repair including all necessary replacements. Lessee shall also keep the walkways in front of the Leased Premises free of any debris, papers, or dirt. Notwithstanding the foregoing, Lessor shall perform all necessary repairs, maintenance and replacement of the foundation, roof and structural parts of the Building. The cost thereof shall be paid by Lessor and reimbursed by Lessee on a pro rata basis in the manner provided in this Lease with respect to Common Area Costs, including amortization of Capital Costs. Lessee's pro rata share shall be a fraction, the numerator of which shall be the number of square feet in the Leased Premises, and the denominator of which shall be the number of square feet in the Building. All such amounts shall be due within ten (10) days after Lessee's receipt of billing. Lessee shall, at its sole cost, keep and maintain all utilities, fixtures and mechanical equipment used by Lessee in good order, condition and repair. In the case of equipment installed by Lessor for Lessee, or installed by Lessee and being or to become the property of Lessor, such as heating, ventilating and air conditioning equipment, or other mechanical equipment, Lessee shall maintain a service contract for its regular maintenance with a service company acceptable to Lessor, at Lessee's expense. Evidence of such a service contract will be provided to Lessor at its request.

B. <u>HVAC System.</u> Notwithstanding the provisions of the preceding Section, Lessor may elect at any time upon written notice to Lessee to perform the maintenance of the heating, ventilating and air conditioning system (hereinafter "HVAC") for the account of Lessee. In such event, Lessee shall pay the full cost of the maintenance contract for the HVAC in the Leased Premises within ten (10) days of receipt of billing therefor from Lessor, as well as for costs of repair or replacement of parts thereof as necessary, in the reasonable judgment of Lessor. Lessor may, at its option, elect to have the HVAC in the Leased Premises maintained in common with other equipment in the Complex. In such event Lessee shall pay its pro rata share of such maintenance costs which share shall be established in an equitable manner by Lessor based upon the relative tonnage in the Leased Premises compared to the total tonnage under contract, or some other reasonable means of allocation as selected by Lessor. Lessor's good faith judgment as to the allocation of the charges described in this paragraph shall be conclusive. Included in the charges to be allocated to Lessee shall be, without limitation: the maintenance contract upon the HVAC, extended warranties and any repairs and replacements not covered by the maintenance contract or warranty. Lessor may elect to replace the HVAC system, if necessary, and in such event the cost thereof shall be amortized in the manner provided in this Lease with respect to amortization of other Capital Costs. Lessee shall pay to Lessor, within ten (10) days after receipt of billing, its pro rata share of such amortization, established on an equitable basis according to the relative tonnage in the Leased Premises as compared to the entire area served by the system.

C. Condition of Premises. Except as to the construction obligations of Lessor, if any, stated in Exhibit "C" to this Lease, Lessee shall accept the Leased Premises in "as is" condition as of the date of execution of this Lease by Lessee, and Lessee acknowledges that the Leased Premises in such condition are in good and sanitary order, condition and repair.

D. Waiver. Lessee waives all rights it may have under law to make repairs at Lessor's expense.

Additional Office Provisions

E. Lessor's Obligations. Subject to the other provisions of this Lease imposing obligations in this respect upon Lessee, Lessor shall repair, replace and maintain the external and Structural parts of the Complex which do not comprise a part of the Leased

Premises and are not leased to others, janitor and equipment closets and shafts within the Leased Premises designated by Lessor for use by it in connection with the operation and maintenance of the Complex, and all Common Areas. Lessor shall perform such repairs, replacements and maintenance with reasonable dispatch, in a good and workmanlike manner; but Lessor shall not be liable for any damages, direct, indirect or consequential, or for damages for personal discomfort, illness or inconvenience of Lessee by reason of failure of such equipment, facilities or systems or reasonable delays in the performance of such repairs, replacements and maintenance, unless caused by the deliberate act or omission of Lessor, its servants, agents, or employees. The cost for such repairs, maintenance and replacement shall be included in Operating Costs in accordance with Section ___ hereof.

F. <u>Negligence of Lessee.</u> If the Building, the elevators, boilers, engines, pipes or apparatus used for the purpose of climate control of the Building or operating the elevators, or if the water pipes, drainage pipes, electric lighting or other equipment of the Building, or the roof or the outside walls of the Building, fall into a state of disrepair or become damaged or destroyed through the negligence, carelessness or misuse of Lessee, its agents, employees or anyone permitted by it to be in the Complex, or through it in any way, the cost of the necessary repairs, replacements or alterations shall be borne by Lessee who shall pay the same to Lessor as additional charges forthwith on demand.

G. <u>Lessee's Obligations.</u> Lessee shall repair the Leased Premises, including without limiting the generality of the foregoing, all interior partitions and walls, fixtures, Leasehold Improvements and alterations in the Leased Premises and all electrical and telephone outlets and conduits, fixtures and shelving, and special mechanical and electrical equipment which equipment is not a normal part of the Leased Premises installed by or for Lessee, reasonable wear and tear, damage with respect to which Lessor has an obligation to repair as provided in Section ___ and Section ___ hereof only excepted. Lessor may enter and view the state of repair and Lessee will repair in a good and workmanlike manner according to notice in writing.

H. Cleaning. Lessee agrees at the end of each business day to leave the Leased Premises in a reasonably clean condition for the purpose of the performance of Lessor's cleaning services referred to herein.

I. Waiver. Lessee waives all rights it may have under law to make repairs at Lessor's expense.

J. Acceptance. Except as to the construction obligations of Lessor, if any, stated in Exhibit "C" to this Lease, Lessee shall accept the Leased Premises in "as is" condition as of the date of execution of this Lease by Lessee, and Lessee acknowledges that the Leased Premises in such condition are in good sanitary order, condition and repair.

Compliance with Laws and Regulations

K. Lessee's Obligations. Lessee, shall, at its sole cost and expense, comply with all of the requirements of all municipal, state and federal authorities now in force, or which may hereafter be in force, pertaining to the Leased Premises, and shall faithfully observe in the use of the Leased Premises all municipal ordinances and state and federal statutes and regulations now in force or which may hereafter be in force, including, without limitation, Environmental Laws (as hereinafter defined), and the Americans with Disabilities Act, 42 U.S.C. §§ 12101-12213 (and any rules, regulations, restrictions, guidelines, requirements or publications promulgated or published pursuant thereto, collectively herein referred to as the "ADA"), whether or not any of the foregoing were foreseeable or unforeseeable at the time of the execution of this Lease. The judgment of any court of competent jurisdiction, or the admission of Lessee in any action or proceeding against Lessee, whether Lessor be a party thereto or not, that any such requirement, ordinance, statute or regulation pertaining to the Leased Premises has been violated, shall be conclusive of that fact as between Lessor and Lessee. Within five (5) days after receipt of notice or knowledge of any violation or alleged violation of any Environmental Law(s), and/or the ADA pertaining to the Complex, any governmental or regulatory proceedings, investigations, sanctions and/or actions threatened or commenced with respect to any such violation or alleged violation, and any claim made or commenced with respect to such violation or alleged violation, Lessee shall notify Lessor thereof and provide Lessor with copies of any written notices or information in Lessee's possession. Lessee shall make, at Lessee's sole cost and expense, any and all alterations, improvements or non-structural changes that are required by laws, statutes, ordinances and governmental regulations or requirements as a result of Lessee's specific use of the Premises or any alterations, additions or improvements made by Lessee. If any alterations, improvements or structural changes are required to be made to the Building in general or are applicable to substantially all lessees in the Building without regard to Lessee's specific use of the Leased Premises or any alterations, additions or improvements made by Lessee, then Lessor shall make such alterations, additions or improvements and the costs thereof shall be included within Operating Costs pursuant to Section ___.

L. <u>Condition of Leased Premises.</u> Subject to Lessor's Work, if any, as referred to in Exhibit ___ to this Lease, Lessee hereby accepts the Leased Premises in the condition existing as of the date of occupancy, subject to all applicable zoning, municipal, county and state laws, ordinances, rules, regulations, orders, restrictions of record, and requirements in effect during the Term or any part of the Term hereof regulating the Leased Premises, and without representation, warranty or covenant by Lessor, express or implied, as to the condition, habitability or safety of the Leased Premises, the suitability or fitness thereof for their intended purposes, or any other matter. Lessor covenants that the Lessor's Work pursuant to Exhibit ___ shall be in material compliance with applicable local and state building codes and ordinances in such manner that any violations or conditions of non-compliance will not result in the inability of Lessee to be issued a building permit for Lessee's Work pursuant to Exhibit ___ ("Code Compliance").

M. <u>Hazardous Materials.</u>

(a) Hazardous Materials Defined. As used herein, the term "Hazardous Materials" shall mean any wastes, materials or substances (whether in the form of liquids, solids or gases, and whether or not air-borne), which are or are deemed to be pollutants or contaminants, or which are or are deemed to be hazardous, toxic, ignitable, reactive, corrosive, dangerous, harmful or injurious, or which present a risk, to public health or to the environment, or which are or may become regulated by or under the authority of any applicable local, state or federal laws, judgments, ordinances, orders, rules, regulations, codes or other governmental restrictions, guidelines or requirements, any amendments or successor(s) thereto, replacements thereof or publications promulgated pursuant thereto (collectively "Environmental Laws"), including, without limitation, any waste, material or substance which is:

(i) defined as "hazardous waste," "extremely hazardous waste," or "restricted hazardous waste" under Sections 25115, 25117 or 25122.7, or listed pursuant to Section 25140, of the California Health and Safety Code, Division 20, Chapter 6.5 (Hazardous Waste Control Law);

(ii) defined as a "hazardous substance" under Section 25316 of the California Health and Safety Code, Division 20, Chapter 6.8 (Carpenter-Presley-Tanner Hazardous Substance Account Act);

(iii) defined as a "hazardous material," "hazardous substance," or "hazardous waste" under Section 25501 of the California Health and Safety Code, Division 20, Chapter 6.95 (Hazardous Materials Release Response Plans and Inventory);

(iv) defined as a "hazardous substance" under Section 25281 of the California Health and Safety Code, Division 20, Chapter 6.7 (Underground Storage of Hazardous Substances);

(v) defined as a "waste" or "hazardous substance" under Section 13050 of the California Water Code, Division 7, Chapter 2 (Porter-Cologne Water Quality Control Act);

(vi) listed as a chemical known to the State of California to cause cancer or reproductive toxicity pursuant to Section 25249.8 of the California Health and Safety Code, Division 20, Chapter 6.6 (Safe Drinking Water and Toxic Enforcement Act of 1986);

(vii) defined as a "hazardous substance" or "pollutant or contaminant" pursuant to Section 101 of the Comprehensive Environmental Response, Compensation and Liability Act of 1980, as amended, 42 U.S.C. § 9601 et seq.;

(viii) listed as an "extremely hazardous substance," "hazardous chemical," or "toxic chemical" pursuant to the Emergency Planning and Community Right-to-Know Act of 1986, 42 U.S.C. § 11001 et seq.;

(ix) listed as a "hazardous substance" in the United States Department of Transportation Table, 49 C.F.R. 172.101 and amendments thereto, or by the Environmental Protection Agency (or any successor agency) in 40 C.F.R. Part 302 and amendments thereto;

(x) defined, listed or designated by regulations promulgated pursuant to any Environmental Law; or

(xi) any of the following: pesticide; flammable explosive; petroleum, including crude oil or any fraction thereof; asbestos or asbestos-containing material; polychlorinated biphenyl; radioactive material; or urea formaldehyde.

In addition to the foregoing, the term Environmental Laws shall be deemed to include, without limitation, local, state and federal laws, judgments, ordinances, orders, rules, regulations, codes and other governmental restrictions, guidelines and requirements, any amendments and successors thereto, replacements thereof and publications promulgated pursuant thereto, which deal with, or otherwise in any manner relate to, air or water quality, air emissions, soil or ground conditions or other environmental matters of any kind.

(b) Use, etc. of Hazardous Materials. Lessee agrees that during the Term, there shall be no use, presence, disposal, storage, generation, leakage, treatment, manufacture, import, handling, processing, release or threatened release of Hazardous Materials on, from or under the Leased Premises except to the extent that, and in accordance with such conditions as, Lessor may have previously approved in writing. The use, presence, disposal, storage, generation, leakage, treatment, manufacture, import, handling, processing, release or threatened release of Hazardous Materials are sometimes hereinafter individually or collectively referred to as "Hazardous Use." It is further agreed that Lessee shall be entitled to use and store only those Hazardous Materials which are necessary for Lessee's business, provided that such usage and storage is in full compliance with Environmental

Laws, and all judicial and administrative decisions pertaining thereto. Lessee shall not be entitled to install any tanks under, on or about the Leased Premises for the storage of Hazardous Materials without the express written consent of Lessor, which may be given or withheld in Lessor's sole arbitrary judgment. For the purposes of this Section ___, the term Hazardous Use shall include Hazardous Use(s) on, from or under the Leased Premises by any and all lessees, occupants, and/or users of the Leased Premises (except Lessor), whether known or unknown to Lessee, and whether occurring and/or existing during or prior to the commencement of the Term.

(c) Hazardous Materials Report; When Required. Lessee shall submit to Lessor a written report with respect to Hazardous Materials ("Report") in the form prescribed in subparagraph (d) below on the following dates:

(i) Within ten (10) days after the Commencement Date,

(ii) Within ten (10) days after each anniversary of the Commencement Date during the Term,

(iii) At any time within ten (10) days after written request by Lessor, and

(iv) At any time when there has been or is planned any condition which constitutes or would constitute a change in the information submitted in the most recent Report, including any notice of violation as referred to in subparagraph (d)(vii) below.

(d) Hazardous Materials Report; Contents. The Report shall contain, without limitation, the following information:

(i) Whether on the date of the Report and (if applicable) during the period since the last Report there has been any Hazardous Use on, from or under the Leased Premises.

(ii) If there was such Hazardous Use, the exact identity of the Hazardous Materials, the dates upon which such materials were brought upon the Leased Premises, the dates upon which the Hazardous Materials were removed therefrom, and the quantity, location, use and purpose thereof.

(iii) If there was such Hazardous Use, any governmental permits maintained by Lessee with respect to such Hazardous Materials, the

issuing agency, original date of issue, renewal dates (if any) and expiration date. Copies of any such permits and applications therefor shall be attached.

(iv) If there was such Hazardous Use, any governmental reporting or inspection requirements with respect to such Hazardous Materials, the governmental agency to which reports are made and/or which conducts inspections, and the dates of all such reports and/or inspections (if applicable) since the last Report. Copies of any such reports shall be attached.

(v) If there was such Hazardous Use, identification of any operation or business plan prepared for any government agency with respect to Hazardous Use.

(vi) Any liability insurance carried by Lessee with respect to Hazardous Materials, the insurer, policy number, date of issue, coverage amounts, and date of expiration. Copies of any such policies or certificates of coverage shall be attached.

(vii) Any notices of violation of Environmental Laws, written or oral, received by Lessee from any governmental agency since the last Report, the date, name of agency, and description of violation. Copies of any such written notices shall be attached.

(viii) Any knowledge, information or communication which Lessee has acquired or received relating to: (x) any enforcement, cleanup, removal or other governmental or regulatory action threatened or commenced against Lessee or with respect to the Leased Premises pursuant to any Environmental Laws; (y) any claim made or threatened by any person or entity against Lessee or the Leased Premises on account of any alleged loss or injury claimed to result from any alleged Hazardous Use on or about the Leased Premises; or (z) any report, notice or complaint made to or filed with any governmental agency concerning any Hazardous Use on or about the Leased Premises. The Report shall be accompanied by copies of any such claim, report, complaint, notice, warning or other communication that is in the possession of or is available to Lessee.

(ix) Such other pertinent information or documents as are requested by Lessor in writing.

(e) Release of Hazardous Materials: Notification and Cleanup. If at any time during the Term Lessee knows or believes that any release of any Hazardous Materials has come or will come to be located upon, about or beneath the Leased Premises, then Lessee shall immediately, either prior to the release or following the discovery thereof by Lessee, give verbal and follow-up written notice of that condition to Lessor. Lessee covenants to investigate, clean up and otherwise remediate any release of Hazardous Materials at Lessee's cost and expense; such investigation, clean-up and remediation shall be performed only after Lessee has obtained Lessor's written consent, which shall not be unreasonably withheld; provided, however, that Lessee shall be entitled to respond immediately to an emergency without first obtaining Lessor's written consent. All clean-up and remediation shall be done in compliance with Environmental Laws and to the reasonable satisfaction of Lessor. Notwithstanding the foregoing, whether or not such work is prompted by the foregoing notice from Lessee or is undertaken by Lessor for any other reason whatsoever, Lessor shall have the right, but not the obligation, in Lessor's sole and absolute discretion, exercisable by written notice to Lessee at any time, to undertake within or outside the Leased Premises all or any portion of any investigation, clean-up or remediation with respect to Hazardous Materials (or, once having undertaken any of such work, to cease same, in which case Lessee shall perform the work), all at Lessee's cost and expense, which shall be paid by Lessee as additional rent within ten (10) days after receipt of written request therefor by Lessor (and which Lessor may require to be paid prior to commencement of any work by Lessor). No such work by Lessor shall create any liability on the part of Lessor to Lessee or any other party in connection with such Hazardous Materials or constitute an admission by Lessor of any responsibility with respect to such Hazardous Materials. It is the express intention of the parties hereto that Lessee shall be liable under this Section _____ for any and all conditions covered hereby which were caused or created by any person or entity whatsoever (except Lessor) whether such condition occurred, was created or caused or existed prior to or after the execution of this Lease and/or prior to or after Lessee's possession of the Leased Premises. Lessee shall not enter into any settlement agreement, consent decree or other compromise with respect to any claims relating to any Hazardous Materials in any way connected to the Leased Premises without first:

(i) notifying Lessor of Lessee's intention to do so and affording Lessor the opportunity to participate in any such proceedings; and

(ii) obtaining Lessor's written consent.

(f) Inspection and Testing by Lessor. Lessor shall have the right at all times during the Term to: (i) inspect the Leased Premises, as well as Lessee's books and records; and (ii) conduct tests and investigations to determine whether Lessee is in compliance with the provisions of this Section. Except in case of emergency, Lessor shall give reasonable notice to Lessee before conducting any inspections, tests, or investigations. The cost of all such inspections, tests and investigations shall be borne by Lessee, if Lessor reasonably believes them to be necessary. Neither any action nor inaction on the part of Lessor pursuant to this Section ___ shall be deemed in any way to release Lessee from, or in any way modify or alter, Lessee's responsibilities, obligations, and/or liabilities incurred pursuant to Section ___ hereof.

N. Indemnity. Lessee shall indemnify, hold harmless, and, at Lessor's option (with such attorneys as Lessor may approve in advance and in writing), defend Lessor and Lessor's officers, directors, shareholders, trustees, partners, employees, contractors, agents and mortgagees or other lien holders, from and against any and all claims, demands, expenses, actions, judgments, damages (whether consequential, direct or indirect, known or unknown, foreseen or unforeseen), penalties, fines, liabilities, losses of every kind and nature (including, without limitation, property damage, diminution in value of Lessor's interest in the Leased Premises or the Complex, damages for the loss or restriction on use of any space or amenity within the Leased Premises or the Complex, damages arising from any adverse impact on marketing space in the Complex, sums paid in settlement of claims and any costs and expenses associated with injury, illness or death to or of any person), suits, administrative proceedings, costs and fees, including, but not limited to, attorneys' and consultants' fees and expenses, and the costs of cleanup, remediation, removal and restoration (all of the foregoing being hereinafter sometimes collectively referred to as "Losses"), arising from or related to any violation or alleged violation of any of the requirements, ordinances, statutes, regulations or other laws referred to in this Article, including, without limitation, Environmental Laws, any breach of the provisions of this Article, or any Hazardous Use on, about or from the Leased Premises caused by the acts or omissions of any persons or entities whatsoever, whether related or unrelated to Lessee, including without limitation any Hazardous Use or release of Hazardous Materials arising, occurring or existing prior to the execution of this Lease and/or Lessee's possession of the Leased Premises. Lessee warrants that it is leasing the Premises "as-is, where-is," that it has thoroughly inspected the Leased Premises prior to execution of this Lease, and that it intends to act as an insurer with respect to any Hazardous Use on, under or about the Leased Premises.

O. <u>Release and Assumption of Risk.</u>

(a) Lessee, for itself, and its officers, directors, shareholders, partners, agents, contractors, attorneys, brokers, servants, employees, sublessees, lessees, invitees, concessionaires, licensees and representatives (hereinafter referred to as "Releasors"), hereby waives, releases, acquits and forever discharges Lessor and its officers, directors, trustees, shareholders, partners, agents, contractors, attorneys, brokers, servants, employees, lessees, invitees, licensees and representatives (hereinafter referred to as "Releasees") of and from any and all Losses, which are in any way connected with, based upon, related to or arising out of (i) any Hazardous Use or Hazardous Materials on or about the Leased Premises or the Complex, (ii) any violation by or relating to the Leased Premises or the Complex (or the ownership, use, condition, occupancy or operation thereof), or by the Releasors or any other persons or entities, of any Environmental or Wetlands Laws affecting the Leased Premises or the Complex, or (iii) any investigation, inquiry, order, hearing, action or other proceeding by or before any governmental agency or any court in connection with any of the matters referred to in clauses (i) or (ii) above (collectively, the "Released Matters"), except to the extent caused by the gross negligence or willful misconduct of the Releasees. Releasors hereby expressly assume any and all risk of Losses based on or arising out of or pertaining to the Released Matters.

(b) Lessee agrees, represents and warrants that the Released Matters are not limited to matters which are known, disclosed or foreseeable, and Lessee waives any and all rights and benefits which are conferred upon Lessee by virtue of the provisions of Section 1542 of the California Civil Code, which provides:

A GENERAL RELEASE DOES NOT EXTEND TO CLAIMS WHICH THE CREDITOR DOES NOT KNOW OR SUSPECT TO EXIST IN HIS FAVOR AT THE TIME OF EXECUTING THE RELEASE, WHICH IF KNOWN BY HIM MUST HAVE MATERIALLY AFFECTED HIS SETTLEMENT WITH THE DEBTOR.

(c) Lessee agrees, represents and warrants that it is familiar with, has read, understands, and has consulted legal counsel of its choosing with respect to California Civil Code Section 1542 and Lessee realizes and acknowledges that factual matters now unknown to it may have given, or may hereinafter give, rise to Losses which are presently unknown, unanticipated and unsuspected. Lessee further agrees, represents and warrants that the provisions of this Section 12.5 have been negotiated and agreed upon in light of that realization and that Lessee nevertheless hereby intends to release, discharge and acquit the Releasees from any such unknown Losses which are in any way related to this Lease or the Complex.

P. <u>Indoor Air Quality.</u> To prevent the generation, growth or deposit of any mold, mildew, bacillus, virus, pollen or other microorganism (collectively, "Biologicals") and the deposit, release or circulation of any indoor contaminants, including, but not limited to, emissions from paint, carpet and drapery treatments, cleaning, maintenance and construction materials and supplies, pesticides, pressed wood products, insulation, tobacco and other materials and products (collectively with Biologicals, "Contaminants"), that could adversely affect the health, safety or welfare of any tenant, employee, or other occupant of the Complex or their invitees (each, an "Occupant"), Lessee shall, at Lessee's sole cost and expense, at all times during the Term: (i) maintain, operate and repair the HVAC system servicing the Leased Premises (to the extent that Lessee is otherwise obligated to perform such maintenance, operation and repair pursuant to this Lease) in a manner consistent with preventing or minimizing the generation, growth, circulation, release or deposit of any Contaminants; (ii) maintain the humidity level and the air exchange rate within the Leased Premises (to the extent that Lessee has control thereof) at a level recommended to prevent or minimize the growth of any Biologicals and the circulation of any other Contaminants; (iii) maintain, operate and repair the Leased Premises in such a manner to prevent or minimize the accumulation of stagnant water and moisture in planters, kitchen appliances and vessels, carpeting, insulation, water coolers and any other locations where stagnant water and moisture could accumulate; and (iv) otherwise maintain, operate and repair the Leased Premises to prevent the generation, growth, deposit, release or circulation of any Contaminants. If any governmental entity or any Occupant alleges that health, safety or welfare has been or could be adversely affected by any such Contaminants, Lessee shall notify Lessor in writing within twenty-four (24) hours of the time the allegation is made. Lessor may then elect to engage the services of an industrial hygiene testing laboratory (or alternatively or concurrently require Lessee to do the same) to determine whether the cause of any alleged adverse health effect is or could be attributable to any Contaminants present within the Leased Premises. Lessee shall be responsible for all such testing costs and for any consequential damages and costs (including, without limitation, any third-party claims, loss of rental, remediation, removal and/or abatement costs, and increases in insurance premiums) resulting from Lessee's failure to comply in whole or in part with the terms of this Section ___. The indemnity set forth in Section ___ above shall apply to Lessee's failure to comply with any of the terms of this Section.

Chapter 8 – Alterations

A. <u>Consent of Lessor; Ownership.</u> Lessee shall not make, or suffer to be made, any alterations to the Leased Premises, or any part thereof, without the written consent of Lessor first had and obtained. Any additions to, or alterations of, the Leased Premises, except trade fixtures, shall upon expiration or termination of the Term become a part of the realty and belong to Lessor. Except as otherwise provided in this Lease, Lessee shall have the right to remove its trade fixtures placed upon the Leased Premises provided that Lessee restores the Leased Premises as indicated below.

B. Requirements. Any alterations, additions or installations performed by Lessee hereinafter collectively "alterations") shall be subject to strict conformity with the following requirements:

1. All alterations shall be at the sole cost and expense of Lessee;

2. Prior to commencement of any work of alteration, Lessee shall submit detailed plans and specifications, including working drawings, (hereinafter referred to as "Plans") of the proposed alterations, which shall be subject to the consent of Lessor in accordance with the terms of Section A above;

3. Following approval of the Plans by Lessor, Lessee shall give Lessor at least ten (10) days prior written notice of commencement of work in the Leased Premises so that Lessor may post notices of nonresponsibility in or upon the Leased Premises as provided by law;

4. No alterations shall be commenced without Lessee having previously obtained all appropriate permits and approvals required by and of governmental agencies;

5. All alterations shall be performed in a skillful and work-manlike manner, consistent with the best practices and standards of the construction industry, and pursued with diligence in accordance with the Plans previously approved by Lessor and in full accord with all applicable laws and ordinances. All material, equipment, and articles incorporated in the alterations shall be new, and of recent manufacture, and of the most suitable grade for the purpose intended;

6. Lessee must obtain the prior written approval of Lessee's contractor from Lessor before commencement of the work.

Lessee's contractor shall maintain all of the insurance reasonably required by Lessor, including commercial general liability, workers' compensation, builder's risk and course of construction insurance;

7. As a condition to approval of the alterations, Lessor may require performance and labor and materialmen's payment bonds issued by a surety approved by Lessor, in a sum equal to the cost of the alterations guarantying the completion of the alterations free and clear of all liens and other charges in accordance with the Plans. Such bonds shall name Lessor as beneficiary;

8. The alterations must be performed in a manner such that there will be no interference with the quiet enjoyment of other premises by the other lessees in the Complex.

C. <u>Liens.</u> Lessee shall keep the Leased Premises and the Complex in which the Leased Premises are situated, free from any liens arising out of any work performed, materials furnished or obligations incurred by Lessee. In the event a mechanic's or other lien is filed against the Leased Premises or the Complex as a result of a claim arising through Lessee, Lessor may demand that Lessee furnish to Lessor a surety bond satisfactory to Lessor in an amount equal to at least one hundred fifty percent (150%) of the amount of the contested lien claim or demand, indemnifying Lessor against liability which may arise therefrom and holding the Leased Premises free from the effect of such lien or claim. Such bond must be posted within ten (10) days following notice from Lessor. In addition, Lessor may require Lessee to pay Lessor's attorney's fees and costs in participating in any action to foreclose such lien if Lessor shall decide it is in its best interest to do so. Lessor may pay the claim prior to the enforcement thereof, in which event Lessee shall reimburse Lessor in full, including attorney's fees, for any such expense, as additional rent, with the next due rental.

D. <u>Restoration.</u> Lessee shall return the Leased Premises to Lessor at the expiration or earlier termination of the Term in good and sanitary order, condition and repair, free of rubble and debris, broom clean, reasonable wear and tear excepted. However, Lessee shall ascertain from Lessor at least thirty (30) days prior to the termination of this Lease, whether Lessor desires the Leased Premises, or any part thereof, restored to its condition prior to the making of permitted alterations, installations and improvements, and if Lessor shall so desire, then Lessee shall forthwith restore said Leased Premises or the designated portions thereof as the case may be, to its original condition, entirely at its own expense, excepting normal wear and tear. All damage to the Leased Premises caused by the removal of such trade fixtures and other personal property that Lessee is permitted to remove under the terms of this Lease and/or such restoration shall be repaired by Lessee at its sole cost and expense prior to termination.

Chapter 9 – Common Areas

A. <u>Definition of Common Areas.</u> The term "Common Areas" as used herein means all areas and facilities outside the Leased Premises, within the exterior boundaries of the Complex, that are provided and designated by Lessor from time to time for the general use and convenience of Lessee and of other tenants of Lessor having the common use of such areas, and their respective authorized representatives and invitees. Common Areas include, without limitation, driveways, parking areas, sidewalks, and landscaped areas [Offices include indoor areas such as lobbies, corridors, etc.], all as generally described on Exhibit "B" attached hereto. Exhibit "B" is tentative and Lessor reserves the right to make alterations thereto from time to time.

B. <u>Rights and Duties of Lessor.</u> Lessor shall, in a manner it deems proper in its opinion, maintain the Common Areas, establish and enforce reasonable rules and regulations concerning such areas, establish parking charges, with or without validation, close any of the Common Areas to whatever extent required in the opinion of Lessor's counsel to prevent a dedication of any of the Common Areas or the accrual of any rights of any person or of the public to the Common Areas, close temporarily any of the Common Areas for maintenance purposes, and make changes to the Common Areas including, without limitation, changes in the location of driveways, entrances, exits, vehicular parking spaces, parking area, the designation of areas for the exclusive use of others, the direction of the flow of traffic or construction of additional Buildings thereupon. Lessee hereby acknowledges that Lessor is under no obligation to provide security for the Common Areas but may do so at its option.

C. <u>Payment by Lessee.</u> Lessee shall pay to Lessor, as additional rent, its proportionate share of Common Area Costs as hereinafter defined, within ten (10) days of receiving a bill therefor from Lessor, but no more frequently than monthly. Lessee's proportionate share (or "pro rata %") shall be that fraction of Common Area Costs the numerator of which is the number of square feet in the Leased Premises and the denominator of which is the number of square feet of Occupied Floor Area of buildings in the Complex having the use of the Common Areas. Lessee's initial pro rata % of Common Area Costs is stated in Section ___. Lessor may bill Lessee estimated charges in accordance with Section E. below. Notwithstanding the preceding provisions of this Section, Lessee's proportionate share as to certain expenses included in Common Area Costs may be calculated differently to yield a higher percentage share for Lessee as to certain expenses in the event Lessor permits other tenants or occupants in the Complex to incur such expenses directly rather than have Lessor incur the expense in common for the Complex. In such case Lessee's proportionate share of the applicable expense shall be calculated as having as its denominator the Occupied Floor Area of all buildings in the Complex less the number of square feet of building area of tenants or occupants who have incurred such expense directly. In any case where Lessee, with Lessor's consent, incurs such expenses directly, Lessee's proportionate share of Common Area Costs will be calculated specially so that expenses of the same character which are incurred by Lessor for the benefit of other tenants in the Complex shall not be pro-rated to Lessee. Nothing herein shall imply that Lessor will permit Lessee or any other tenant of the Complex to incur Common Area Costs. Any such permission shall be in the sole discretion of Lessor, which Lessor may grant or withhold in its arbitrary judgment.

D. <u>Definition of Common Area Costs.</u> "Common Area Costs" means all sums (including "Capital Costs" as hereinafter defined and to the extent stated herein) expended by Lessor, its agents, contractors and employees for operating, maintaining, repairing and administering of the Shopping Center including, without limitation, equipping, policing and protecting, lighting, providing sanitation and sewer and other services, providing a music and public address system, insuring (including self-insurance and the payment of deductible amounts under insurance policies), repairing, replacing and maintaining the (1) common areas and (2) all buildings and roofs within the Complex, and (3) all other areas, facilities and buildings, vertical transportation facilities, retention ponds (if applicable), and any and all facilities and improvements connecting the Complex to off-site buildings or areas, which are used in connection with the maintenance and/or operation of, and whether located within or outside of, the Complex; such costs and expenses shall include, but shall not be limited to, the full cost of: illumination and maintenance of Complex signs, whether located on or off the Complex; refuse disposal, water, gas, sewage, electricity and other utilities (without limitation), including any and all usage, service, hook up, connection, availability and/or standby fees or charges pertaining to same, and including all costs associated with the provision, maintenance and operation of any central telephone service for the Complex; the operation, maintenance, repair and replacement of all or any part of the parking areas; snow removal, maintenance and operation of any temporary or permanent utility, including a sewage disposal system, within or without the Complex, built, together with hook up or connection fees and service charges; compliance with rules, regulations and orders of governmental authorities pertaining to air pollution control, including the cost of monitoring air quality; maintenance for wooded areas, retention ponds, lakes and shoreline areas (if applicable); cleaning, lighting, striping and landscaping; curbs, gutters, sidewalks, drainage and irrigation ditches, conduits, pipes and canals located on or adjacent to the Complex; premiums for liability, casualty, and property insurance; personal property taxes; licensing fees and taxes, audit fees and expenses; supplies; the cost and expense of supplying music to the Complex; all real estate taxes and assessments and substitutions and replacements thereof levied or assessed by municipal, county, state, federal or other taxing or assessing authority upon, against or with respect to the Common Areas and/or the land thereunder and the land on which the Complex buildings are located, and all property (including any land upon which may be located any temporary or permanent utility, including a sewage disposal system, within or without the Complex built, operated and/or maintained for the specific purpose of servicing the Complex) provided by Landlord which may at any time comprise or serve the Complex, whether located on or off the site of the Complex, irrespective of whether the same is taxed or assessed as real or personal property; cost, lease payment or depreciation of any equipment, improvements or facilities used in the operation or maintenance of the common areas or project areas; total compensation and benefits (including premiums for workers' compensation or any other insurance or other retirement or employee benefits, and including all costs incurred in providing such benefits) paid to or on behalf of employees involved in the performance of the work specified in this Section or employees otherwise providing services to tenants or customers of the Complex; and public transit or carpooling facilities of the Complex; and the public transit or carpooling facilities, management fees paid to independent contractors, reserve accounts established for the purchasing and/or replacement of equipment; property owner's association dues and assessments which may be imposed upon Lessor by virtue of any recorded instrument affecting title to the Complex, plus an allowance of fifteen percent (15%) of such sums to Lessor for administrative fee. Capital Costs are defined as those expenditures which do not normally recur more frequently than at five (5) year intervals in the normal course of operation and maintenance of the Complex. Notwithstanding anything above which may be to the contrary, Common Area Costs shall include a portion of all Capital Costs, representing any costs of capital improvements made by Lessor to the Complex for the purpose of reducing recurring expenses or utility costs and from which Lessee can expect a reasonable benefit, or that are required by governmental law, ordinance, regulation or mandate, not applicable to the Complex at the time of the original construction. The portion thereof to be included each year in Common Area Costs shall be that fraction allocable to the calendar year in question calculated by amortizing the cost over the reasonably useful life of such improvement, as determined by Lessor, with interest on the unamortized balance at ten per cent (10%)

per annum or such higher rate as may have been paid by Lessor for funds borrowed for the purpose of constructing such improvements, but in no event to exceed the highest rate permissible by law.

E. Estimated Payments. Lessor shall have the right, at its option, to estimate Lessee's pro rata share of Common Area Costs due in the future from Lessee and to collect from Lessee on a monthly or quarterly basis, as Lessor may elect, the amount of Lessee's estimated pro rata share of such costs. Lessor shall provide Lessee with a reconciliation of Lessee's account at least annually, and if such reconciliation shall indicate that Lessee's account is insufficient to satisfy Lessee's pro rata share of Common Area Costs for the period estimated, Lessee shall immediately pay to Lessor any deficiency. Any excess in such account indicated by the reconciliation shall be credited to Lessee's account to reduce the estimated payments for the next ensuing period.

Chapter 10 – Operating Costs

A. "Operating Costs" means the total amounts paid or payable, whether by Lessor or others on behalf of Lessor, in connection with the ownership, maintenance, repair, replacement and operations of the Complex (including, without limitation, all areas and facilities within the exterior boundaries of the Complex) as determined in a manner consistent with generally accepted accounting principles ("GAAP"). Operating Costs shall include, but not be limited to, the aggregate of the amount paid for all electricity and fuel used in heating and air conditioning of the Building; the amount paid or payable for all electricity furnished by Lessor to the Complex; the cost of periodic relamping and reballasting of Building Standard lighting fixtures; the amount paid or payable for all hot and cold water (other than that chargeable to lessees by reason of their extraordinary consumption of water); the amount paid or payable for all labor and/or wages and other payments including cost to Lessor of workers' compensation and disability insurance, payroll taxes, welfare and fringe benefits made to janitors, caretakers, and other employees, contractors and subcontractors of Lessor (including wages of the Building manager) involved in the operation, maintenance and repair of the Complex; painting for exterior walls of the buildings in the Complex; managerial and administrative expenses; the total charges of any independent contractors employed in the repair, care, operation, maintenance, and cleaning of the Complex; the amount paid or payable for all supplies occasioned by everyday wear and tear; the costs of VAC (as defined in Section ___) of the Complex, (except to the extent paid by Lessee, or other lessees, for VAC provided to the Leased Premises, or other leased premises, in respect of VAC provided outside the Climate Control Hours defined in Section ___), window and exterior wall cleaning, telephone and utility costs; the cost of accounting services necessary to compute the rents and charges payable by lessees and keep the books of the Complex; fees for management, legal, accounting, inspection and consulting services; the cost of operating, repairing and maintaining and replacing the Building escalators and elevators and the utility systems, including Lines, of the Complex including the cost of inspection and service contracts; the cost of porters, guards and other protection services; the cost of establishing and maintaining the Building's directory board; payments for general maintenance and repairs to the plant and equipment supplying climate control; the cost of supplying all services pursuant to Article ___ hereof to the extent such services are not paid by individual lessees; amortization of the costs, including repair and replacement, of all maintenance and cleaning equipment and master utility meters and of the costs incurred for repairing or replacing all other fixtures, equipment and facilities serving or comprising the Complex which by their nature require periodic or substantial repair or replacement, and which are not charged fully in the year in which they are incurred, at rates on the various items determined from time to time by Lessor in accordance with GAAP; the cost of the Shuttle Service described in Article ___ hereof; the cost of operating the parking facility in the Complex and the cost of parking fees and rents paid to the owner of another parcel for use of certain parking spaces therein (collectively "Parking Costs") net of parking fees and rents collected by Lessor in connection herewith provided, however, Lessor shall not be obligated to credit any sums received in excess of the actual Parking Costs; the cost and expenses for insurance for which Lessor is responsible hereunder or which Lessor reasonably deems necessary in connection with the operation of the Complex (including, without limitation, self-insurance and the payment of deductible amounts under insurance policies); community association dues or assessments and property owners' association dues and assessments which may be imposed upon Lessor by virtue of any recorded instrument affecting title to the Complex; and costs of complying with all governmental regulations, rules, laws, ordinances and codes, including Environmental Laws as such term is defined in Article ____. In addition, Operating Costs shall include any Real Estate Taxes as defined in Paragraph ____ hereof. Operating Costs shall also include, without limitation, the repair and replacement, resurfacing and repaving of any paved areas, curbs, gutters or other surfaces or areas within the Complex, the repair and replacement of any equipment or facilities located within or serving the Complex, and the cost of any capital repairs, replacements or improvements made by Lessor to the Complex ("Capital Costs"). However, certain Capital Costs (the "Restricted Capital Costs") shall be includable in Operating Costs each year only to the extent of that fraction allocable to the year in question calculated by amortizing such Restricted Capital Costs over the reasonably useful life of the improvement resulting therefrom, as determined by Lessor, with interest on the unamortized balance at the higher of (1) ten percent (10%) per annum; or (2) the interest rate as may have been paid by Lessor for the funds borrowed for the purpose of performing the work for which the Restricted Capital Costs have been expended, but in no event to exceed the highest rate permissible by law. The Restricted Capital Costs subject to such amortization procedure are the following: (x) those costs for capital improvements to the Complex of a type which do not normally recur more frequently than every five (5) years in the normal course of operation and maintenance of facilities such as the Complex (specifically excluding painting of all or a portion of the Complex); (y) costs incurred for the purpose of reducing other operating expenses or utility costs, from which Lessee can expect a reduction in the amounts it would otherwise expend, or reimburse Lessor, and (z) expenditures by Lessor that are required by governmental law, ordinance, regulation or mandate, including, without limitation, any Environmental Laws (as such term is defined in Article ____), which were not applicable to the

Complex at the time of the original construction. Operating Costs shall not include legal or accounting expenses incurred expressly for negotiating a lease with a particular lessee, or as a result of a default of a specific lessee, which negotiation or default does not affect the operation of the Complex.

B. "Proportionate Share" or "Pro Rata Percent" shall be that fraction (converted to a percentage) the numerator of which is the Rentable Area of the Leased Premises and the denominator of which is the number of square feet of Rentable Area of all floors (or leased premises if the Complex is on a single floor) rentable to lessees in the Complex. Lessee's Proportionate Share as of the commencement of the Term hereof is specified in Section ___. Said Proportionate Share shall be recalculated as may be required effective as at the commencement of any period to which the calculation is applicable in this Lease. Notwithstanding the preceding provisions of this Section, Lessee's Proportionate Share as to certain expenses may be calculated differently to yield a higher percentage share for Lessee as to certain expenses in the event Lessor permits other lessees in the Complex to directly incur such expenses rather than have Lessor incur the expense in common for the Complex (such as, by way of illustration, wherein a lessee performs its own janitorial services). In such case Lessee's Proportionate Share of the applicable expense shall be calculated as having as its denominator the Rentable Area of all floors (or leased premises if the Complex is on a single floor) rentable to lessees in the Complex less the Rentable Area of lessees who have incurred such expense directly. Furthermore, in the event Lessee consumes extraordinary amounts of any provided utility or other service as determined in Lessor's good faith judgment, Lessee's Proportionate Share for such utility or service may, at Lessor's election, be based on usage as opposed to Rentable Area, that is, Lessee's Proportionate Share of such a utility or service would be calculated as having as its denominator the total usage of such utility or service in the Complex (or Building as the case may be), and having as its numerator Lessee's usage of such utility or service, as determined by Lessor in its sole good faith judgment. In any case in which Lessee, with Lessor's consent, incurs such expenses directly, Lessee's Proportionate Share will be calculated specially so that expenses of the same character which are incurred by Lessor for the benefit of other lessees in the Complex shall not be prorated to Lessee. If repairs are required for systems exclusively serving the Leased Premises (whether within or outside of said Leased Premises), Lessee shall pay one hundred percent (100%) of such repair costs. Nothing herein shall imply that Lessor will permit Lessee or any other lessee of the Complex to incur any Common Area Costs or Operating Costs. Any such permission shall be in the sole discretion of the Lessor, which Lessor may grant or withhold in its arbitrary judgment.

(See provisions for Chapter 5-Rent, Additional Rent supplement, paragraph B above for payment of Operating Costs by Tenant.)

Chapter 11 – Assignment and Subletting

A. <u>Lease is Personal.</u> The purpose of this Lease is to transfer possession of the Leased Premises to Lessee for Lessee's personal use in return for certain benefits, including rent, to be transferred to the Lessor. Lessee's right to assign or sublet as stated in this Article is subsidiary and incidental to the underlying purpose of this Lease. Lessee acknowledges and agrees that it has entered into this Lease in order to acquire the Leased Premises for its own personal use and not for the purpose of obtaining the right to convey the leasehold to others.

B. <u>"Transfer of the Leased Premises" Defined.</u> The terms "Transfer of the Leased Premises" or "Transfer" as used herein shall include any assignment of all or any part of this Lease (including assignment by operation of law), subletting of all or any part of the Leased Premises or transfer of possession, or granting of the right of possession or contingent right of possession of all or any portion of the Leased Premises including, without limitation, license, concession, mortgage, devise, hypothecation, agency, franchise or management agreement, or suffering any other person (the agents and servants of Lessee excepted) to occupy or use the Leased Premises or any portion thereof; and the party to whom the Transfer is to be effected is hereinafter referred to as the "Transferee." If Lessee is a corporation which is not deemed a public corporation, or is an unincorporated association or partnership, or Lessee consists of more than one party, the transfer, assignment or hypothecation of any stock or interest in such corporation, association, partnership or ownership interest, in the aggregate in excess of twenty-five percent (25%), shall be deemed a Transfer of the Leased Premises.

1. No Transfer Without Consent. Lessee shall not suffer a Transfer of the Leased Premises or any interest therein, or any part thereof, or any right or privilege appurtenant thereto without the prior written consent of Lessor, and a consent to one Transfer of the Leased Premises shall not be deemed to be a consent to any subsequent Transfer of the Leased Premises. Any Transfer of the Leased Premises without such consent shall (a) be voidable, and (b) terminate this Lease, in either case, at the option of Lessor.

2. When Consent is Granted.

(a) The consent of Lessor to a Transfer may not be unreasonably withheld, provided that it is agreed to be reasonable for Lessor to consider any of the following reasons, which list is not exclusive, in electing to consent or to deny consent:

(i) Financial strength of the proposed Transferee is not at least equal to that of Lessee at the time of execution of this Lease;

(ii) A proposed Transferee whose occupation of the Leased Premises would cause a diminution in the reputation of the Complex or the other businesses located therein;

(iii) A proposed Transferee whose impact on the common facilities or the other occupants of the Complex would be disadvantageous to the operation and management of the Complex including increasing the cost of operation and management;

(iv) A proposed Transferee whose use presents a risk of violation of Article ___;

(v) A proposed Transferee whose occupancy will require a variation in the terms of this Lease (for example, a variation in the use clause) or which otherwise adversely affects any interest of Lessor;

(vi) That there be no uncured notices of default under the terms of this Lease; or

(vii) A proposed Transferee who is or is likely to be, or whose business is or is likely to be, subject to compliance with additional laws or other governmental requirements beyond those to which Lessee or Lessee's business is subject.

(b) Notwithstanding the foregoing, Lessee shall have the right, without the consent of Lessor, but upon prior written notice to Lessor, to assign this Lease to a company incorporated or to be incorporated by Lessee, provided that Lessee owns or beneficially controls all the issued and outstanding shares of capital stock of the company; further provided, however, that in the event that at any time following such assignment, Lessee wishes to sell, mortgage, devise, hypothecate or in any other manner whatsoever transfer any portion of the ownership or beneficial control of the issued and outstanding shares in the capital stock of such company, such transaction shall be deemed to constitute a Transfer and shall be subject to all of the provisions of this Article ___ with respect to a Transfer of the Premises including, by specific reference, the provisions of Section ___.

3. Procedure for Obtaining Consent.

(a) Lessor need not commence its review of any proposed Transfer, or respond to any request by Lessee with respect to such, unless and until it has received from Lessee adequate descriptive information concerning the Transferee, the business to be conducted by the Transferee, the Transferee's financial capacity, and such other information as may reasonably be required in order to form a prudent judgment as to the acceptability of the proposed Transfer, including, without limitation, the following:

(i) Reasonable financial information concerning the

proposed Transferee including the past two years' audited annual Balance Sheets and Profit and Loss statements, certified correct by a Certified Public Accountant;

(ii) Banking references of the proposed Transferee;

(iii) A resume of the business background and experience of the proposed Transferee;

(iv) At least five (5) business references for the proposed Transferee;

(v) An executed copy of the instrument by which Lessee proposes to effectuate the Transfer;

(vi) A certified statement, including the calculation, of the amount of unamortized cost of Lessee's Tenant Improvements to the Leased Premises.

(b) Lessee shall reimburse Lessor as additional rent for Lessor's reasonable costs and attorneys' fees incurred in conjunction with the processing and documentation of any proposed Transfer of the Leased Premises, whether or not consent is granted.

4. Recapture.

(a) By written notice to Lessee (the "Termination Notice") within twenty (20) business days following submission to Lessor by Lessee of the information specified in Section ___, Lessor: (1) may terminate this Lease in the event of an assignment of this Lease or sublet of the entire Leased Premises; or (2) if such proposed subletting will result in more than fifty percent (50%) of the entire Leased Premises being sublet (in the aggregate with any previous subleases), terminate this Lease as to all or any portion of the Leased Premises. Any termination pursuant to clause (2) above shall be subject to the rights of any sublessees under any existing subleases provided Lessor has previously consented to the sublease in accordance with the terms of this Lease. In the event Lessor elects to terminate this Lease as to that portion of the Leased Premises to be sublet, an amendment to this Lease shall be executed whereby the description of the Leased Premises is restated and Lessee's obligations for rent and other charges are reduced in proportion to the reduction in Rentable Area of the Leased Premises caused thereby.

(b) In the event that Lessor terminates this Lease or terminates this Lease as to a portion thereof, Lessor may, if it elects, enter into a new lease covering the Premises or a portion thereof with the intended transferee on such terms as Lessor and such transferee may agree or enter into a new lease covering the Premises with any other party; in such event, Lessee shall not be entitled to any portion of the profit if any which Lessor may realize on account of such termination and reletting. From and after the date of such termination of this Lease, the parties shall have no further obligations to each other under this Lease except for matters occurring or obligations arising prior to the date of such termination.

5. Reasonable Restriction. The restrictions on Transfer described in this Article ____ are acknowledged by Lessee to be reasonable for all purposes, including, without limitation, the provisions of California Civil Code (the "Code") Section 1951.4(b)(2). Lessee expressly waives any rights which it might otherwise be deemed to possess pursuant to applicable law, including, without limitation, Section 1997.040 of the Code, to limit any remedy of Lessor pursuant to Section 1951.2 or 1951.4 of the Code by means of proof that enforcement of a restriction on use of the Leased Premises would be unreasonable.

6. Effect of Transfer. If Lessor consents to a Transfer (or if a Transfer occurs without Lessor's consent in accordance with Section ____) the following conditions shall apply:

(a) Each and every covenant, condition or obligation imposed upon Lessee by this Lease and each and every right, remedy or benefit afforded Lessor by this Lease shall not be impaired or diminished as a result of such Transfer.

(b) Lessee shall pay to Lessor on a monthly basis, eighty percent (80%) of the excess of any sums of money, or other economic consideration received by Lessee from the Transferee in such month (whether or not for a period longer than one month), including higher rent, bonuses, key money, or the like over the aggregate, of (1) the Amortized Portion, as defined below, of the reasonable expenses actually paid by Lessee to unrelated third parties for brokerage commissions, tenant improvements to the Leased Premises, or design fees incurred as a direct consequence of the Transfer, and, (2) the total sums which Lessee pays Lessor under this Lease in such month, or the prorated portion thereof if the Leased Premises transferred is less than the entire Leased Premises. The amount so derived shall be paid with Lessee's payment of Minimum Rent. The term "Amortized Portion" is that portion of the applicable expenses derived by dividing such expenses by the number of months in the original term of the Transfer transaction.

(c) No Transfer, whether or not consent of Lessor is required hereunder, shall relieve Lessee of its primary obligation to pay the rent and to perform all other obligations to be performed by Lessee hereunder. The acceptance of rent by Lessor from any proposed Transferee shall not be deemed to be a waiver by Lessor of any provision of this Lease or to be a consent to any Transfer of the Leased Premises.

(d) If Lessor consents to a sublease, such sublease shall not extend beyond the expiration of the Term.

(e) No Transfer shall be valid and no Transferee shall take possession of the Leased Premises or any part thereof unless, within ten (10) days after the execution of the documentary evidence thereof, Lessee shall deliver to Lessor a duly executed duplicate original of the Transfer instrument in form satisfactory to Lessor which provides that: (1) the Transferee assumes Lessee's obligations for the payment of rent and for the full and faithful observance and performance of the covenants, terms and conditions contained herein; (2) such Transferee will, at Lessor's election, attorn directly to Lessor in the event Lessee's Lease is terminated for any reason on the terms set forth in the instrument of transfer; and (3) such instrument of transfer contains such other assurances as Lessor reasonably deems necessary.

Chapter 12 – Insurance and Indemnity

Property Insurance

A. Use of Premises. No use shall be made or permitted to be made on the Leased Premises, nor acts done, which will increase the existing rate of insurance upon the Building in which the Leased Premises are located or upon any other Building in the Complex or cause the cancellation of any insurance policy covering the Building, or any part thereof, nor shall Lessee sell, or permit to be kept, used or sold, in or about the Leased Premises, any article which may be prohibited by the standard form of all-risk fire insurance policies. Lessee shall, at its sole cost and expense, comply with any and all requirements pertaining to the Leased Premises, of any insurance organization or company, necessary for the maintenance of reasonable property damage and public liability insurance, covering the Leased Premises, the Building, or the Complex.

B. Increase in Premiums. Lessee agrees to pay to Lessor, as additional rent, any increase in premiums on policies which may be carried by Lessor on the Leased Premises, the Building or the Complex, or any blanket policies which include the Building or Complex, covering damage thereto and loss of rent caused by fire and other perils above the rates for the least hazardous type of occupancy for retail operations. Lessee further agrees to pay Lessor, as additional rent, any increases in such premiums resulting from the nature of Lessee's occupancy or any act or omission of Lessee.

C. Pro Rata Share of Premiums.

1. Lessee shall pay to Lessor, during the term hereof, as additional rent, its pro rata share of the insurance premiums for any property insurance carried by Lessor covering the Complex (the "Complex Insurance Premium"). Such pro rata share is defined as that fraction of the insurance

premiums the numerator of which is the total square footage in the Leased Premises and the denominator of which is the total square footage in all Occupied Floor Area to which the Complex Insurance Premium is applicable. In the event that the property insurance carried by Lessor covering the Complex is a blanket policy in which other properties not related to the Complex are included, the Complex Insurance Premium shall be calculated as that portion of such blanket policy insurance premium which, in Lessor's good faith judgment, is properly allocable to the Complex. The sum due under this subsection shall be in addition to that which may be due under the previous Section of this Lease.

2. Lessee shall pay any such premium portion to Lessor within ten (10) days after receipt by Lessee of Lessor's billing therefor.

D. <u>Estimated Payments.</u> Lessor may, at its option, estimate the amount of insurance premiums for property insurance to be due in the future from Lessee and collect from Lessee on a monthly or quarterly basis, at Lessor's option, the amount of Lessee's estimated insurance premium obligation. Prior to March 1 of each year, Lessor shall provide Lessee with a reconciliation of Lessee's account along with a billing for any shortage in the event of a deficiency or statement for credit applicable to the next ensuing insurance premium payments, if an overpayment has been made by Lessee.

E. <u>Personal Property Insurance.</u> Lessee shall maintain in full force and effect on all of its fixtures and equipment in the Leased Premises a policy or policies of fire and casualty insurance in "all risk" form to the extent of at least ninety percent (90%) of their replacement cost, or that percentage of the replacement cost required to negate the effect of a co-insurance provision, whichever is greater. No such policy shall have a deductible in a greater amount than One Thousand Dollars ($1,000.00). Lessee shall also insure in the same manner the physical value of all its leasehold improvements in the Leased Premises. During the term of this Lease, the proceeds from any such policy or policies of insurance shall be used for the repair or replacement of the fixtures, equipment, and leasehold improvements so insured. Lessor shall have no interest in said insurance, and will sign all documents necessary or proper in connection with the settlement of any claim or loss by Lessee. Lessee shall also maintain insurance for all plate glass upon the Leased Premises.

Liability Insurance

F. <u>Lessee's Insurance.</u> Lessee shall, at Lessee's expense, obtain and keep in force during the term of this Lease, a commercial general liability insurance policy insuring Lessee against the risks of personal injury and property damage arising out of the ownership, use, occupancy, or maintenance of the Leased Premises and all areas appurtenant thereto. Such insurance shall be a combined single limit policy in an amount not less than ONE MILLION DOLLARS ($1,000,000.00) per occurrence and an umbrella policy of THREE MILLION DOLLARS ($3,000,000.00) combined single limit per occurrence. Lessor shall be named as an additional insured. The policy shall contain cross liability endorsements and shall insure performance by Lessee of the indemnity provisions of this Lease; shall cover contractual liability, and products liability; shall be primary, not contributing with, and not in excess of coverage which Lessor may carry; shall state that Lessor is entitled to recovery for the negligence of Lessee even though Lessor is named as an additional insured; shall provide for severability of interest; shall provide that an act or omission of one of the insured or additional insureds which would void or otherwise reduce coverage shall not void or reduce coverages as to the other insured or additional insured; and shall afford coverage after the term of this Lease (by separate policy or extension if necessary) for all claims based on acts, omissions, injury or damage which occurred or arose (or the onset of which occurred or arose) in whole or in part during the term of this Lease. The limits of said insurance shall not limit any liability of Lessee hereunder. Not more frequently than every three (3) years, if, in the reasonable opinion of Lessor, the amount of liability insurance required hereunder is not adequate, Lessee shall promptly increase said insurance coverage as required by Lessor.

G. <u>Worker's Compensation Insurance.</u> Lessee shall carry Workers Compensation insurance as required by law, including an employer's contingent liability endorsement.

Insurance Policy Requirements

H. <u>General Requirements.</u> All insurance policies required to be carried by Lessee hereunder shall conform to the following requirements:

> (1) The insurer in each case shall carry a designation in Best's Insurance Reports as issued from time to time throughout the term as follows: Policy holders' rating of A; financial rating of not less than X;

> (2) The insurer shall be qualified to do business in the state in which the Leased Premises are located;

> (3) The policy shall be in a form and include such endorsements as are acceptable to Lessor;

> (4) Certificates of insurance shall be delivered to Lessor at commencement of the term and certificates of renewal at least thirty (30) days prior to the expiration of each policy;

> (5) Each policy shall require that Lessor be notified in writing by the insurer at least thirty (30) days prior to any cancellation or expiration of such policy, or any reduction in the amounts of insurance carried;

Lessee Insurance Default

I. <u>Rights of Lessor.</u> In the event that Lessee fails to obtain any insurance required of it under the terms of this Lease, Lessor may, at its option, but is not obligated to, obtain such insurance on behalf of Lessee and bill Lessee, as additional rent, for the cost thereof. Payment shall be due within ten (10) days of receipt of the billing therefor by Lessee.

Indemnification, Waiver of Claims, and Subrogation

J. <u>Intent and Purpose.</u> This Article ___ is written and agreed to in respect of the intent of the parties to assign the risk of loss whether resulting from negligence of the parties or otherwise, to the party who is obligated hereunder to cover the risk of such loss with insurance. Thus, the indemnity and waiver of claims provisions of this Lease have as their object, so long as such object is not in violation of public policy, the assignment of risk for a particular casualty to the party carrying the insurance for such risk, without respect to the causation thereof.

K. Waiver of Subrogation. Lessor and Lessee release each other, and their respective authorized representatives, from any claims for damage to any person or to the Leased Premises and the Building and other improvements in which the Leased Premises are located, and to the fixtures, personal property, Lessee's improvements and alterations of either Lessor or Lessee, in or on the Leased Premises and the Building and other improvements in which the Leased Premises are located, including loss of income, that are caused by or result from risks insured or required under the terms of this Lease to be insured against under any property insurance policies carried or to be carried by either of the parties.

L. Form of Policy. Each party shall cause each such insurance policy obtained by it to provide that the insurance company waives all rights of recovery by way of subrogation against either party in connection with any damage covered by such policy. Neither party shall be liable to the other for any damage caused by fire or any other risks insured against under any property insurance policy carried under the terms of this Lease. If any such insurance policy cannot be obtained with a waiver of subrogation without payment of an additional premium charge above that charged by the insurance companies issuing such policies without waiver of subrogation, the party receiving the benefit shall elect to either forfeit the benefit or shall pay such additional premium to the insurance carrier requiring such additional premium.

M. Indemnity. Lessee, as a material part of the consideration to be rendered to Lessor, shall indemnify, defend, protect and hold harmless Lessor against all actions, claims, demands, damages, liabilities, losses, penalties, or expenses of any kind which may be brought or imposed upon Lessor or which Lessor may pay or incur by reason of injury to person or property, from whatever cause, all or in any way connected with the condition or use of the Leased Premises, or the improvements or personal property therein or thereon, including without limitation any liability or injury to the person or property of Lessee, its agents, officers, employees or invitees. Lessee agrees to indemnify, defend and protect Lessor and hold it harmless from any and all liability, loss, cost or obligation on account of, or arising out of, any s uch injury or loss however occurring, including breach of the provisions of this Lease and the negligence of the parties hereto. Nothing contained herein shall obligate Lessee to indemnify Lessor against its own sole or gross negligence or willful acts, for which Lessor shall indemnify Lessee.

N. <u>Defense of Claims.</u> In the event any action, suit or proceeding is brought against Lessor by reason of any such occurrence, Lessee, upon Lessor's request will at Lessee's expense resist and defend such action, suit or proceeding, or cause the same to be resisted and defended by counsel designated either by Lessee or by the insurer whose policy covers the occurrence and in either case approved by Lessor. The obligations of Lessee under this Section arising by reason of any occurrence taking place during the Lease term shall survive any termination of this Lease.

O. <u>Waiver of Claims.</u> Lessee, as a material part of the consideration to be rendered to Lessor, hereby waives all claims against Lessor for damages to goods, wares, merchandise and loss of business in, upon or about the Leased Premises and for injury to Lessee, its agents, employees, invitees or third persons in or about the Leased Premises from any cause arising at any time, including breach of the provisions of this Lease and the negligence of the parties hereto.

P. <u>References.</u> Wherever in this Article the term Lessor or Lessee is used and such party is to receive the benefit of a provision contained in this Article, such term shall refer not only to that party but also to its officers, directors, employees, partners and agents.

Chapter 13 – Destruction and Condemnation

Destruction

A. <u>Rights of Termination.</u> In the event the Leased Premises suffers (a) an uninsured casualty, or (b) a casualty which cannot be repaired within one hundred twenty (120) days from the date of destruction under the laws and regulations of state, federal, county or municipal authorities, or other authorities with jurisdiction, Lessor may terminate this Lease as at the date of the damage upon written notice to Lessee following the casualty. In the event of a casualty to the Leased Premises which cannot be repaired within one hundred ninety five (195) days of the occurrence thereof, Lessee shall have the right to terminate the Lease by written notice to Lessor within twenty (20) days following notice from Lessor that the time for restoration shall exceed one hundred ninety five (195) days. For Purposes hereof, an "uninsured casualty" is a casualty arising from a peril not covered by the standard form of fire policy with extended coverage endorsement.

B. Repairs. In the event of a casualty which may be repaired within one hundred twenty (120) days from the date of the damage, or, in the alternative, in the event the parties do not elect to terminate this Lease under the terms of Section A above, then this Lease shall continue in full force and effect and Lessor shall forthwith undertake to make such repairs to reconstitute the Leased Premises to as near the condition as existed prior to the casualty as practicable. Such partial destruction shall in no way annul or void this Lease except that Lessee shall be entitled to a proportionate reduction of Minimum Monthly Rent following the casualty and until the time the Leased Premises are restored. Such reduction shall be an amount that reflects the degree of interference with Lessee's business. So long as Lessee conducts its business in the Leased Premises there shall be no abatement until the parties agree on the amount thereof. If the parties cannot agree within forty-five (45) days of the casualty, the matter shall be submitted to arbitration under the rules of the American Arbitration Association. Upon the resolution of the dispute, the settlement shall be retroactive and Lessor shall within ten (10) days after receipt of a written copy of the arbitration award decision refund to Lessee any sums due in respect of the reduced rental from the date of the casualty. Lessor's obligations to restore shall in no way include any construction originally performed by Lessee or subsequently undertaken by Lessee, but shall include solely that property constructed by Lessor prior to commencement of the term hereof.

C. Repair Costs. The cost of any repairs to be made by Lessor, pursuant to Section B shall be paid by Lessor utilizing available insurance proceeds. Lessee shall reimburse Lessor upon completion of the repairs for any deductible for which no insurance proceeds will be obtained under Lessor's insurance policy, or if other premises are also repaired, a pro rata share based on total costs of repair equitably apportioned to the Leased Premises. Lessee shall, however, not be responsible to pay any deductible or its share of any deductible to the extent that Lessee's payment would be in excess of $10,000 if Lessee's consent has not been received by Lessor, unless such denial of consent by Lessee is unreasonable.

D. <u>Waiver.</u> Lessee hereby waives all statutory or common law rights of termination in respect to any partial destruction or casualty which Lessor is obligated to repair or may elect to repair under the terms of this Article. Further, in event of a casualty occurring during the last two (2) years of the original term hereof or of any extension, Lessor need not undertake any repairs and may cancel this Lease unless Lessee has the right under the terms of this Lease to extend the term for an additional period of at least five (5) years and does so within thirty (30) days of the date of the casualty.

E. <u>Lessor's Election.</u> In the event that the Complex or Building in which the Leased Premises is situated be destroyed to the extent of not less than thirty-three and one-third percent (33-1/3%) of the replacement cost thereof, Lessor may elect to terminate this Lease, whether the Leased Premises be injured or not, in the same manner as in Section A above. At all events, a total destruction of the Complex of which the Leased Premises form a part, or the Leased Premises itself, shall terminate this Lease.

Condemnation

F. <u>Definitions.</u>

1. "Condemnation" means (a) the exercise of any governmental power, whether by legal proceedings or otherwise, by a condemnor and/or (b) a voluntary sale or transfer by Lessor to any condemnor, either under threat of condemnation or while legal proceedings for condemnation are pending.

2. "Date of taking" means the date the condemnor has the right to possession of the property being condemned.

3. "Award" means all compensation, sums or anything of value awarded, paid or received on a total or partial condemnation.

4. "Condemnor" means any public or quasi-public authority, or private corporation or individual, having the power of condemnation.

G. <u>Total Taking.</u> If the Leased Premises are totally taken by condemnation, this Lease shall terminate on the date of taking.

H. <u>Partial Taking; Common Area.</u>

1. If any portion of the Leased Premises is taken by condemnation, this Lease shall remain in effect, except that Lessee can elect to terminate this Lease if 33-1/3% or more of the total number of square feet in the Leased Premises is taken.

2. If any part of the Common Areas of the Complex are taken by condemnation, this Lease shall remain in full force and effect so long as there is no material interference with the access to the Leased Premises, except that if thirty percent (30%) or more of the Common Area is taken by condemnation, either party shall have the election to terminate this Lease pursuant to this section.

3. If fifty percent (50%) or more of the Building in which the Leased Premises are located is taken, Lessor shall have the election to terminate this Lease in the manner prescribed herein.

I. <u>Termination or Abatement.</u> If either party elects to terminate this Lease under the provisions of Section ____, (such party is hereinafter referred to as the "Terminating Party") it must terminate by giving notice to the other party (the "Nonterminating Party") within thirty (30) days after the nature and extent of the taking have been finally determined (the "Decision Period"). The Terminating Party shall notify the Nonterminating Party of the date of termination, which date shall not be earlier than sixty (60) days after the Terminating Party has notified the Nonterminating Party of its election to terminate nor later than the date of taking. If Notice of Termination is not given within the Decision Period, the Lease shall continue in full force and effect except that Minimum Monthly Rent shall be reduced by subtracting therefrom an amount calculated by multiplying the Minimum Monthly Rent in effect prior to the taking by a fraction the numerator of which is the number of square feet taken from the Leased Premises and the denominator of which is the number of square feet in the Leased Premises prior to the taking.

J. Restoration. If there is a partial taking of the Leased Premises and this Lease remains in full force and effect pursuant to this Article, Lessor, at its cost, shall accomplish all necessary restoration so that the Leased Premises is returned as near as practical to its condition immediately prior to the date of the taking, but in no event shall Lessor be obligated to expend more for such restoration than the extent of funds actually paid to Lessor by the condemnor.

K. Award. Any award arising from the condemnation or the settlement thereof shall belong to and be paid to Lessor except that Lessee shall receive from the award compensation for the following if specified in the award by the condemning authority, so long as it does not reduce Lessor's award in respect of the real property: Lessee's trade fixtures, tangible personal property, goodwill, loss of business and relocation expenses. At all events, Lessor shall be solely entitled to all award in respect of the real property, including the bonus value of the leasehold. Lessee shall not be entitled to any award until Lessor has received the above sum in full.

Chapter 14 – Default And Other Provisions

Default

A. Definition. The occurrence of any of the following shall constitute a material default and breach of this Lease by Lessee:

1. Any failure by Lessee to pay the rental or to make any other payment required to be made by Lessee hereunder when due;

2. The abandonment or vacation of the Leased Premises by Lessee in violation of Section _____ hereof;

3. A failure by Lessee to observe and perform any other provision of this Lease to be observed or performed by Lessee, where such failure continues for ten (10) days after written notice thereof by Lessor to Lessee; provided, however, that if the nature of the default is such that the same cannot reasonably be cured within the ten (10) day period allowed, Lessee shall not be deemed to be in default if Lessee shall, within such ten (10) day period, commence to cure and thereafter diligently prosecute the same to completion;

4. Either (a) the appointment of a receiver (except a receiver appointed at the instance or request of Lessor) to take possession of all or substantially all of the assets of Lessee, or (b) a general assignment by Lessee for the benefit of creditors, or (c) any action taken or suffered by Lessee under any insolvency or bankruptcy act shall constitute a breach of this Lease by Lessee. In such event, Lessor may, at its option, declare this Lease terminated and forfeited by Lessee, and Lessor shall be entitled to immediate possession of the Leased Premises. Upon such notice of termination, this Lease shall terminate immediately and automatically by its own limitation;

5. Any two (2) failures by Lessee to observe and perform any provision of this Lease during any twelve (12) month period of the term, as such may be extended, shall constitute, at the option of Lessor, a separate and noncurable default.

Remedies upon Default

B. <u>Termination and Damages.</u> In the event of any default by Lessee, then in addition to any other remedies available to Lessor herein or at law or in equity, Lessor shall have the immediate option to terminate this Lease and all rights of Lessee hereunder by giving written notice of such intention to terminate. In the event that Lessor shall elect to so terminate this Lease, then Lessor may recover from Lessee:

1. The worth at the time of award of any unpaid rent which had been earned at the time of such termination; plus

2. The worth at the time of award of the amount by which

the unpaid rent which would have been earned after termination until the time of award exceeds the amount of such rental loss Lessee proves could have been reasonably avoided; plus

3. The worth at the time of award of the amount by which the unpaid rent for the balance of the term after the time of award exceeds the amount of such rental loss that Lessee proves could be reasonably avoided; plus

4. Any other amount necessary to compensate Lessor for all the detriment proximately caused by Lessee's failure to perform its obligations under this Lease or which in the ordinary course of events would be likely to result therefrom; and

5. At Lessor's election, such other amounts in addition to or in lieu of the foregoing as may be permitted from time to time by the applicable law in the state in which the Leased Premises are located.

C. Definitions.

1. The term "rent", as used in this Lease, shall be deemed to be and to mean the Minimum Monthly Rent and all other sums required to be paid by Lessee pursuant to the terms of this Lease.

2. As used in Sections B (1) and (2) above, the "worth at the time of award" is computed by allowing interest at the rate of ten percent (10%) per annum. As used in Section B (3) above, the "worth at the time of award" is computed by discounting such amount at the discount rate of the Federal Reserve Bank for the region in which the Complex is located at the time of award plus one percent (1%).

D. Personal Property.

1. In the event of any default by Lessee, Lessor shall also have the right, with or without terminating this Lease, to reenter the Leased Premises and remove all persons and property from the Leased Premises; such property may be removed and stored in a public warehouse or elsewhere at the cost of and for the account of Lessee.

2. In the event of default, all of Lessee's fixtures, furniture, equipment, improvements, additions, alterations and other personal property, shall remain upon the Leased Premises and in that event, and continuing during the length of such default, Lessor shall have the sole right to take exclusive possession of such property and to use it, rent or charge free, until all defaults are cured or, at Lessor's option, at any time during the term of this Lease, to require Lessee to forthwith remove such property. The rights stated herein are in addition to Lessor's rights described in Section ___ (forfeiture of property).

E. Recovery of Rent; Reletting.

1. In the event of the vacation or abandonment of the Leased Premises by Lessee or in the event that Lessor shall elect to reenter as provided in Section D above, or shall take possession of the Leased Premises pursuant to legal proceeding or pursuant to any notice provided by law, then if Lessor does not elect to terminate this Lease as provided in Section A above, Lessor may from time to time, without terminating this Lease, either recover all rental as it becomes due or relet the Leased Premises or any part thereof for such term or terms and at such rental or rentals and upon such other terms and conditions as Lessor in its sole discretion, may deem advisable with the right to make alterations and repairs to the Leased Premises.

2. In the event that Lessor shall elect to so relet, then rentals received by Lessor from such reletting shall be applied: first, to the payment of any indebtedness other than rent due hereunder from Lessee to Lessor; second, to the payment of any cost of such reletting; third, to the payment of the cost of any alterations and repairs to the Leased Premises; fourth, to the payment of rent due and unpaid hereunder; and the residue, if any, shall be held by Lessor and applied in payment of future rent as the same may become due and payable hereunder. Should that portion of such rentals received from such reletting during any month, which is applied by the payment of rent hereunder, be less than the rent payable during that month by Lessee hereunder, then Lessee shall pay such deficiency to Lessor immediately upon

demand therefor by Lessor. Such deficiency shall be calculated and paid monthly. Lessee shall also pay to Lessor as soon as ascertained, any costs and expenses incurred by Lessor in such reletting or in making such alterations and repairs not covered by the rentals received from such reletting.

3. No reentry or taking possession of the Leased Premises or any other action under this Section shall be construed as an election to terminate this Lease unless a written notice of such intention be given to Lessee or unless the termination thereof be decreed by a court of competent jurisdiction. Notwithstanding any reletting without termination by Lessor because of any default by Lessee, Lessor may at any time after such reletting elect to terminate this Lease for any such default.

F. <u>No Waiver.</u> Efforts by Lessor to mitigate the damages caused by Lessee's default in this Lease shall not constitute a waiver of Lessor's right to recover damages hereunder, nor shall Lessor have any obligation to mitigate damages hereunder.

G. <u>Curing Defaults.</u> Should Lessee fail to repair, maintain, and/or service the Leased Premises, or any part or contents thereof at any time or times, or perform any other obligations imposed by this Lease or otherwise, then after having given Lessee reasonable notice of the failure or failures and a reasonable opportunity, which in no case shall exceed ten (10) days, to remedy the failure, Lessor may perform or contract for the performance of the repair, maintenance, or other Lessee obligation, and Lessee shall pay Lessor for all direct and indirect costs incurred in connection therewith within ten (10) days of receiving a bill therefor from Lessor.

H. <u>Cumulative Remedies.</u> The various rights, options, election powers, and remedies of Lessor contained in this Article and elsewhere in this Lease shall be construed as cumulative and no one of them exclusive of any others or of any legal or equitable remedy which Lessor might otherwise have in the event of breach or default, and the exercise of one right or remedy by Lessor shall not in any way impair its right to any other right or remedy.

Forfeiture of Property and Lessor's Lien

I. <u>Removal of Personal Property.</u> Lessee agrees that as at the date of termination of this Lease or repossession of the Leased Premises by Lessor, by way of default or otherwise, it shall remove all personal property to which it has the right to ownership pursuant to the terms of this Lease. Any and all such property of Lessee not removed by such date shall, at the option of Lessor, irrevocably become the sole property of Lessor. Lessee waives all rights to notice and all common law and statutory claims and causes of action which it may have against Lessor subsequent to such date as regards the storage, destruction, damage, loss of use, and ownership of the personal property affected by the terms of this Article. Lessee acknowledges Lessor's need to relet the Leased Premises upon termination of this Lease or repossession of the Leased Premises and understands that the forfeitures and waivers provided herein are necessary to aid said reletting, and to prevent Lessor incurring a loss for inability to deliver the Leased Premises to a prospective lessee.

J. <u>Lessor's Lien.</u> Lessee hereby grants to Lessor a lien upon and security interest in all fixtures, chattels and personal property of every kind now or hereafter to be placed or installed in or on the Leased Premises and agrees that in the event of any default on the part of Lessee, Lessor shall have all the rights and remedies afforded the secured party by the chapter on "Default" of Division 9 of the Uniform Commercial Code of the state in which the Leased Premises are located and may, in connection therewith, also (1) enter on the Leased Premises to assemble and take possession of the collateral, (2) require Lessee to assemble the collateral and make its possession available to Lessor at the Leased Premises, and (3) enter the Leased Premises, render the collateral, if equipment, unusable and dispose of it in a manner provided by the Uniform Commercial Code of the state in which the Leased Premises are located. Lessee hereby designates Lessor as his attorney-in-fact for purposes of executing such documents as may be necessary to perfect the lien and security interest granted hereunder.

Lessor's Exculpation

K. <u>Limited Liability.</u> In the event of default, breach, or violation by Lessor (which term includes Lessor's partners, co-venturers, co-tenants, officers, directors, employees, agents, or representatives) of any Lessor's obligations under this Lease, Lessor's liability to Lessee shall be limited to its ownership interest in the Leased Premises (or its interest in the Complex, if applicable) or the proceeds of a public sale of such interest pursuant to foreclosure of a judgment against Lessor. Lessor may, at its option, and among its other alternatives, relieve itself of all liability under this Lease by conveying the Leased Premises to Lessee. Notwithstanding any such conveyance, Lessee's leasehold and ownership interest shall not merge.

L. <u>No Recourse.</u> Lessor shall not be personally liable for any deficiency beyond its interest in the Leased Premises.

INDEX

C

D

E

F

N

O

P

Q

Quality, and alterations, 91

R

Radius clause, and percentage rent, 58
Range of clauses, use, 30-31
Reasonable consent, and assignment and
    subletting, 121
Rebates, property taxes, 213
Recapture, lease, 126
Records, percentage rent and, 57,
    173-174, 207-208
Recovery of rent, default, 256-257
Regional mall leases, 2
Regional shopping centers, landlords and
    use clause, 27-29
Reimbursements and offsets, percentage
    rent, 54-55
Relative cost, tax allocation, 71-72
Remedies
    default, 155, 254-257
    for late term delivery, 38-39
    repair and deduct or sue,
    maintenance, 49, 83
Removal, of alterations, 92-93
Rent
    abatements or offsets, 48-49,
    141-143
    additional, 173, 206-208, 209-211
    calculation of, 11, 47-48, 53-58
    cost-of-living adjustments in, 43-44
    cotenancy, 49-50, 171-172
    covenant of continuous operation,
    58, 208-209
    fair market value adjustments in,
    44-46
    fixed increases in, 42-43
    free rent, 50-51
    increases in, 204-205
    minimum, 171-172
    and option to expand, 22-23
    payment frequency, 56-57
    percentage, 51-58, 173-175,
    206-208

unit costs and, 8
Rentable area, 8-9
Rental adjustments, 43-46, 47-48
Rental income insurance, 132
Repair and deduct remedy, maintenance,
    49, 83
Repair and sue remedy, maintenance, 83
Repair costs, following destruction,
    250-251
Repair/replacement maintenance
    question, 76-79
Repairs, following destruction, 194, 250
Repair versus maintenance, and landlord
    responsibility, 110
Replacement cost
    and tax allocation, 71
    endorsement, insurance, 132
Restoration
    following alteration, 229-230
    following condemnation, 253
Restrictions on use, shopping center,
    28-29
Retail premises substitution, 20
Right of early return, security deposit,
    160
Right of first offer, tenant expansion,
    24-26
Right of first refusal, tenant expansion,
    23-24
Right of use, common areas, 182
Right to cancel, construction and, 169
Right to change use, 30-32
Rollover date, and premises delivery,
    38-39, 168-169
Roof or roofing maintenance question,
    76
R/U ratio, and usable to rentable space
    conversion, 11-13

S

Safes and other heavy equipment,
    201-202
Sample lease clauses
    alterations, 181-182, 227-230
    assignment and subletting, 186-187,

T

W

U